PURSUIT

ALSO BY CLINT JOHNSON

The Politically Incorrect Guide to the South (and Why It Will Rise Again)

Colonial America and the American Revolution: The 25 Best Sites

The 25 Best Civil War Sites

In the Footsteps of Robert E. Lee

In the Footsteps of Stonewall Jackson

In the Footsteps of J.E.B. Stuart

Touring Virginia's and West Virginia's Civil War Sites

Touring the Carolinas' Civil War Sites

Civil War Blunders

Bull's-Eyes and Misfires: 50 People Whose Obscure Efforts Shaped the American Civil War

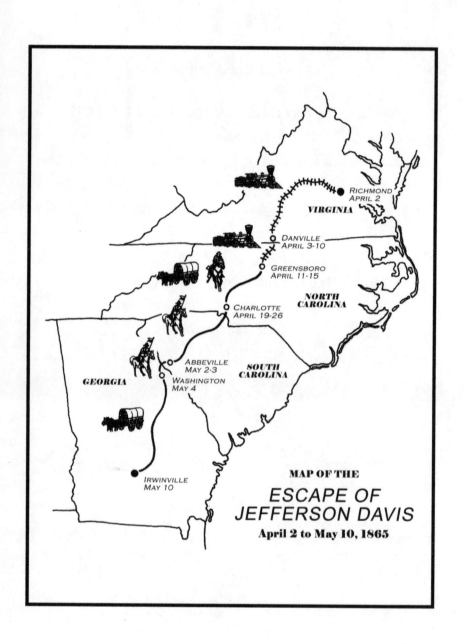

RICHMOND
APRIL 2

VIRGINIA

DANVILLE
APRIL 3-10

GREENSBORO
APRIL 11-15

NORTH
CAROLINA

CHARLOTTE
APRIL 19-26

ABBEVILLE
MAY 2-3

SOUTH
CAROLINA

GEORGIA

WASHINGTON
MAY 4

IRWINVILLE
MAY 10

MAP OF THE

ESCAPE OF JEFFERSON DAVIS

April 2 to May 10, 1865

PURSUIT

The Chase, Capture, Persecution,
and Surprising Release of Confederate
President Jefferson Davis

CLINT JOHNSON

CITADEL PRESS
Kensington Publishing Corp.
www.kensingtonbooks.com

CITADEL PRESS BOOKS are published by

Kensington Publishing Corp.
850 Third Avenue
New York, NY 10022

All Kensington titles, imprints, and distributed lines are available at special quantity discounts for bulk purchases for sales promotions, premiums, fund-raising, educational, or institutional use. Special book excerpts or customized printings can also be created to fit specific needs. For details, write or phone the office of the Kensington special sales manager: Kensington Publishing Corp., 850 Third Avenue, New York, NY 10022, attn: Special Sales Department; phone 1-800-221-2647.

First printing: June 2008

10 9 8 7 6 5 4 3 2 1

Printed in the United States of America

Library of Congress Control Number: 2008922833

ISBN-13: 978-0-8065-2890-8
ISBN-10: 0-8065-2890-7

For all the men and women who fought The War.
No one was right. No one was wrong.

Contents

PURSUIT

CHAPTER 1

"Nothing Short of Dementation"

AT THE DISMAL DAWNING of 1865, more than one quarter of the one million men who had enlisted in the South's armies over the previous three years were dead. Another 125,000 were wounded, their shattered arms and missing legs virtually ensuring that they would be unable to return to their prewar occupations as farmers and laborers. Another quarter million Southerners were languishing in widely scattered prisoner-of-war camps like "Hell-Mira" in Elmira, New York, and "40 Acres of Hell" in Camp Douglas, outside Chicago.

Southern civilians were not faring much better. The two largest cities in Virginia, Richmond and Petersburg, were slowly strangling, their communications and their food supplies being cut off by Lieutenant General Ulysses S. Grant's Army of the James and the Army of the Potomac. The Shenandoah Valley, once the breadbasket of the Confederacy, had been burned so completely that one Union general boasted to another that a crow flying over the devastated farms would have to pack his own lunch.

The situation elsewhere in the South was even worse. Western Confederate state capitals like Nashville, Tennessee; Little Rock, Arkansas; Jackson, Mississippi; and Baton Rouge, Louisiana, had been captured years earlier. Atlanta, Georgia, had been shelled into submission in the summer of 1864 and then burned to the ground when General William T. Sherman and his 63,000 angry young men left on their destructive March to the Sea. Savannah and its wealth of unshipped cotton were presented to President Lincoln as a gift at Christmas 1864 by Sherman just a few weeks earlier. Now Sherman was preparing to cross the Savannah River to unleash his battle-tested veterans in South Carolina, the state these Midwesterners blamed for starting the war.

Just up the coast from Savannah, a massive sea bombardment and land invasion force were bearing down on Wilmington, North Carolina, the war's most successful blockade-running port. Though Wilmington was still open despite four years of the smothering Union blockade, the government leaders in Richmond knew if Fort Fisher fell, the end of the Confederate nation would soon follow. That was an inevitable truth as most of the Army of Northern Virginia's supplies came ashore at Wilmington and were loaded on railroad cars for off-loading in Petersburg. If that rail line was captured south of Petersburg, then the end of the war could come quickly because the army would run out of food and ammunition.

Disaster piled upon defeat throughout the South. There seemed to be no hope that anything could be salvaged from the piles of rubble that were already there and the even larger mounds of debris that soon would be.

Yet there was one man in the South who confidently, almost cheerfully, still believed the Confederate States of America would triumph in the four-year war with the North. He was Jefferson F. Davis, the seceded nation's president.

February 6, 1865—three weeks after the capture of Fort Fisher, North Carolina—an event Davis knew very well meant disaster for resupplying Lee's army, Davis gave a morale boosting speech:

> Does any one who has seen the Confederate soldiers believe they are willing to fail? If so, the suspicion is most unjust! Go to our camps; go to our guarded lines; go where our pickets hold their dangerous watch, and to the posts where our sentinels tread their weary rounds, and you will find in none of those the place for grumblings and complaints. The resolutions of our soldiers exclaim with Patrick Henry, "Victory or death!"

Those who knew Davis only casually might have thought his resolute, confident attitude about winning the war was a surprisingly sunny position for the president to take. After all, Davis had stepped onto the national stage of secessionist politics in a sour mood, warning both sides of the dangers of war between the regions.

Those who knew Davis well were not at all surprised that the president truly believed the war was still winnable. He had convinced himself years earlier that the war was politically ethical, morally right, and, most important of all, absolutely legal under the U.S. Constitution. He would die believing in his cause.

☆ ☆ ☆

FROM CHILDHOOD, Davis had displayed one personality trait that would stay constant in his life. That quirk would continually infuriate his parents, his brothers, his sisters, his wife, his personal friends, and his political enemies. He considered it strength of character.

Everyone else found it maddening.

Once Davis made up his mind that the course he had chosen in his politics, or in his personal or business affairs was correct, he never wavered from that decision. Once his decision was made, he never changed his mind despite the best efforts of his supporters to offer their own differing opinions.

Davis not only believed he was right all the time, he also believed he was the only person he knew who was prescient about the course of history. Sometimes he was tragically correct.

For at least three years preceding the opening of the war, Davis believed that a war between the North and the South was inevitable unless both sides listened to a voice of reason. He firmly, if humbly, believed that he was the one to voice those warnings, and if his voice was ignored, there would be hell to pay.

In an 1858 speech in Faneuil Hall to the citizens of Boston Davis hinted at civil war if the federal government continued to trample on the sanctity of states' rights. Throughout the speech Davis coyly suggested that Massachusetts political heroes like Samuel Adams and John

Hancock had invented the concept that states were the primary political unit in the nation. Such a view was in accordance with his belief that the Constitution was an instrument designed to govern a
voluntary Union of all states.

Davis cleverly explained his bedrock belief in states' rights over federal control of those states by reminding the Bostonians that Massachusetts Governor Hancock once refused to call on President George
Washington who was visiting the state. Hancock believed that the nation's president should defer to the assumed power of the state governor he was visiting and that Washington should have called, hat in
hand, on him.

Davis warned that any action based on the belief that the federal
government was superior to the states' power would have dire consequences.

Skillfully working in references that it was in Faneuil Hall that
Massachusetts' political leaders had plotted secession from England,
Davis said:

> Thus, it is that the peace of the Union is disturbed; thus it is that
> brother is arrayed against brother; thus it is that the people come
> to consider, not how they can promote each other's interests, but
> how they can successfully make war upon them.

Firebrands on both sides ignored the warnings from Davis, the best
known and most popular in the North of all the Southern senators.
Nearly three years after his widely reported Boston speech, the debate
between the states' rights advocates for the South and the unbreakable
Union advocates for the North ended in December 1860 when South
Carolina left the Union. Starting in January 1861, six other Deep
South states followed South Carolina out of the Union, just as Davis
had predicted.

After Mississippi became the second state to secede from the Union,
Davis assured his Senate colleagues in his January 21, 1861, resignation speech that people in the South "hope for peaceful relations with
you, though we must part." Knowing his suggestions had been ignored

in the past, Davis also gravely warned that "the reverse will bring disaster on every part of the country."

For days after leaving Washington on January 22, 1861, all Davis could think about was the coming calamity of war. After arriving in the capital city of Jackson, the governor of Mississippi appointed him major general of volunteers and suggested that the purchase of 75,000 muskets would be sufficient to defend the state.

Davis scoffed: "We will need all and many more than we can get, I fear."

After accepting visitors in his hotel room who were confident of a successful, peaceful severing of ties with the Union, Davis wailed to his wife, "God help us, war is a dreadful calamity even when it is made against aliens and strangers. They know not what they do!"

When the seceded states planned their constitutional convention for early February in Montgomery, Alabama, Davis must have known, even before leaving Washington, that his name would be brought up as a potential president for the proposed "confederacy" of slaveholding states. As a humble but true Mexican War hero, a popular United States Secretary of War in the Franklin Pierce administration, a former congressman, and most recently a widely respected senator, Davis was one of the most government-experienced Southerners on the national scene.

But Davis had always been a reluctant politician. He hated shaking hands and meeting common voters. He hated the backslapping and the toasting to other politicians' health. He hated the backroom dealing and trading of votes to get bills passed and money appropriated. He hated everything about nineteenth-century politics except making laws and protecting the South's interests.

With the secession of Mississippi and his resignation from the Senate, Davis was suddenly free of public service for the first time in more than fifteen years. He no longer had to participate in the grubbiness he detested, which almost certainly would be a part of the forming of the new nation. He had never expressed any interest in even discussing how to form this new country, nor had he asked any of the Mississippi delegates to the secession convention to put his name into nomination. He did not even ask them to keep him informed. In fact,

Davis gave a letter to one delegate specifically stating that he did not think himself suited for the job as president in the event his name came up for nomination.

His name did come up. Davis was the only presidential candidate seriously discussed after former United States senator Robert Toombs from Georgia made a spectacle of himself openly drinking to excess at the convention hotel. The Mississippi delegate whom Davis had asked to discourage his nomination never took Davis's letter from his vest pocket. After former United States senator Alexander Stephens from Georgia was nominated for the vice president's slot, Davis was unanimously nominated and elected by the delegates to a single six-year term as president on February 9, 1861.

Davis had not told anyone he wanted the job. He had not campaigned for it. He had done everything he could to avoid being considered for it. Yet as he had feared, his career as the most famous and successful of Southern politicians in the late 1850s had doomed him to fill the slot.

A courier who had ridden hard from Montgomery with an important letter in his satchel found Davis on February 10 tending his rose garden at Brierfield, one of the Davis family's plantations near Vicksburg, Mississippi. The man handed Davis a sealed telegram.

For the fleeting instant it took Davis to unfold the paper, he must have hoped that the message agreed with his own belief that the Confederacy did not need the services of a perpetually ill, fifty-three-year-old man who had already served his previous nation for nearly two decades. But knowing the firebrands who were taking the Southern states out of the United States, they would demand something of its most famous politician. Davis held out hope that he would be offered a generalship in the still-forming army. And, if he were to take that post, he wanted to do more than recruit and train militia. He wanted a field command, something that would take him back to the thrill of leading men under fire.

When Davis read the telegraph's few lines congratulating him on his unanimous election to the post of president of the Confederate States of America, his hands quivered and his face darkened. Davis looked so stricken with grief that his wife, Varina, thought that the message had informed her husband of a death in the family.

Varina remembered: "After a few minutes of painful silence, he told me, as a man might speak of a sentence of death. As he neither expected nor desired the position, he was more depressed than before."

Despondent but ever certain that a man did not shirk from duty thrust upon him, Davis departed for Montgomery the day after receiving the telegram. He would take the job that he did not want. He would take the job that would quickly make him one of the most hated men in the United States and the Confederate States.

☆ ☆ ☆

Now, four years into his single six-year term, Davis felt virtually alone. His instincts were right. Though his cabinet still supported him—at least in cabinet meetings and in their public statements—Davis's political adversaries, newspaper editorial writers, his personal friends, and the common citizens of the Confederacy had begun to question his leadership.

Frustrated with the president's insistence that he act as chief war strategist as well as commander in chief, the Confederate Congress had begun to challenge Davis more vigorously on war planning. For the first time, Confederate Congress passed a law forcing Davis to name a general in chief. That was a war measure the United States had passed more than a year and a half earlier with the appointment of Grant to direct war strategy on all fronts.

Davis, who fancied himself a military expert since he had graduated from West Point and had served under fire, resisted the legislation. He finally accepted the law when his friends in the Confederate Congress watered it down so that he could still make such an appointment himself rather than leave it to Congress to name its own favorite person to such an important position. Davis wisely chose the only commander who had been able to stand up to Grant's continuous, yearlong onslaught, Robert E. Lee.

Lee was an acceptable choice to Davis's critics. Newspaper editorial writers, always among the most fierce of Davis's political critics and who normally mocked his military acumen, breathed a sigh of relief that Davis had not chosen his best friend, General Braxton Bragg. The *Richmond Examiner* published a headline in October 1864 when it learned Davis had appointed Bragg to the defense of Wilmington, North Carolina: "Bragg Is Going To Wilmington. Good-bye Wilmington." In the body of the article the newspaper expanded on its headline with: "General Bragg's presence wherever he has controlled, has been felt as a disaster, an omen of impending evil like a dark, cold, dreary cloud."

In some ways, it was remarkable that Davis had not chosen Bragg. He might have slotted Bragg into the position just to spite his political enemies, who had objected to his leadership style since his inauguration four years ago. Davis fought back against them by ignoring them, doing the opposite of what they wanted, or wasting his time by often writing them long, complicated letters condemning them for their complaints.

Davis could strike back at the political elites who had nominated him to run the government that they now complained about, but he had no power other than speeches to influence what the average Southern citizen thought of him and his conduct of the war.

John B. Jones, a clerk in the Confederate War Department, never had the ear of Davis, but he had the common man's pulse on what the public felt about the chief executive as the end of the Confederacy was becoming apparent to all but its president. Jones kept a diary for most of the war where he made observations about all he saw happening around his little desk.

On December 17, 1864, Jones noted that a wild rumor was circulating in the streets that Davis had died. He wrote: "Alas for President Davis's government! It is now in a painful strait." He ended the day's entry with a final comment about the rumor he personally discounted: "His death would excite sympathy," but he also noted that Davis's "enemies are assailing him bitterly, and attributing all our misfortunes to his incompetence."

Jones believed that so many men in high positions now hated the president that they were considering a coup against him. On Christmas day Jones wrote that "a large number of the croaking inhabitants censure the President for our misfortunes and openly declare for General Lee as Dictator." On New Year's Eve, Jones wrote again of the supposed plot:

It can only be done by revolution and the overthrow of the Constitution. Nevertheless, it is believed many executive officers, some high in position, favor the scheme.

But while common clerk Jones had sympathy for Davis, he also did not think he made a good president. On January 1, 1865, Jones wrote down what many of Davis's enemies were thinking and saying:

The President is considered really a man of ability, and eminently qualified to preside over the Confederate States, if independence were attained and we had peace. But he is probably not equal to the role he is now called upon to play. He has not the broad intellect requisite for the gigantic measures needed in such a crisis, nor the health or the physique for the labors devolving onto him.

Jones continued his observations that all the politicians who voted Davis into office in 1860 now "desire to see General Lee at the head of affairs [but] the President is resolved to yield the position to no man during his term of service."

☆   ☆   ☆

DAVIS WOULD NOT YIELD to any man in the Confederacy, and he would not yield to any man in the United States, including Lincoln, whose troops were closing in on the capital city of Richmond from the east and the south.

On February 3, 1865, Davis sent three commissioners, including Vice President Stephens, to talk over peace terms with Lincoln and Secretary of State William H. Seward. Davis himself did not go because Lincoln had declared in a December 1864 speech to the United States Congress that he would never recognize Davis as a head of state, but

he was open to the possibility of meeting with lower ranking Confederate officials.

The meeting took place aboard the Union transport ship *River Queen*
at Hampton Roads, Virginia, within shouting distance of Fortress Monroe, a U.S. fort on the tip of the peninsula between the James and the
York rivers that had never fallen into Confederate hands. The meeting's eventual outcome was telegraphed to all attending within a few
minutes of it starting when Lincoln noticed that Davis had changed
Lincoln's original letter asking for the meeting to discuss "securing
peace to the people of our one common country." Davis had written
his own reply, using Lincoln's own sentence structure, but substituted
"our two countries" for Lincoln's "common country." Although most
of the Confederacy was already occupied and the rest in imminent
danger of being overrun by overwhelming Union forces, Davis still insisted that any peace would hinge on the United States recognizing
the continuing existence of the Confederacy.

Lincoln said to the Confederates when he noted the change in wording:

> The restoration of the Union is a *sine qua non* [Latin legal term
> for an indispensable action] with me, and hence my instructions
> that no conference was to be held except upon that basis.

The commissioners listened as Lincoln offered some surprisingly
liberal terms, such as allowing the Confederate states immediately back
into the House and Senate, and some terms that they knew were un-
acceptable to the Confederate Congress and its citizens. Lincoln offered
$100 per slave compensation to owners who would willingly free them,
less than ten percent of the prewar range between $1,000 and $1,500
for a fit field hand. Lincoln and Seward also confused the Confederate commissioners by hinting that the Emancipation Proclamation was
a wartime measure that might be found unconstitutional by the U.S.
Courts. In another part of the discussion, Lincoln told the Confederates that the U.S. Congress (minus the Southern states) had just passed
the Thirteenth amendment outlawing slavery. Seward suggested that if the

Southern states quickly reentered the Congress, they might be able to rally their own state legislatures to defeat the ratification of the amendment.

Grant would later remember that he was surprised at the liberal terms offered to the Confederates by Lincoln.

Grant wrote:

> They would have to agree on two points; one being that the Union should be preserved and the other that slavery should be abolished; and if they were ready to concede those two points, he was almost ready to sign his name to a blank piece of paper and permit them to fill in the balance of the terms upon which we could live together.

The Confederate commissioners, their heads swimming in confusion over what they had just heard, left the meeting with no assurances that the war would end unless the surviving Southern states gave up and returned to the Union. That much they understood from the meeting because Lincoln had not permitted any notes to be taken to produce an official transcript as to who said what and who offered what to whom.

It had been a promising meeting where peace was discussed, but the Confederate commissioners returned to Richmond knowing no matter what the Union had offered, Davis would not agree to surrender the idea of the Confederacy as a separate nation from the Union. He was committed to an independent Confederacy.

On the evening of February 6, 1865, not long after the commissioners had returned, the president addressed a large crowd in the auditorium of Richmond's African Church, a church that slave owners had built so that their people could worship in the city. On every other day but Sunday, the African Church was a favorite speaking spot for politicians because it featured a large auditorium, larger than any white church in the city.

Davis, a man normally taciturn in his dealings with the public, came alive with a rousing, extemporaneous speech condemning Lincoln for demanding the surrender of the Confederacy.

At one point Davis exclaimed:

We must lock shields together and go forward to save our country, or sink together to honorable graves. . . . If our disagreements result from passion we must exorcise it, and make the good of our country our sole aim. If we will all do our duty, we shall reap a brilliant reward. If the absentees from our armies will return, and if the local assistance be rendered which may be readily afforded, the noble Army of Northern Virginia will read General Grant a yet severer lesson than it taught him from the Rapidan to the James; while the gallant Beauregard will cause Sherman's march across Georgia to be his last.

Immediately after hearing Davis's speech, Vice President Stephens left Richmond for his Georgia home. He did not share Davis's optimism that the South could rise again. In his 1870 book, *A Constitutional View of the War*, Stephens remarked that Davis's speech was "not only bold and undaunted in tone, but had that loftiness of sentiment and rare form of expression, as well as magnetic influence in its delivery by which the people are moved to their profoundest depths."

Stephens was not the only person inspired by Davis, who previously had a reputation for giving slow-moving policy speeches. The president's off-the-cuff remarks were wildly applauded by the audience and reported favorably by newspapers that usually criticized the administration's handling of the war.

Stephens himself refused to offer any rousing speeches.

Stephens said:

I could not undertake to impress upon the minds of the people the idea that they could do what I believed to be impossible, or to inspire in them hopes which I did not believe could be realized.

While Stephens remembered being impressed with the speech in his 1870 book, he made an earlier assessment of it while languishing as a political prisoner in the summer of 1865 in Fort Warren, a cold stone fort in Boston's harbor. Stephens twice wrote in his diary that he thought Davis must have lost his mind to be so optimistic when the nation's capital was almost cut off from the rest of the Confederacy. One diary entry recorded on June 21, 1865, reads: "When he made that speech in Richmond, brilliant though it was, I looked upon it as nothing short of dementation."

☆ ☆ ☆

By April 2, 1865, the burst of Confederate patriotism bolstered by Davis's widely reported February speech had faded with the reality that talk did nothing to throw back the armies of Grant and Sherman. In the fifty-five days since Davis had given his African Church speech, at one point predicting that "before another summer solstice falls upon us, it will be the enemy that will be asking us for conferences," the Confederacy had been dealt even more blows. It would be a long, cold, hard spring before the solstice Davis predicted would arrive.

In those fifty-five days, the war in the upstate of the Carolinas, a section of the South that had seen few battles or even scouting forays by the Federals, turned heavily against the Confederacy. Sherman had crossed the Savannah River into South Carolina and then slashed his way northward, burning farms and towns until he captured the state capital of Columbia on February 17. Much of the capital city burned to the ground that same night. On that same day, Charleston, the city where the war had started, surrendered after nearly two years of constant shelling of its civilian population.

North Carolina was not faring any better. Wilmington surrendered on February 22. After securing the town, another Union force was on the march west toward the interior of the state, intending to link up with Sherman's forces. Sherman burned the armory at Fayetteville, and then headed north. Along the way he defeated the Confederate general Joseph E. Johnston's cobbled-together forces at the three-day Battle of Bentonville from March 19 to 21. Johnston's army limped away to the west after the battle, lucky that it was not totally destroyed.

Now, three weeks later, nothing stood between Sherman and North Carolina's capital at Raleigh but the battered and bruised forces of Johnston. His men could not survive another battle with Sherman. Both generals knew that fact.

Confederates in Virginia were also fighting losing battles. On March 2, the last of the Confederate forces in the Shenandoah Valley was defeated. There was so little Confederate opposition left in the Valley that Union general Phillip Sheridan abandoned the region and moved east to join Grant for the final assaults on the Army of Northern Virginia.

Grant, who had lost tens of thousands of men assaulting Confederate lines over the past year as Lee slowly retreated toward Richmond, was now content to starve the Confederates into submission as they lay in their muddy trenches. Grant knew Lee's men still had fight left in them. On March 25 Lee's men briefly broke through Grant's lines at Fort Stedman near Petersburg, but they were pushed back, effectively demonstrating to Lee that Grant's army was too strong to be defeated.

The end was near. Everyone but Davis could sense it, could feel it, and could see it.

THE FINAL FATE of the Confederacy was sealed an hour before the sun rose on April 2, 1865, when Grant ordered an assault on the Confederate trenches on the south side of Petersburg. At 4:40 a.m. the Union Sixth Corps under Major General Horatio Wright boiled out of the ground like yellow jackets in the direction of the Confederate trenches along the Boydton Plank Road. The 10,000 Federals rushing the Confederate trenches were grateful for the darkness. It made them harder targets.

Though some Union men suspected this to be the last big fight they would ever have with the Confederates they had been harassing for more than a year, others believed it was just one more futile attack on a well-dug-in enemy. The Federals had been told repeatedly over those last nine months that one day soon the Confederates would give up because the Petersburg civilians were demoralized by the constant shelling. They had been told the Confederates were starving, reduced to eating rats for meat, and boiling their own shoe leather for soup.

But each day of the first three months of 1865 had passed without any sign of a white flag being raised over the Confederate trenches.

These Sixth Corps men were going to be careful with their lives.

All it would take was one hard, concentrated volley from the Confederate trenches, and the first wave of the assault would drop dead on the ground like harvested, blue-clad wheat.

But as the corps rushed forward over the shell-pocked, grass-barren ground, there was no concentrated musket volley from the Confederate trenches, no hailstorm of canister coming from Lee's cannons. Confederate deserters had confessed to Grant and Wright that their trenches were barely manned after months of siege, disease, and desertions. The Confederate defenders were standing ten feet apart rather than shoulder to shoulder, as they should have been.

To their surprise and relief, Wright's corps swept over and into the Confederate trenches with little opposition. They captured four cannons that were loaded with canister but which the gunners had not had time to set off. Wright ordered his brigades to fan out toward Petersburg to crush any remaining opposition.

The Union's piercing of the Confederate line came so quickly that Lee himself was still napping when an aide rushed into his headquarters bedroom reporting the news. As the weary, bleary-eyed Lee was putting on the topcoat of his uniform, his First Corps commander Lieutenant General James Longstreet opened the front door of the house they were using as a headquarters. The proof of the collapse of the Confederate lines was right in front of them.

"As far as the eye could cover the field, [was] a line of skirmishers in quiet march toward us," Longstreet later wrote.

It was still before 7:00 a.m. when Lee telegraphed his first message to the Confederate secretary of war John C. Breckinridge. That telegram was forwarded to Breckinridge's superior, President Davis.

Lee wrote:

I see no prospect of doing more than holding my position here till night. I am not certain that I can do that. It is absolutely necessary that we should abandon our position tonight, or run the risk of being cut off in the morning. . . . Please give all orders that you find necessary in and about Richmond.

As Lee rode away from his headquarters back toward Petersburg, he turned in his saddle and watched as Union explosive shells set the house afire.

"I told those politicians in Richmond that this would happen. I told them," Lee said to an aide. Lee had once complained that all Congress—the Confederate Congress—was capable of doing was "chewing tobacco and eating peanuts."

Richmond's residents on the south side of the city heard the cannons booming some twenty-five miles to their south around Petersburg, but that was a sound they had grown accustomed to for more than a year and a half. They had no idea that Petersburg's lines had been pierced, and Lee's army protecting Richmond from Union attack from the south would soon be marching away to the west.

The day dawned bright and cloud free, a welcome respite from days of rain that had left the streets of Richmond deep with mud. Were it not for the knowledge that the Federals could almost hear the city's church bells, the citizens of Richmond would have been reveling in what promised to be the portent of a wonderful, colorful spring.

By 10:30 that morning, Davis had already spent several hours at his desk in the Executive Mansion poring over maps and reading Robert E. Lee's gloomy Saturday night report describing the recent loss of The Battle of Five Forks on April 1. Five Forks, a crossroads community to the southwest of Petersburg, was near the Southside Railroad, the last link the Confederacy had to supply lines extending into North Carolina. Once those rail lines were cut, all supplies coming into Petersburg and Richmond from the south would be lost. Davis had not yet received Lee's telegram detailing the predawn attack on Petersburg itself. Alone with his thoughts for now, Davis knew that the end for Richmond could now be measured by hours, not the days, weeks, and months that he had been using as guidelines since Grant had placed his forces to the east of both Richmond and Petersburg in the summer of 1864.

Frustrated that there was no fresh news from Lee, Davis rose from his desk and called to his aide, former Texas governor Frank Lubbock. Davis had promised his wife that he would not neglect going to church no matter how much work piled up on his desk.

As Davis walked down the hill toward the church with his head down and his hands clasped behind him, he ignored his surroundings while Lubbock, a man used to dry, brown, sometimes treeless Texas, reveled in their surroundings. Every house yard seemed to have a dozen or more dogwood trees bursting into bloom. The neighborhoods were awash with white petals and a fragrance that masked the streets' stench of horse manure and drying mud.

The cold, dismal winter had ended weeks ago. Now the nights were still cool, but the days were rapidly warming, bringing forth the buds on the trees and the flower bulbs from the ground. Today was shaping up to be a day where one's eyes were drawn to blue sky and the white-petaled trees in front yards.

The two were still strolling to morning worship services at St. Paul's Episcopal Church when a breathless Postmaster General John Reagan ran up. The portly Reagan, his face flushed with excitement, concern, and overexertion, handed Davis a telegram from Lee addressed to the newly installed secretary of war Breckinridge. It was just twenty minutes before church would begin at 11:00 a.m.

Davis read the telegram with a seemingly unconcerned look on his face. He scribbled a reply to Lee for Reagan to take back to the telegrapher at the War Department. He then continued his leisurely walk toward church.

Reagan, a 47-year-old former U.S. congressman who had argued against secession until his own state, Texas, voted to leave the Union, was flabbergasted. He had read the telegram. Its meaning was indisputable. Yet, the inscrutable Davis had read it without even changing the expression on his face. Neither had Davis asked Reagan, his own cabinet member, what course he thought the cabinet should take now that Federal forces appeared poised to capture the capital itself. Reagan watched Davis and Lubbock continue their meander down the hill for a few moments while he got his second wind. Reagan rushed back to the War Department to send Davis's reply to Lee.

As the sun climbed higher in the sky, Richmond's residents were filling the sidewalks on their way to church. Dryer streets meant the men were pulling on their good, low-cut, Sunday shoes rather than their boots. They were wearing their best knee-length frock coats, no longer worrying that passing carriages would fling mud from wheels onto their sleeves. Their wives were reaching back into the closets and bringing out long, formal, spring dresses. Those who still had silk dresses that had not been donated early in the war to make fine flags were smoothing the wrinkles. Such a nice day demanded nice clothes.

It was a great, cheerful day, but it was more than just a sunny Sunday. It was communion Sunday. One week away was Palm Sunday, and there were two weeks until the holiest day of the year for Christians, Easter. It was a perfect time for men and women to pray for deliverance of their nation.

Passersby nodded to Davis and he only nodded to them. If anyone spoke, it was only to say "Good morning." Richmond's residents knew Davis was not a gregarious man. Governing a nation at war with an enemy at its doorstep was not a task for the lighthearted.

It was now at least four hours since the fighting had broken the Confederate trenches in Petersburg. While Lee was still riding toward downtown Petersburg, a courier found him with a telegraphed reply from Davis to his earlier message. Aides watched Lee's eyes darken and his face flush and tighten as he read Davis's reply that Reagan had telegraphed back to Lee.

"To move tonight will involve the loss of many valuables, both for the want of time to pack and transportation," Davis had answered.

Petersburg and Richmond were about to be captured, having been threatened for weeks, and Davis was complaining about not having sufficient warning. With a stub of pencil, Lee wrote out another telegram to Davis briefly describing the military situation. Lee was done with suggestions to the politicians. He now had to save his army.

By 11:00 a.m., Davis was seated in the pew he sponsored at St. Paul's Episcopal Church at the corner of Grace and Ninth Streets, just steps from the State Capitol. He was dressed in his signature gray suit, white shirt, and black tie. His broad-brimmed hat lay beside him on the pew. He was alone, a circumstance that surprised those who had not heard that Varina and the children had left Richmond by train three nights earlier.

Residents just now finding out about Varina's leaving of the city knew it was a bad sign. If a nation's president evacuates his family from the capital, there must be bad news coming that he has not yet announced. Yet Davis sat placidly, calmly waiting for the service to begin.

The upper-crust ladies of St. Paul's had known through their own grapevine that Mrs. Davis had been planning an evacuation weeks before she actually left. She had put her finest possessions such as her collection of silk dresses and leather gloves on consignment in the shops in the city that specialized in fine ladies attire. Richmond's leading matrons, many of whom had never liked the Mississippi native, suspected those actions hinted that the Confederacy's First Lady had no plans to return to Richmond and reclaim her prized possessions.

Standing in St. Paul's pulpit was the thin-faced, diminutive Reverend Dr. Charles Minnigerode. Minnigerode had emigrated from Germany to the United States in 1839 when he began to suspect that his activism against the land-hoarding feudal system would result in his eventual death at the hands of lords who were not interested in having their subjects rebel against them. He had taken a job as a language professor at William & Mary College in Williamsburg, Virginia, in 1842 and had been ordained a priest in 1847.

It was while acting as a private tutor in Williamsburg that Minnigerode, homesick for Germany, started an American tradition. Coaxed by the children he was teaching to tell them about how he celebrated Christmas back in Germany, Minnigerode went into the forest, cut down a pine tree, and brought it into his employer's house to decorate with paper ornaments and lighted candles. By 1860 decorating Christmas trees was already an American tradition in the North and the South.

Minnigerode became rector at St. Paul's in 1852. He had always been an advocate for secession and a strong supporter of the Confederacy. Under his leadership the church had grown in numbers and influence in the city. The man himself had become something of a tourist attraction, attracting out-of-towners to standing-room-only services. One diarist once counted fourteen generals seated in two pews, including noted Presbyterian Thomas "Stonewall" Jackson. Minnigerode had officiated at the graveside service for General J. E. B. Stuart in May

1864, and then both the wedding and funeral several days later of General John Pegram after he was killed in combat south of Petersburg.

Davis had been baptized by Minnigerode in 1862. Since then Davis had attended church regularly. He enjoyed the rector's rousing, challenging sermons, which always supported his role as president. Just three months ago, a month before Davis had made his African Church speech, Minnigerode had asked his congregation:

What is it that makes the present crisis so painful?

Our reverses? *No*, Brethren! For great as they have been (and no honest man would hide their extent), we have had reverses before, and God always has blessed them to us, made them the source of greater harmony among ourselves, roused us to new and greater exertions, and taught us to bear them and repair them as men. What makes the present crisis so painful and so perilous lies not in what the enemy has done to us with his armies, but in what our own coward, faithless, selfish hearts may do.

Davis liked this reverend and his sermons. That message of pushing ahead with a cause no matter how many people were against it resonated with the president.

The service had just begun with a hymn and a prayer, when an excited clerk from the War Department yanked open the huge doors and rushed into the vestibule. He started to walk down the aisle when a sexton stopped him with a hand to the chest. The prayer was still underway. When Minnigerode finished, the sexton took the folded paper from the messenger's hand and strode down the aisle to Davis's pew.

Davis read the note. It was the second telegram from Lee that morning, the one an irritated Lee had written after being admonished by Davis that "many valuables would be lost."

"I advise that all preparation be made for leaving Richmond tonight. I will advise you later, according to circumstances," Lee had written.

Lee had not even bothered addressing Davis's earlier admonition that the general had not given the government time to pack its "valuables."

Without saying a word to Lubbock, or even nodding an apology to

Minnigerode, Davis rose from his seat, turned up the aisle, and walked quickly out of church. The congregation turned and watched. Unknowing of what the note said and unsure as to how they should react to their president rudely walking out of a church service, they exchanged worried glances and whispers. What could be so important that the president of the nation could not wait an hour before disrupting church?

Opinions differed among the congregation as to how Davis reacted when he read the telegram.

Constance Cary, the fiancée of Burton Harrison, Davis's private secretary, remembered that the president's "cold calm eye, the sunken cheeks, the compressed lip, were all as impenetrable as an iron mask."

But another member of the church said, "I plainly saw the sort of gray pallor that came over his face as he read a scrap of paper."

One person recalled that Davis "was noted to walk unsteadily out of the church."

But another watched Davis rise from his seat and walk "softly down the aisle, erect and quiet."

When Davis walked out of the church clutching the telegram in his hand, he glanced to his right toward the Virginia State Capitol lawn. What he saw would have troubled the president of any other nation: clerks building bonfires of paper money and bonds. Much of the remaining wealth of the Confederacy was either burning to ashes or blowing down the street, but no one bothered to rescue any of the $50 bills that featured Davis's idealized portrait showing an unlined, youthful, pleasant, clean-shaven face.

The real Davis, skeletal in frame, blind in one eye, and pale, with a face sometimes paralyzed by neuralgia, should have been furious at the destruction of the assets of the Confederate treasury. He had not ordered it—at least not yet. But the president seemed curiously unmoved watching bills emblazoned with his face being consumed by the fire.

CHAPTER 2

"The Direful Tidings"

BAD NEWS TRAVELS FAST. Before Davis had even completed his two-block walk from the church to his office and before he could summon his cabinet, the people of Richmond were reacting to the news that Lee was abandoning Petersburg.

The newspaper the *Richmond Whig* reported this on the following day: "Suddenly, as if by magic, the streets became filled with men walking as though for a wager, and behind them excited Negroes with trunks, bundles, and baggage of every description. All over the city it was the same—wagons, trunks, bandboxes, and their owners, a mass of hurrying fugitives."

John B. Jones, the ever-observant clerk who had a good grasp of military matters (*A Rebel War Clerk's Diary*), recognized the military predicament in which the Confederacy now found itself.

"General Lee may not have troops sufficient to defend both the city and the Danville Road [railroad] at the same time," Jones noted to himself that Sunday. Jones also observed the reaction of some other interested parties when they heard the news: "The negroes stand about mostly silent, as if wondering what will be their fate. They make no demonstrations of joy."

Jones was probably misreading the reactions of the slaves. Slaves rarely displayed their emotions. Showing joy that the South was losing the war or even feigning fear that Federals were approaching might irritate their owners. Some may have feared for their lives after hearing stories that slaves faired poorly when captured and used by Union forces. The slaves in Richmond kept their emotions in check. They waited to see which side prevailed.

Jones, normally accurate in his diary entries, was not above recording wild rumors even if he was the only intended audience: "The President told a lady that Lieutenant General Hardee was only twelve miles distant, and might get up in time to save the day."

In reality, Hardee's little force of fewer than eight thousand men was still in North Carolina with General Johnston's army, more than two hundred miles away. Davis would not have been discussing the displacement of his nation's armed forces with Richmond's matrons, but both hopeful and dire rumors were sweeping the city.

Most Richmonders who heard the news about Petersburg's fall were realists who had no illusions that Davis's leaving the church service was anything other than what it was—the end of Confederate Richmond.

Diarist Sallie Ann Brock Putnam wrote:

The direful tidings spread with the swiftness of electricity. From lip to lip, from men, women, children and servants, the news was bandied, but many received it first as only a Sunday sensation rumor. Friend looked into the face of friend to meet only an expression of incredulity; but later in the day, as the truth, stark and appalling, confronted us, the answering look was that of stony, calm despair. Late in the afternoon the signs of evacuation became obvious to even the most incredulous.

Richmond had reason to fear.

In the spring of 1862, a Union force had burned Winton, North Carolina, to the ground, the first incident of what would become a common Union method of undermining Southern civilian morale. In the summer of 1863, Vicksburg, Mississippi, had been shelled into submission with the civilian population being the primary targets. Charleston, South Carolina's civilians had been shelled for two years. All of Atlanta, Georgia, including its residential sections, had been burned by

General William T. Sherman's troops during the summer of 1864. The citizens of Columbia, South Carolina, heard their fate just two months earlier in February 1865 when Sherman's Fifteenth Corps crossed the Santee River chanting: "Hail, Columbia, happy land. If I don't burn you, I'll be dammed."

The residents of Richmond would not be surprised if the Confederate capital city was also slated to be wiped from the earth.

No one unaware of the telegram who saw the erect Confederate president striding his way along the sidewalk toward his office would have suspected anything out of the ordinary. Davis had always been inscrutable. He had a face that belied any public emotion whatsoever, a manner that was cold, distant, and formal with everyone but his closest friends and family. He treated good news for the Confederacy and bad the same way—with casual indifference.

But if Davis thought he was fooling people about the future of the city by keeping up his passive front, he was mistaken. It was now two months since his flaming speech at the African Church evoking patriotism for the cause. The reality of Richmond's situation had become real again to citizens who had forgotten the rhetoric.

Food was expensive and in short supply. According to Jones's diary, barrels of flour were selling for $700, bacon for $20 a pound. Truthfully, there was food to be had if one was willing to eat it. At a nearby hospital, the nurses and doctors regularly enjoyed a meal of a particular kind of roasted meat. One guard invited to partake passed on the offer, preferring to get his nourishment from whatever bread he could find to sop up his gruel.

"Having seen the rats in the morgue running over the bodies of dead soldiers, I had no relish for them," said the guard.

Mrs. William A. Simmons, a woman whose husband was stationed in the trenches east of Richmond, did not have much to eat, but she kept her sense of humor:

Our Confederate money is getting so reduced in value that it is a common remark when one goes out to buy, "You can carry your money in your market basket, and bring home your provisions in your purse." Even our bacon and greens lack the bacon. The one topic everywhere and on occasions is eating. Even the ministers in the pulpit consciously preach of it.

Hope too was in short supply.

The prescient Mrs. Simmons noted in her April 1 diary entry, the day before the breakthrough at Petersburg: "The air is full of strange rumors, events are thickening around us. It is plain that General Lee cannot hold out much longer. With a force smaller than is reported and almost destitute, it is impossible to hold our long lines stretching below Petersburg, along which for a mile or two, at some places, there is not a sentinel on guard."

By noon most of Davis's cabinet had gathered in his office. Present were Secretary of War John C. Breckinridge, Secretary of the Navy Stephen Mallory, Secretary of State Judah P. Benjamin, Postmaster General John Reagan, and Secretary of the Treasury George Trenholm. Listening on the sidelines were Richmond's Mayor Joseph Mayo, Virginia's governor William Smith, and former governor John Letcher. Those men would have to deal with the federal authorities after the departure of the cabinet.

Davis looked around the room at the men with whom he would share the Confederacy's fate. After four years of mixing and matching men into positions to which previous officeholders were unsuited, Davis had finally assembled what he considered a capable cabinet. He did not dwell on the irony that the Confederacy was collapsing just as his cabinet was jelling.

Breckinridge was described by female admirers as the "handsomest man in the Confederacy" thanks to his 6-foot-2-inch frame, deep blue eyes, and huge handlebar mustache that framed his angular cheeks. A former lawyer, congressman, and senator, Breckinridge had also served as vice president of the United States under James Buchanan. He had finished third in the 1860 presidential race running as a Southern Democrat. Though untrained in military affairs, Breckinridge proved to be a capable general on battlefields from Mississippi to Kentucky to Virginia. He had been appointed secretary of war in February 1865, so he had not made many worthwhile suggestions to the war effort even if Davis was inclined to give up any of his own power to direct war strategy.

While Davis may have won the Confederate presidency in 1861, Breckinridge, whose name was never brought up as a prospective president, was the more experienced politician. Now after serving as a general, during which he had won some notable battles, the former U.S. vice president had more battlefield experience than the Confederate president, who had no one shooting at him for nearly twenty years.

Mallory, former U.S. senator from Florida, no longer had much to do in his cabinet position. Most of the Confederate navy had been captured or sunk. In his earlier days, however, Mallory had proved innovative, always willing to try new ideas such as building the ironclad CSS *Virginia*, and financing the European construction of commerce raiders like the CSS *Alabama*. Mallory was fifty-two years old with a thick body and a beard that ran under his chin, but he grew no mustache. Mallory was the first Catholic to serve in any presidential cabinet, United States or Confederate. He was also a diarist and a keen observer of the personalities of the men with whom he would be keeping company on the escape from Richmond.

Benjamin sat smoking a cigar and playing with his gold-headed cane, seemingly without a care in the world. The former U.S. senator from Louisiana, Benjamin had served Davis as attorney general and as secretary of war before his present position. Davis trusted Benjamin implicitly, one of the few people he did. Benjamin was the first person of Jewish heritage to serve the government in high capacity in either the United States or the Confederacy. He had always ignored any anti-Semitic remarks he heard about himself, just as Davis ignored any about his choice of a Jew for a cabinet member.

The 53-year-old Benjamin was rotund, dark bearded, and dark skinned, and he always smiled even when he was worried about what was happening around him. Benjamin's smile often irritated those who believed he was unwilling to tell Davis bad news. Mallory looked at Benjamin and noted that the secretary of state's casual expression made him resemble "the last man outside of the ark, who assured Noah of his belief that it would not be such a hell of a shower, after all."

On the previous evening of April 1 when it was obvious even before the receipt of the Lee telegrams that Richmond would soon fall, Benjamin had even infuriated General Samuel Cooper, the ranking general in the Confederate army who had never taken a field command. Cooper walked into the secretary of state's office to find Benjamin's clerks packing boxes of records. Instead of helping sort through the valuable and the mundane, Benjamin was sitting on top of a box singing and whistling an improvisational tune he called "The Exit from Shockhoe Hill." Cooper was incensed that the secretary of state would be cracking jokes about the impending flight of high-ranking Confederates from the city they had sworn to protect.

Benjamin's jolly appearance was really a front to hide his nervousness about what would happen to the Confederate cabinet if and when it fell into the hands of the United States. After the war, the French counsel to the Confederacy, Alfred Paul, wrote that the last time he saw Benjamin was immediately after the cabinet meeting.

"I found him extremely agitated, his hands shaking, wanting and trying to do and say everything at once," Paul recalled.

The jolly demeanor Benjamin had posed in front of his fellow cabinet officers was gone in front of a single friend.

Reagan of Texas, 46, was a postmaster general and a master administrator though he too had little to do with more of the South falling into Union hands every day. Not only had Reagan built a postal system from scratch that could deliver a letter from one end of the Confederacy to the other in a few weeks, it also made money for the Confederate government. He too was a former U.S. congressman.

Trenholm, fifty-eight, had been secretary of the treasury less than a year. He knew how to make money in his civilian life as he had built a personal fortune running goods into the South from a fleet of blockade-runners. On the other hand, Trenholm's skills at managing a system of collecting taxes and setting up realistic government budgets had bested him as it had previous treasury secretaries. Though the government still had considerable hard assets in the bank vaults of Richmond, his duties were more important than ever if the government was to survive. Unfortunately, Trenholm was very ill. He suffered, like Davis, from neuralgia, a neurological condition that would frequently send shockwaves of paralyzing pain into his face without warning.

Rather than hold up the meeting, Davis sent an aide to inform the missing Attorney General George Davis (no relation to the president) to be at the train station that night. Davis, 45, was a reluctant secessionist from North Carolina but a good lawyer. Like Trenholm, he had not held a high elective office in the United States government before the formation of the Confederacy. But again like Trenholm, Attorney General Davis proved to be a valuable asset because he gave unbiased advice based on his experience as a private businessman. All the other cabinet members were politicians who gave fawning advice filtered through years of public service of pandering to other office-holders and to a fickle voting public.

Davis called the meeting to order and quickly got to business. He read Lee's telegram and told his cabinet to pack all critical papers and be prepared to leave that night. The meeting was over in a matter of minutes.

Few of the men were surprised that the evacuation of Richmond as a Confederate capital had come. Davis himself had spent the previous night helping aides box records so that they would be ready to be transported or destroyed on his order.

The cabinet's choice of where to flee was limited to one direction. Since the Southside Railroad just west of Petersburg had been captured, that left only the recently completed Richmond & Danville Railroad leading to Danville, Virginia, 140 miles to the southwest. That city was on the North Carolina border, linked by rail to Greensboro, about 40 miles south of Danville. At that moment Johnston's army, shattered and demoralized after the Battle of Bentonville two weeks earlier, was encamped at Smithfield, North Carolina, about 110 miles or five days march to the east of Greensboro. That army, as weak and recently defeated as it was, would play into Davis's vision of continuing the fight for the Confederacy.

Once Davis dismissed the meeting, the sickly Trenholm and other clerks rushed to pack what was left of the Confederate treasury. At least $600,000 in gold was packed into wooden boxes. Most of the money was in gold coins minted in both Mexico and the United States.

The coins had been deposited into the treasury early in the war by merchants and financiers confident in the long-term survival of the Confederacy. They exchanged their coins for paper notes so that the Confederate treasury could honestly tell its citizens that the paper money and bonds being issued were backed by hard assets of gold and silver held in vaults in the Confederate capital.

Davis went back to the Confederate White House where he told the servants to pack up the valuables of the residence and to give them to neighbors for safekeeping. Though he did not want to leave behind anything of true value, Davis also ordered that they do the stripping carefully. Always a perfectionist, Davis wanted the house to look presentable to any Union officer who would occupy it. It was what Southern gentlemen of his generation had been taught—to be polite even to your enemies.

He gave his servants precise instructions, including removing the family cow from the backyard so that she would not be butchered by the invading Federals. Davis followed through on a promise to Varina by crating a bust of him that she favored. That bust was sent to a neighbor who promised to hide it. Another neighbor refused to take Varina's carriage out of fear that Union troops would harm his family or property if Davis's possessions were discovered in his care.

Though the servants were confused over what to pack and what to leave, Davis coolly kept his head, even taking time to think of people who might benefit from some of the things he wanted removed from the house. He sent his favorite easy chair to the Franklin Street home where Mrs. Robert E. Lee had been living for the past several months. Crippled with rheumatoid arthritis, Mrs. Lee needed a wheelchair to get around. Davis thought she would welcome the addition of an easy chair to her home.

Into the midst of the maelstrom of activity at the Executive Mansion arrived former U.S. senator Clement Clay, of Alabama. When Davis expressed surprise at seeing his former Senate colleague, Clay, 48 years old and heavily bearded, joked: "I am probably the last man in the Confederate service to seek to enter Richmond. The trend of Confederate travel seems to be in just the opposite direction."

While the thought apparently never crossed his mind, Davis might have more closely considered his immediate offer to Clay to join the Confederate cabinet on the escape from the city. His association with Clay throughout 1864 and now at this late date of the war would give the U.S. government reason to believe the two old friends were more like criminal collaborators.

While the first leg of the cabinet's escape would be by rail, escape from the Confederacy by ocean had been an occasional topic with Davis. Before Varina had left with the children, her husband told her to "make for the Florida coast and from there board a ship to a foreign country."

It may not have been by chance that two of the men who would be accompanying Davis to Danville had skills that could come in handy should the party make it to a coast.

One was Confederate navy commander John Taylor Wood, Davis's nephew by his first wife and grandson of former president Zachary Taylor. The 34-year-old Taylor, a Minnesota native, had declined to follow his father into the army. Instead, he joined the United States Navy as a 17-year-old midshipman. He later won an appointment to the United States Naval Academy, graduating in 1853. He spent the next eight years at sea chasing slave-trading ships and as an instructor at the academy. In 1861 he resigned from the United States Navy and joined the Confederate navy as one of its most experienced officers.

After early, wasted appointments commanding shore batteries, Taylor was assigned to the CSS *Virginia*, the ironclad that fought the USS *Monitor*. After leading several raids to capture Union vessels in 1862, exploits so dangerous and successful that he won the rare official thanks of the Confederate Congress, Taylor was invited by his uncle to be a military aide. Davis rewarded his nephew with the rank of colonel of cavalry. The unusual dual rank in two different services, plus the fact that he was the president's nephew, gave Wood a level of trust between him, politicians, and officers in the two services. It was in 1864 that Wood found his true calling as a formidable sea raider. While commanding the CSS *Tallahassee*, he took more than thirty-three Union vessels.

Not on the same train, but soon to follow the cabinet to Danville was the most famous of sailors for both the North and the South, Admiral Raphael Semmes. Semmes was a 55-year-old native of Maryland who practiced looking flamboyant by keeping a waxed mustache whose ends sprang several inches from each side of his face. He had gone to sea with the United States Navy when he was 14 and had spent more than 35 years in the service of his country, including winning commendations for trying to save his ship during a violent storm off Mexico in 1846. Early in 1861 he resigned his commission as a commander and cast his lot with the Confederacy.

Semmes was famous in the South and infamous in the North for his command of first the CSS *Sumter* and later the CSS *Alabama*, two fast raider ships designed to run down Northern commercial vessels such as cargo and whaling ships. In the course of two years, Semmes' two commands accounted for the capture of eighty-seven Union vessels. No Union ship captain left port without fearing that he would one day see Semmes' sails rushing over the horizon toward him. Semmes was also a formidable foe when he had to do battle. He sank the warship USS *Hatteras* off Texas in a battle that lasted just thirteen minutes.

Semmes made the mistake of fighting the USS *Kearsage* off the coast of France on June 19, 1864, when the CSS *Alabama* was badly in need of an overhaul and fresh gunpowder. The *Alabama* had been at sea so long that she leaked at several points in her hull, and her powder was so damp that her cannons were not firing as hot as they should have been. When the *Alabama*'s stern was shot away, Semmes jumped into the sea, but he was quickly pulled from the water by a British ship. Eventually he returned to Richmond and continued to command the ships and ironclads making up the last remnants of the James River Squadron.

Not only were two of the South's most famous sea captains planning to escape south with Davis, there were at least a dozen skilled ship captains and sailors, refugees from the James River Squadron, who were also retreating toward Danville. If Davis needed an experienced crew of sailors to go wherever he wanted in the world reachable by the seven seas, all he had to do was walk through the train cars and recruit from the flower of the Confederate navy.

As for his long-range plans after escaping from Richmond, Davis seemed determined to head for the vastness of the Trans-Mississippi Theater (Arkansas, Texas, Missouri, Indian Territory, and parishes of Louisiana west of the river) where he hoped to find troops still in the field who had not lost the will to fight. He intended to meet up with General Edmund Kirby Smith around Galveston, Texas, an island just a few miles from the coast from which blockade-runners still successfully slipped in and out of port. Ideally, Davis wanted to stop along the way to Texas and link up with another nephew, General Richard Taylor, who was leading a small army quartered near the coastal (but captured) city of Mobile, Alabama.

While Davis would never have admitted it, trying to reach Taylor and Kirby Smith by taking a land route would be virtually impossible because much of the territory between Virginia and Texas was already occupied by Union troops. The best way for the cabinet to reach both of these armies quickly would be by sea. But finding a fast ship large enough to accommodate the cabinet was no longer as easy as it had been just a few months earlier. The big blockade running ports of Charleston, South Carolina, and Wilmington, North Carolina, had been captured. Owners of many of the most successful blockade-runners that had routinely run back and forth to Bermuda and to Nassau, Bahamas, were now holding them in foreign ports, finally convinced that their profitable ventures of trading cotton for war material were over.

It was still possible but not promising to make for the Atlantic coast of the Carolinas. If a small party could slip between Grant's army around Petersburg, Virginia, and Sherman's army around Smithfield, North Carolina, they could make for the coastal network of numerous small rivers and streams. Once on the coast, they might find loyal citizens willing to give them a boat seaworthy enough to run to the Bahamas or Bermuda. A small craft, disguised as a fishing boat operating along the Carolina coast, might escape the attention of the Union blockaders who would be concentrating on watching for larger blockade-runners still trying to make a profit.

If the cabinet could survive Atlantic storms in a small boat and reach a neutral country like Bermuda or the Bahamas, they could then board safer, foreign-flagged ships bound for Europe. Or if they still felt loyalty to Davis and the Confederacy, they could risk their freedom by following him and boarding a blockade-runner that would make for Alabama and Texas. One possibility that could have crossed Davis's mind was reaching and boarding the CSS *Stonewall*, a French-built, iron-hulled raider that was supposed to be on its way across the Atlantic to Havana, Cuba. No Union wooden blockading ship would have been able to stand against the *Stonewall*, a ship designed to break the Union blockade. All Davis would have known on April 2 was that the *Stonewall* should be at sea on its way to Cuba.

But Davis did not try for the shorter escape route toward the Carolina coast. The option Davis apparently chose without conferring with his cabinet was a combination land and sea escape. He chose a longer route that would take them even further from the coast, first into upstate South Carolina and then into Georgia with coastal Florida assumed as the final destination.

The longer route seemed plausible. Florida was still mostly unmolested by Union forces. The third state to secede from the Union had been a blockade-runner's haven early in the war. But since it was also the smallest of the Confederate states in population, fewer than 45,000 people, there had been little buildup of prewar infrastructure such as railroads or even large towns or ports, so large quantities of supplies could not be brought into Florida and then easily shipped north. The blockade-runners based in Florida were mostly small boats and schooners that could carry a few bales of cotton to Cuba or the Bahamas while carrying loads of lead and arms back to the peninsula that local forces would use.

However, while Florida did not have large blockade-runners, it did have the longest coastline of any state in the Union or the Confederacy at nearly 2,300 miles. Hidden along both the Atlantic and the Gulf of Mexico coast were scores of inlets and rivers that were too numerous for the United States Navy to patrol continuously. With prior word sent ahead by courier, loyal Confederates could have prepared large boats and small ships for the Confederate cabinet's use.

But, the escape plan would take weeks to effect, even if nothing went wrong. If the cabinet could successfully avoid Union capture by taking trains south through North Carolina, switching to wagons and horses through unoccupied upstate South Carolina, and then going through unoccupied upstate Georgia, there was a chance they could stay ahead of any pursuing Union troops and disappear into Florida's still unoccupied panhandle. From north Florida, they would make their way through the upper center of the state before splitting off into one of two directions, either to the southeast below Union-occupied St. Augustine on the east coast or to the southwest toward the Gulf of Mexico on the west coast.

Heading southeast to Florida's Atlantic coast was the less desirable direction. While the Union blockade on that side of the state was light because there were few coastal towns below St. Augustine that could have engaged in blockade-running, there would also be fewer people living near the coast who could be called on to help with the escape. Leaving for Alabama from Florida's Atlantic coast would also have added hundreds of miles and days of risky ocean sailing before Davis could reach Mobile.

Leaving from Florida's west coast had its own problems, principally that those waters were more heavily guarded because Union ships blanketed the Gulf to capture blockade-runners trying to use Mobile and Galveston. Still there was opportunity there. While Florida's small, blockade-running port of Cedar Key had been captured in 1862, the coastline north of Cedar Key was still in Confederate hands and actively used for making salt that was shipped to Confederate armies. This part of the coast bending upward and westward was just too long for the Union navy to patrol fully. Florida natives living close to the coast and still loyal to the Confederacy would know where boats and ships capable of open-sea travel would be hidden up small creeks and canals. If the cabinet's boat could hug the coast disguised as a fishing vessel, they could escape detection all the way to finding Taylor's army.

The hard part facing the cabinet was getting to Florida. The state line lay 600 miles from Richmond. The sparsely settled Gulf Coast, the ideal starting point for a voyage to Mobile, was another 150 miles beyond the border. An unimpeded, continuous trek by train, wagon, and horse would take nearly a month.

One wild card was available in the deck of the last game the Confederacy was playing that could be thrown on the table by the Union at any time. If it landed close to him, Davis would have to fold.

That wild card was the month-long, 6,000-man cavalry raid of Union major general George Stoneman who had left Knoxville, Tennessee on March 25 and who was now somewhere in the North Carolina mountains. Stoneman's horse soldiers were burning Confederate warehouses and factories. No one in the Confederacy had any idea where Stoneman's men might turn up or how quickly. Both Grant's and Sherman's armies were tied down by slow-walking infantry, but Stoneman's cavalry could cover up to 50 miles in a day. If a Union telegram or a courier reached Stoneman detailing that Davis and the cabinet were moving south and had not yet even entered North Carolina, an interception would have been possible.

If Davis had given any thought or planning to how quickly the cabinet would move from one location to another, he kept it to himself. All his cabinet and the public knew was that they would be leaving Richmond on the night of April 2. The cabinet gathered at the rail station around 6:00 p.m., along with scores of Richmonders, all of whom heard that the cabinet was leaving the city and who hoped that they too would be able to take a refugee train out of town. It soon became clear to the citizens, however, that only two trains would be leaving the city that night. Only important government employees would be joining the cabinet's flight. Average citizens would have to face whatever wrath the Yankees intended to inflict on the city.

There were some thirty locomotives left in the city by the end of the war but few that were fully operational. Most had been taken out of service due to lack of parts. The best locomotives and rolling stock had already been evacuated or captured by Union cavalry raiders. The one selected for evacuating the cabinet seemed to be the best of the worst left in Richmond. Its wood-fueled firebox leaked, as did its boiler, meaning it took longer to make enough steam to pull any cars. Under normal circumstances the locomotive assigned to pull the cars carrying the cabinet would have been dismantled for parts, but the railroad president had no choice. It would have to be pressed into service to rescue the Confederate government. A second engine was found to pull the treasury train loaded with the gold and bills that had been gathered from Richmond's banks.

Perhaps surprisingly, no military escort was gathered to protect the train on which the Confederate nation's most important officials would be traveling.

While either Davis or Breckinridge could have ordered an escort to be put together, Lee, who sent the telegram suggesting the cabinet leave Richmond, never offered any of his 30,000 troops scattered between Richmond and Petersburg for the job. All of Lee's messages to his generals in Richmond revolved around how they should rendezvous with the rest of the Army of Northern Virginia leaving Petersburg somewhere to the west of both cities.

Lee knew that Davis and the others would be using the railroad line as an escape route as Breckinridge had asked him in one telegram how much longer the Danville Railroad would be open.

"I think the Danville Road will be safe until tomorrow," was Lee's terse if indefinite reply in his only known telegram that seemed to have anything to do with the pending evacuation of the cabinet.

In reality, Lee had no idea if the Danville Railroad was safe. His troops had lost control of Five Forks and Sutherland Station in successive days. By midnight on April 2, a time when the cabinet train might be passing through Amelia Court House, no one in the Confederate army could guarantee that Union cavalry would not be astride the Danville tracks, waiting to see what they could capture from any trains passing their way. On the morning of April 2, the way toward the Danville line was wide open if the Federals chose to move on it.

With his lines broken at Petersburg, Lee did not have time to contemplate the fate of his boss, President Davis. Lee just wanted to evacuate his army. Lee's last telegram to Breckinridge read: "All troops will be directed to Amelia Court House," a railroad station some forty miles to the southwest, a two-day march for troops.

Amelia Station was on the Danville line, and the cabinet would pass through the small town that night on its escape, a fact that Davis would have to deal with in a postwar controversy involving getting food to Lee's army.

At a time when Davis could have been working with Breckinridge to find military units in the city who could cover his escape, he was more interested in packing up or dispersing the family's personal possessions to keep them out of the hands of advancing Federals. Davis seems to have given little thought to his own safety.

There was cavalry available in Richmond who could have ridden in front of, and beside, the Danville-bound train Davis had already decided would be the cabinet's best option for leaving the city. Brigadier general Martin Gary, a thin, bald man who had been given the nickname "The Bald Eagle" for his high-pitched voice that could be heard above all battle noise, commanded at least 1,000 fully equipped cavalrymen made up of the remnants of cavalry regiments from South Carolina, Georgia, and Virginia. Gary, a Harvard-educated trial lawyer before the war, had been one of South Carolina's legislators who had carried the state out of the Union in December 1860. He was one of the few officers still alive and still unwounded who had fought in virtually every major battle in Virginia starting with First Manassas in July 1861. Gary remained an ardent secessionist in 1865 and presumably would have welcomed the opportunity to escort the president of the Confederacy to safety—if only he had been asked.

The only troops specifically assigned to leave Richmond as part of the cabinet's entourage would not be on the same train as Davis, nor would they be soldiers. They were not even men.

The first military escort even close to Davis on the escape south would be little more than teenaged boys who had never faced Union forces. At the cabinet meeting earlier in the day, Mallory volunteered the services of the sixty midshipmen of the Confederate Naval Academy to be assigned as escorts—not for the president and the cabinet—but for the Confederate treasury that would leave Richmond on a separate train.

Mallory's volunteering of the midshipmen—most between the ages of 14 and 18—at least gave him something constructive to do in his cabinet post in the waning days of the Confederacy. Most of the Confederate navy's coastal and river-based ironclads and ocean-going commerce raiders had been either sunk by their own crews or captured.

One of the few surviving ships was the side-wheeler CSS *Patrick Henry*, the naval academy school ship on which the boys practiced their seamanship.

The midshipmen had no warning that they would soon be real land soldiers rather than practicing blue water sailors. Their 39-year-old commander, Lieutenant William H. Parker, a native New Yorker who resigned his United States Navy lieutenancy at the beginning of the war, must have suspected something was up when he found Mallory on April 1 pacing up and down the sidewalk in front of his house practicing the cocking and firing of a revolver. Suspicious at the naval secretary's behavior, Parker asked about any war-front news, but Mallory assured him that "the news that day from General Lee was good, and that affairs around Petersburg looked promising." Parker, satisfied, then asked to spend the night in town, which Mallory granted.

The next day, April 2, Parker was back on board the CSS *Patrick Henry* when he received a vague order from Mallory for the cadets to report to the Danville train depot at 6:00 p.m. A curious Parker started walking to Mallory's house to get him to elaborate on the order. Along the way he noted Union prisoners being transported in daylight rather than at night, which had been the custom throughout the war. Within a block he stopped a panicked government clerk who told him that the cabinet was leaving. On his own, without any orders from Mallory, Parker evacuated all the midshipmen from the *Patrick Henry* and ordered it burned later that night to keep it out of the hands of the Federals. He then put his cadets on the march toward the train station. He had not anticipated that Mallory's order meant the cadets would be leaving Richmond and the muskets, with which they had probably rarely trained, were to be used to protect the Confederacy's last stocks of wealth.

Parker was struck by how quiet the city seemed to be, particularly since everyone knew the Yankees would soon be entering it.

"Perhaps the pale, sad faces of the ladies aided to bring it about [the 'peculiar quiet']. They knew it was impossible for them to leave, and they prepared to share the fate of their beloved city with the same heroism they had exhibited during the past four years," Parker wrote.

The midshipmen guarded the treasure train with the fierce determination of youth, keeping curious citizens and potential thieves back with all the looks of seriousness they could muster on their whiskerless faces. All the boys had been told what was in the wooden boxes, but they had no thoughts of stealing it. They were more interested in winning their place in the history of the war.

Parker and the boys waited at the station for the departure of the first train in line that would be carrying the cabinet. He observed that Davis "preserved his usual calm and dignified manner" and that Breckinridge "was as cool and gallant as ever," but the rest of the cabinet's nervousness was showing: "[They] had the air of wishing to be off."

Finally, around 11:00 p.m. on the night of April 2, more than three hours after the deadline Lee had set for the cabinet to leave the city, Davis's train pulled out of the station. The treasury train was delayed until all of Richmond's banks had loaded their paper money. Parker warned his boys to be ready for trouble because the social order of the city was breaking down as deserters and street ruffians sensed that no one in authority was left to keep them from breaking into warehouses.

Someone in authority ordered that the city's whiskey barrels be broken and turned over to prevent just the sort of unruliness that was starting to sweep the city. Parker watched in disgust as men and women used their own shoes and boots to scoop up whiskey flowing down street gutters.

Just before his train was ready to leave, Parker heard a series of explosions that marked the end of the James River Squadron, including his own CSS *Patrick Henry*. Not long after the explosions, Parker noticed that fires had begun to break out around the city, a result of the insistence by General Richard Ewell, commander of the Confederate forces protecting the city, that cotton bales stored in the city's warehouses be burned rather than just pouring turpentine over them to make them worthless.

Finally, four hours after the cabinet's train had left, Parker's treasure train pulled out of the station.

Left on the platform were Richmonders who now knew they would have to return to their homes and face the Yankees who were expected to arrive at any minute. Parker described it as a "horror" to leave so many friends behind to an unknown fate.

Among those still standing on the platform were fifty slaves. Just before the second train left, a slave trader named Lumpkin approached the platform with a chain gang of fifty black men and women that he hoped to sell to someone down the line. When Lumpkin was turned away at rifle point by the midshipmen, the man simply unlocked the chains and shooed his happy former property into the darkness. At a prewar cost of at least $1,000 per able field hand, Lumpkin had just given up more than $50,000.

Within a few minutes of the treasure train passing over the rail bridge over the James River and within a few hours of the Confederate cabinet leaving the city, civilization seemed to dissolve in Richmond.

As the Seventh South Carolina Cavalry, part of Gary's cavalry brigade rear guard, pushed through the Rocketts section of Richmond on its way to the southwest side of the city to cross the James, Lieutenant Colonel Edward M. Boykin noted:

The peculiar population of that suburb were gathering on the sidewalk; bold, dirty looking women, who had evidently not been improved by four years' military association, dirtier (if possible) looking children, and here and there skulking, scoundrelly looking men, who in the general ruin were sneaking from the holes they had been hiding in.

As he rode, Boykin noted "bare-headed women" looting warehouses as he watched:

A scene that beggars description, and which I hope never to see again—the saddest of many of the sad sights of the war—a city undergoing pillage at the hands of its own mob, which the standards of an empire were being taken from its capitol, and the tramp of a victorious enemy could be heard at its gate.

Richmond had collected within its walls the refuse of the war—thieves and deserters, male and female, the vilest of the vile were there, but strict military discipline had kept it down. Now, in one moment, it was all removed—all restraint was taken off—and you may imagine the consequences.

As he rode down Franklin Street (past the house where Mrs. Robert E. Lee was living), Boykin sadly observed:

At the windows we could see the sad and tearful faces of the kind Virginia women, who had never failed the soldier in four long years of war and trouble, ready to the last to give him devoted attendance in his wounds and sickness, and to share with his necessities the last morsel.

As Gary himself passed over the Mayo Bridge, he called out to the man assigned to demolish the bridge: "Blow her to Hell!"

As generals Gary and Ewell rode away, they stopped on a high plain on the south bank of the James and watched as fires seemed to spring up at dozens of places within the city. Ewell's orders to burn the military warehouses had been carried out, but as the citizens feared, the fires were already getting out of control and spreading to the residential areas. Richmond, the city that had withstood numerous Union campaigns that brought the blue-coated enemy so close they could hear the city's church bells, had not fallen to an enemy attack. It was set ablaze by the men who had spent the last four years defending the capital city.

The Union soldiers would put out the fires and push into the city within hours of the last Confederates passing over the bridges. Among the first Union soldiers to put down their muskets and pick up fire hoses and axes would be several regiments of United States Colored Troops, freed slaves who had joined the Union army to free other blacks. Instead of letting the Confederate capital burn to the ground, these black men who had every reason to hate Richmond helped save it.

With the two escaping trains huffing and puffing down the Danville line into the darkness with its unknown dangers, Davis and the Confederate cabinet were now officially on the run. The attempt to continue the war without a capital city to defend had begun.

CHAPTER 3

"My Husband Will Never Cry for Quarter"

BEFORE HE LEFT FOR THE TRAIN STATION that Sunday night, April 2, President Jefferson Davis took time out of completing his official duties to attend to some personal business. Even with tens of thousands of Union soldiers marching on Richmond and with all the details of evacuating the cabinet and the Confederate treasury to be tended to, Davis sat down at his desk to write a letter to his wife, Varina.

Davis loved writing and receiving letters, and he expected everyone in his family to share his desire to communicate. The written word helped him express thoughts and emotions that he often could not— or would not—say in public. Even short absences and short distances from the family required the person who was leaving to write a letter back to Davis. Just two weeks before this frantic evening, the president had written to his seven-year-old son Jefferson, Jr., who had insisted on visiting the trenches in Petersburg. Over his wife's concerned objections about letting the boy visit a war zone where snipers watched for movement in the trenches and where cannon shells were regularly lobbed into the city, Davis granted his son permission to play visiting inspector of the troops.

"I was very happy that my dear boy was able to write to me about himself and to give me news from the trenches," Davis wrote to his son, who was less than twenty-five miles away and coming home soon. "Your Mother and the children are well and are anxious to have you back. It made me glad to hear from your Cousin Joe that you were a good boy," the president wrote, ending the letter, "With much love, your father, Jeff'n Davis."

Ignoring the rushed movements and irritated shouts of the servants trying to pack the family's possessions, Davis sat down at his desk on the second floor of the Executive Mansion. As he dipped the pen into the inkwell, he hesitated, thinking about what he was about to say to his wife. As he composed in his head, another thought crept into his consciousness. He knew where Varina was, but the Union army did not. With the Federals closing in on Richmond, he worried that any courier making his way through enemy lines could be captured and the letter would tip off the Federals to his family's location. If Varina and the children fell into Federal hands, he would have no choice but to trade himself for their freedom and safety. Davis put his pen down, resolving to write to this wife from Danville the next day. Lee had promised that town was safe for now, and the way south from there should be free of Union soldiers.

☆　☆　☆

VARINA WAS A PERCEPTIVE WOMAN whose assessment in 1843 on first meeting her future husband at a Christmas party was that he "has a way of taking for granted that everyone agrees with him, which offends me."

Despite Davis's irritating cocksureness that he was master of every subject, Varina sensed while still at the party that she had found the man she would marry. She claimed not to be able to tell how old he was, though he was obviously much older than her 17 years. When she first saw him before speaking to him, he was on horseback, riding so confidently that she described him being "free and strong." He was tall with blue-gray eyes. He had thick hair and a prominent, sharp nose. He kept a radiant smile hidden behind his thin lips except for when he was talking to her. There appeared to be only one thing truly wrong with him. He was of the wrong political party.

"Would you believe it, he is refined and cultivated, yet he is a Democrat!" she exclaimed to her mother in the same letter. Her family was Whig.

The political differences were only the first of the problems her parents saw with any budding romance. Varina was still a teenager. Their daughter's would-be beau was more than twice her age at 35. He was also a widower. As she would discover from asking mutual friends, Davis still carried a ten-year guilt for taking his first wife home to Mississippi in the middle of malaria season. She died before the honeymoon was over.

Davis also appeared to be unhealthy and too reserved for genial public discourse. While Varina described her beau as "slim," her parents thought him cadaverous in appearance. While he might have a sweet voice and engaging smile for her, they thought him too formal and superior when addressing anyone he did not already know. He was not at all the charming, amusing, young, and lively son-in-law that parents dream of becoming their daughter's husband. They tried to steer her away from Davis, but they quickly learned that their daughter and her beau possessed at least one common trait: both were stubborn. She refused to be dissuaded by her parents that she should keep looking for a better first love. He refused to believe that any other woman besides this headstrong teenager could ever make him happy again.

In some respects the two were polar opposites. Varina was dark-skinned, while Davis was pale. She was vivacious and outgoing in public, while he was shy and withdrawn. She loved to attend parties. He preferred surrounding himself with a few close friends. She loved to eat fine foods, enough to make her pleasingly plump, while he ate sparingly and only then when forced to fuel his body so he could continue to work.

But for every trait that irritated Varina, her beau had one that complemented her own personality. They were both well educated; he being a graduate of the United States Military Academy and she having studied Latin and English at a girl's finishing school in Philadelphia. They both respected honesty and held back nothing about their pasts when learning about each other. He readily told her of his first wife's death and his years of mourning her. She told him that her father's business had driven the family into bankruptcy. They shared a deep interest in politics even if they were on opposite sides of the political spectrum.

They both enjoyed jousting with their peers in lively conversation over a wide variety of topics.

The couple courted just over a year, with her mother continually though fruitlessly pointing out the age differences and his character flaws and with Varina herself pondering his overbearing tendencies. Nothing dissuaded her. She went into the marriage knowing that he would always assert that he was right and everyone else was always wrong. Davis was, above everything else that was part of his character, self-confident in his own abilities. It was a trait he had displayed since his childhood in Kentucky and later Mississippi.

As a seven-year-old, Jefferson and his younger sister were walking along a dark trail on their way to school when they heard someone or something coming down the same path. Jefferson could see what he thought were chair legs about six feet above the ground, indicating that the coming terror was a drunken chair mender who terrified children in the region by his unusual and rude behavior. As his sister started to run into the woods, Jefferson grabbed her hand and told her that he was not scared of the man, and he would protect her from harm. Together, the two children waited for the man to approach them. As the chair legs grew closer, Jefferson saw that the chair was actually a buck deer's antler rack. The deer itself turned into the woods when it saw the two small children. For the first time in his life, the future president of his nation had stared down what he perceived to be a danger to himself and family. He had told his sister that he would take care of her and he had.

Keeping promises would be a hallmark of Davis's life.

After transferring from Transylvania College in Lexington, Kentucky, into the United States Military Academy in 1824, Davis learned for the first time in his life that authority figures often expected him to follow their rules rather than his. Davis did not like anyone telling him—not even academy instructors—what to do. On several occasions he found himself in trouble, usually involving minor offenses such as not being in his room for the head count, but also for more serious problems such as being caught off campus in a local bar called Benny Havens.

At a court martial that could have resulted in his expulsion, Davis maintained that while a superior officer had seen him in the bar, the officer had not seen him drinking alcohol, so the officer's assumption that he had been drinking could not be proved. Impressed with Davis's quick thinking of coming up with an improbable defense, the court martial judges declined to dismiss Davis from the academy.

Davis proved his coolness and bravery in the face of real danger later in the year when a laboratory accident nearly caused an explosion as the class was experimenting with chemicals. After the instructor ran from the room when the experiment went wrong and the chemicals began an unexpected reaction, Davis calmly threw the materials out the window. The same officers who had been willing to dismiss him now gave him credit for saving lives and academy property. Davis never became a favorite of the academy officers, nor did he try any harder to fit into the system. He graduated twenty-ninth out of thirty-seven cadets in 1828.

Despite his discipline problems, Davis remembered that "the four years I remained at West Point made me a different creature from that which nature had designed me to be," he wrote to a sister after his graduation.

Davis proved to be a good infantry officer, overcoming his reputation as a stubborn student. When he assisted in the 1832 capture of Black Hawk, an Indian chief who led an uprising in Illinois, the Indian proved prophetic when he spoke admirably of the "good and brave young chief" who treated him with respect while Davis was taking him to a fort where he would be imprisoned.

One good thing came out of the Black Hawk war for Lieutenant Davis. He met Sarah Knox Taylor, the daughter of his commander, Colonel Zachary Taylor. After clashing with another officer and undergoing another court martial that resulted in his acquittal, Davis resigned from the army to marry Sarah. His young wife would be dead from malaria within a few weeks of moving to her new home in steamy Mississippi. His former father-in-law would blame Davis for his daughter's sudden death. They would not make peace with each other until another war brought them together.

Devastated and guilt ridden that he had somehow contributed to his bride's death for taking her into a region known for malaria, Davis threw himself into his civilian life for the next ten years by building his plantations. He did it as he did everything else he had always done in his life—his way.

Davis and his brother Joseph ran their plantations in a different way than any of their neighbors. They believed themselves to be responsible for their slaves' long-term well-being. Davis forbade whipping as discipline for slaves, and he encouraged his people to create their own government and courts to deal with minor offenses such as stealing from each other. Other slaveholders looked askance at his liberal attitude toward slaves, but Davis ignored them.

☆　☆　☆

THEN CAME THAT DAY when the sober, successful planter met the 17-year-old visitor at the party. He had ignored the opportunity to meet other women for more than a decade. Now, something about her bold, mature ways surprised him and helped change him from the recluse he had been since Sarah's death.

About the same time Davis met Varina, he took up his brother Joseph's challenge to get involved in politics. After failing to win a state House seat, but winning the attention of party elders, Davis came back the next year and captured a seat in the United States House of Representatives in 1844. Davis found that voters enjoyed his speeches, even though he did not like meeting them personally.

Davis learned that politicians never counted little white lies as being dishonest. On at least one occasion during his House campaign, Davis told the crowd that if elected, he would be proud to serve "Mississippi—the land of my birth." He had been born in Kentucky.

Davis arrived in Washington in 1845 nationally unknown, but he did not go unnoticed. One fellow freshman representative, Henry W. Hilliard of Alabama, vividly remembered Davis's arrival in the capitol with a description that would follow him for the rest of his life: "His appearance was prepossessing. Tall, slender, with a soldierly bearing; a fine head, an intellectual face; there was a look of culture and refinement about him that made a favorable impression from the first."

The newcomer did not follow protocol from the opening days of the Congress. Instead of sitting back and watching the incumbents conduct business while keeping his freshman mouth shut, Davis rose repeatedly to offer his and Mississippi's opinions on issues facing the United States. He was in favor of speeding up the process of allowing foreigners to become American citizens. He was against allowing Great Britain to expand its colonies in the far northwestern territory of Oregon. He was all in favor of the idea of manifest destiny, that the nation had a God-given right to expand from the Atlantic to the Pacific.

Davis was such a good speaker that on at least one occasion, Varina remembered that he attracted the attention of an elderly congressman from Massachusetts who sat transfixed, watching Davis talk.

"We shall hear more from this young man, I fancy," said former president John Quincy Adams, who loved governing so much that he spent the rest of his life in the House of Representatives.

It was while in Congress that Davis showed future political friends and enemies that he never backed down from a position. Once in a debate where Davis was trying to win appropriations to build forts along the Gulf Coast, a congressman from the North who was seeking appropriations for his own district along the Great Lakes asked if Davis were willing to trade votes.

Davis stared at his fellow Congressman and then carefully in measured tones made his position clear: "Sir, I make no terms. I accept no compromises."

In the spring of 1846, Davis turned his attention to modernizing the United States Army. He suggested issuing rifles to two regiments of the peacetime army, replacing the older, short-range, smoothbore flintlock muskets that were the standard, but obsolete, weapon the army still used. The bill passed. A few months later, the need for a modern army would manifest itself when on April 25, the Mexican Army crossed the Rio Grande River into Texas. They eventually clashed with a U.S. force under the overall command of General Zachary Taylor, Davis's former father-in-law. Blood was drawn. On May 9, 1846, President James K. Polk declared war.

Davis made known his war views when he wrote a letter to the editor of the *Vicksburg Sentinel and Expositor* saying: "Let the treaty of peace be made at the city of Mexico," meaning that he felt the

United States had the right to invade Mexico and capture its capital to end the war. He also hinted that if Mississippians were willing to form a volunteer regiment, he would be willing to leave Congress to lead it. The editor added to Davis's message by leading the cheer for volunteers and asserting that Davis was "the native, gallant, glorious son of our soil" ready to "lead you to your country's service."

Once again it appeared in print that Davis was a native of Mississippi rather than Kentucky. He did not write a letter back to Vicksburg to correct the editor's mistake. He had been in Mississippi so long, Davis himself might have forgotten his own roots.

Varina was appalled at her husband's plans to volunteer for a distant war. He had not discussed with her the idea of putting on a uniform nearly ten years after he had taken it off. She tried arguing him out of it, but even her frantic and copious tears failed to dissuade him: "I have cried until I am stupid," she told her mother.

Her concern was not necessarily that Davis would be killed on the battlefield. She worried that he might not even make it to Texas before expiring from one of the medical conditions he already had. She worried about recurring bouts of malaria, which had almost killed him ten years earlier. She worried about him eating. She had enough trouble making Davis take his meals when she would see him at home, once commenting that he "ate no more than a child." She worried about his left eye. That eye was continually infected and inflamed from what was probably herpes simplex, the same virus that causes fever blisters. She worried about his neuralgia, which could cause him immobilizing pain when he suffered attacks. He was a sickly man, although he would admit it to no one. Varina had written her mother when they first came to Washington that she worried about her husband exhausting himself without telling her how seriously ill he felt: "You know how patiently Jeffy always bears suffering."

If the afflictions common to Jefferson Davis had belonged to any other man, he would have been under the constant care of a doctor. But they were part of who Jefferson Davis was, and he did not listen to man or woman. He certainly was not going to allow any physical infirmity to keep him from leading his Mississippians against Mexico, which had attacked his country.

Before he left Congress for his volunteer assignment, Davis made a speechifying mistake on the House floor, one that would come back to haunt him in 1865. Several pacifist congressmen had previously made speeches decrying the need for West Point and professionally trained officers. When Davis rose to praise some victories won by his father-in-law Taylor, he asked, jokingly, if such victories could have been won by a blacksmith or a tailor.

Davis meant no harm in the statement, only to emphasize that professional military training was necessary to win military victories. But at least one former blacksmith and one former tailor who were now high and mighty congressmen took offense at the implication that their previous professions were not honorable. The tailor was Tennessee's representative Andrew Johnson, who now had an instant reason to take an intense dislike to his Mississippi colleague. On the House floor, Johnson denounced a bewildered, then increasingly irritated, Davis for being part of an aristocracy that looked down on the working class.

Davis and Johnson would have more differences with each other in about twenty years.

When Davis received his appointment of colonel of volunteers, he immediately asked the United States government to supply his 1,000 men with the latest in military technology. He wanted the same type of percussion cap rifles he had suggested for the regular army in 1846. Percussion rifles were a tremendous leap in technology from the antiquated, smoothbore, flintlock muskets the regular army was still using because of decades of congressional resistance to creating a modern army. President James Polk agreed with Davis, although General Winfield Scott suggested that the massed firepower of muskets was still preferable to the rifles.

Before he left his Mississippi plantation, Davis assigned its care to his oldest, best, and most trusted friend, James Pemberton, a slave highly skilled in managing large numbers of acres and the people it took to farm them.

On February 22, 1847, Davis and his regiment, commonly known as the Mississippi Rifles after the new weapons he had demanded for them, won fame at the Battle of Buena Vista, though they also suffered more than a third killed and wounded. Davis himself was wounded in the right foot, but he stayed in the saddle until the battle was over. The stand of the Mississippians led by their brave volunteer congressman who refused to leave the field even after he was wounded was too big a newspaper story to ignore. Davis slowly recovered from his wound, unaware that newspapers across the nation, North and South, were making him into a national hero.

When Davis returned to Mississippi, he discovered men were already planning his future for him. Without much debate, he was appointed U.S. senator, replacing one who had conveniently died at almost the same moment Davis had returned home.

Davis served less than a year as a senator before resigning to run for Mississippi governor, a race he lost to a bitter political enemy, Senator Henry Foote. Foote would later serve in the Confederate Congress where he would continue his enmity toward Davis. Though now without political office himself, Davis stayed interested in politics, campaigning for New Hampshire native Franklin Pierce for president in 1852. Pierce rewarded Davis's work by appointing him secretary of war.

Davis made the most of a post that allowed him to play politics, but in which he did not have to campaign in front of the public, a necessity with which he never got comfortable. He pushed for enlarging the army in total regiments, as well as equipping them with the rifles that his own Mississippi regiment had proved highly accurate.

Though he would never admit it, Davis did make some mistakes in his post. He insisted on importing a few dozen camels from Africa that he believed would replace horses in the western deserts. The soldiers hated the smelly, cantankerous, spitting beasts, and they were never fully tested when Davis left office in 1857. The new administration of James Buchanan ignored Davis's camel corps.

While Pierce failed to get renominated for the presidency, Davis did win the election to the United States Senate in 1858, where he became one of the nation's most famous, respected, and experienced politicians. He had served his country fighting Indians and Mexicans in the House, in the Senate, as secretary of war, and, now again, in the Senate. He had won and lost elections and had been appointed to high office by men who trusted him. Varina, who had sometimes felt abandoned by her husband early in their marriage when he was campaigning for office or campaigning on the battlefield, thought that he had finally found a home in the Senate.

It would be a home that Davis would experience for only two years.

☆   ☆   ☆

WITH THE ELECTION OF ABRAHAM LINCOLN in November 1860, Varina joined in the South's view that Lincoln was "elected with the express understanding that he would rule in hostility over the minority, while ostensibly acting as the guardian of the whole country."

She did not sleep the night before her husband stood to give his farewell address to the Senate early in 1861. She wondered from her seat if the senators and other spectators "saw beyond the cold exterior of the orator—his deep depression, his desire for reconciliation, and his overweening love of the Union in whose cause he had bled, and to maintain which he was ready to sacrifice all but liberty and equality."

Within a few days, the Davis family left Washington for Mississippi. It would be only a few more days before Davis would receive that unwelcome telegram calling on him to report to Montgomery.

After Davis was sworn in as president of the Confederacy in Montgomery, the early leaders of the new nation decided that the Alabama city was too far removed from Washington. Without thinking of the military advantages Montgomery had by being so deep in the South, the fire-eaters of the Confederacy voted to move the Confederate capital to Richmond, just one hundred miles south of Washington. Davis did not have much say in the matter. The Confederates who had elected him wanted to be close to the U.S. capital so they could negotiate peace terms after they won any single battle that they were certain would settle the issue of secession for the last time.

While Varina had been just another Senate wife in the U.S. capital, she found herself in the spotlight in Richmond, the Confederacy's capital. It was not necessarily a welcoming light. At the fancy ball that was supposed to welcome the new power couple to the elite of Richmond society, the wife of a Confederate colonel up for promotion to general whispered around to her friends that the pregnant Varina looked like an "Indian squaw." Varina heard the remark being spread among the ladies, passed it along to her husband, and Colonel Abraham Myers remained a colonel for the rest of his Confederate career. It would not be the first time that Varina intentionally or unintentionally influenced the president. She knew she could never win any arguments with him, but she could sometimes mold his opinion.

As First Lady of the Confederacy, Varina was in a unique position as a civilian to learn things that normally would have been military secrets. She knew the end of the war and the end of the Confederate nation was coming from the conversations she overheard during her daily ritual of taking lunch to Davis in his office.

Davis would often work through lunches and suppers without eating anything unless she personally brought the food to him and berated him into eating to keep up his strength. One day in March 1865, she walked in on a conference with Lee and heard her husband discussing the lack of supplies in the east and then saying that "beef and supplies of all kinds were abundant" in the Trans-Mississippi. Foreseeing the end in Virginia, the president was already thinking ahead and looking for uncaptured regions of the Confederacy where the government could move so the nation could live on to fight another day.

Varina assumed that all the Davis family, including Jefferson, would be leaving the city when he chose to evacuate. It came as a shock when her husband took her aside on the morning of March 30, 1865 and spoke quietly into her ear so the children and the servants would not overhear:

> "You must leave here today. My headquarters must be in the field, and your presence will only embarrass and grieve me rather than comfort me," he said. "I have confidence in your capacity to take care of our babies, and understand your desire to assist and comfort me, but you can do this in but one way, and that is by going yourself and taking our children to a place of safety."

To her horror, her husband then placed into her hands a small Colt revolver, one of the items he had requested a day earlier from Ordnance Department general Josiah Gorgas.

"You can at least, if reduced to the last extremity, force your assailants to kill you," her husband said.

As he talked, Davis demonstrated how to load the Colt, tearing a paper cartridge and pouring the black powder into one of the revolver's cylinder chambers. It was while loading the pistol, a type of weapon she had probably never fired, that Davis also told her to "make for the Florida coast," a vague request which he would not elaborate on with her or with his cabinet on their own journey south.

Varina was speechless as her solemn husband continued his demonstration of how to work the loading lever to jam the round lead balls down on top of the powder in each of the Colt's six chambers. She tried to protest that she would need no revolver, but her husband held up one hand to silence her. His next words chilled her. She had heard him say nothing like it over the past four years:

If I live you can come to me when the struggle is ended, but I do not expect to survive the destruction of constitutional liberty.

Varina's eyes grew wide with fright and comprehension over what was happening. In twenty years of marriage, her husband had never before even displayed a firearm in her presence. Now he had handed her a loaded revolver, instructing her to defend their children to her own death. He then told her in an almost casual tone of voice that he might soon die. He had not made clear if he meant that his enemies would kill him or if he would take his own life rather than submit to capture.

The First Lady knew that nothing she could say would change the President's mind about the family leaving his side. His first obligation was to make sure that his family was safe, but his second obligation was to continue being president of the Confederacy. As strong willed as she was, Varina knew her husband's mind was already made up. She and the children would be leaving the city, just as he insisted. And despite her pleas that he should accompany them out of town, she also knew that he would refuse. He had another bigger job to do.

Almost uncontrollably excited after having her husband talk about both their deaths, Varina began rushing around the Executive Mansion deciding what to pack. She moved first for the silverware. Her husband stopped her, explaining that she must travel light in the event that she would have to switch from the train in which she would leave Richmond to wagons later in her journey. He kept shaking his head and telling her no as she reached for favorite house adornments such as the life-size bust of him.

"Then food. I must pack those barrels of flour," she said, turning for the basement steps. She had used the money made from selling her dresses to buy flour that she had always intended on taking with her on any flight from the capital city.

The president took her arm: "No. You cannot remove anything in the shape of food from here. The people want it, and you must leave it here."

Food had been chronically short in the capital for more than two years. Davis realized it would only cause further panic among the people if they saw his wife loading flour, bacon, and soft bread aboard a train. Few people in the city could still afford to buy the flour that Varina had been purchasing and hoarding for the past year for just the sort of hungry circumstances that were finally gripping the city.

"Only clothes. Take only clothes for you and the children and Jim Limber," Davis said. "Leave everything else behind. It can all be replaced in time."

The children were Maggie, the oldest at 8; Jefferson, Jr., at 7; Willie, 4; and the newest addition to the family, nine-month-old Varina Anne, whom everyone called "Pie Cake." One other member of the Davis family who would be leaving was a four-year-old named Jim Limber. The last name of Limber may have been made up by him or the Davises because a limber during the Civil War was a two-wheeled ammunition wagon on which artillery pieces were hitched.

Jim Limber was a black child whom Varina had rescued the previous year from the streets of Richmond when she saw him being beaten by an older black man. She scooped up the child, put him in her carriage, and took him home to the Executive Mansion where he blended in with the children as a brother and playmate. Though no court papers were apparently filed to make his adoption legal, the Davis family treated Jim Limber as just another child in the household, even to the point of having his photograph taken. The president, the First Lady and the Davis children all considered Jim Limber to be as much a Davis as anyone in the family. He would not be left behind on any flight to safety.

☆　☆　☆

THE ONLY DAVIS CHILD who would be left behind in Richmond this day was Joseph.

On a Saturday evening eleven months before, 5-year-old Joseph Davis had fallen to his death from the second-floor balcony of the Confederate White House. Joseph, named for the president's older brother, had reportedly been following his own older brother, Jefferson, Jr., as the 6-year-old dared his younger sibling to join him in a game of follow the leader. The boys' Irish-born nurse, Catherine, was tending to the younger Davis daughter and had not noticed that the two boys had slipped out the door of their nursery and onto the balcony. It was a twenty-foot drop to a granite walkway where Joseph cracked his skull and broke both legs. Catherine did not learn of the accident until neighboring women rushed into the house carrying Joseph bleeding from his mouth and nose.

Within minutes a messenger delivered an urgent note from neighbors to the president at his office three blocks away. Varina was also there begging her husband to eat his supper rather than work on into the night as was his custom. When both read the note, food was forgotten. They rushed to the side of their son.

Joseph died two hours later with his shocked and grieving parents at his bedside. Davis, always the stoic in public, stood silently during the wake, watching over his youngest son. He said nothing, only nodding as neighbors and friends patted him on the back and whispered condolences. That night, in the privacy of his bedroom above the dining room, visiting close friends heard the tread of the president's feet walking back and forth in his bedroom. For the first time, they heard Davis remark on the loss of his willful son Joe who Varina told everyone in earshot was most like his father of all their children.

"Not mine, O Lord, but thine," Davis said repeatedly to himself and his God from behind his closed door. Sending his son to Heaven was the only comfort the president could find in the tragedy. He took that comfort alone in his room while his wife watched over her son's body one floor below.

The next day, Monday, Joseph was buried in Richmond's Hollywood Cemetery, surrounded by hundreds of child mourners who already knew after three years of war in the South what death was about. One little girl boldly walked up to Mary Chesnut, the wife of a general and a keen observer of political and personal goings-on in Richmond, to ask that she cover Joe's body with her bouquet because she knew him so well.

That afternoon, May 1, 1864, Davis resumed his duties in his office, leaving his wife and remaining children to mourn and reflect on Joe's funeral in their own fashion. The president's method of dealing with the loss of his son was to go back to work. In his mind, the Confederacy needed him more than his family did.

☆ ☆ ☆

NOW, ONE YEAR LATER, his family, which had grown to include his second daughter and last child, needed him more than the Confederacy.

It was after 9 p.m. when Davis escorted his wife and children to the railroad station. Rain was coming down in torrents as it had been for days. Most people in Richmond were praying for the rain to end, but Davis welcomed it this night. It would mask his family's departure.

The decision to remove Varina and the children had been made so quickly that there had been no time to outfit a special train suited to the wife of the president. Waiting for the Davis family was one wheezing, wood-fired engine, one elderly passenger car with cracked leather seats infested with fleas, and a single leaky baggage car on which Varina's carriage and two horses were loaded. Davis said nothing when he saw the dilapidated condition of the railcars. At least they were rolling.

Varina also eyed the cars, but she too knew that the family was lucky to have what they had. The first stop would be Danville, Virginia, before pushing on to Charlotte, North Carolina, where Davis hoped a rental house was waiting for his family to live in until he could join them. He was sending his family to an unfamiliar city where they knew no one. He did not know when he would be able to find them again if he—or they—were captured by the Federals.

It was a small party, consisting only of Varina; the children; Maggie Howell, Mrs. Davis's sister; Burton Harrison, Davis's personal secretary; two daughters of Secretary of the Treasury George Trenholm; two trusted black servants named Ellen and James Jones; and a young midshipman named James Morgan, who would act as the sole armed guard for the party. Though Federal forces were threatening the capital city and Union cavalry was roaming the countryside, Davis did not assign a military escort to protect his family. Varina, biographer of her husband, never speculated in print as to why the family did not rate a guard of soldiers when it would be venturing close to enemy-held territory. The president may have thought two things: if a military train was leaving Richmond with his family, it could create more notice and potential public panic, and second, if the train was approached by Union cavalry and the Confederate escort resisted, the Union soldiers might indiscriminately fire on the train without realizing that it carried only women and children.

Davis knelt and warmly embraced his children, showering them with kisses. The few bystanders standing on the station's landing were shocked at his behavior. In public Davis was always reserved, barely acknowledging strangers and expressing reluctance even to shake hands. But in the presence of his own family or in the privacy of the Executive Mansion, he was an attentive, affectionate father, instantly on his knees to be eye to eye with his children. At home Varina had repeatedly admonished him to change out of his dress suits before rolling on the floor with his children. He had worn out many pairs of expensive dress pants crawling around on all fours playing with his children.

As the president stood and regained his public face, a tearful Maggie wrapped herself around his leg, begging him to come along with them, not to leave them alone. Jefferson, Jr., grabbed the other leg, begging to stay in Richmond with his father so he could help fight back the Yankees that even the small boy knew were coming soon. Jefferson, Jr., saw the fighting in the trenches at Petersburg and knew what death meant. Though he was only 7, he wanted to be a man. He wanted to stay behind and help his father save the Confederacy.

Davis, fighting back his own tears, hugged his children again and whispered in their ears that he would see them again soon. He pulled out his purse and emptied it into Varina's handbag. He kept only a five-dollar gold piece for himself. In his pocket was an uncashed check for $28,000, money Varina had raised by selling off most of her good jewelry and dresses in Richmond's stores. There had been no time to cash it before the banks closed that day. The check would never be cashed.

It was nearly 10:00 p.m. The rain continued down in torrents, making final, whispered good-byes impossible because the rain crashing into the clay tiles of the train station's roof made quiet conversation difficult.

As the train chugged away, belching smoke from the green, unseasoned wood its crews were forced to burn because all the dried wood had long since been burned or captured, Davis waved at his family. A rare smile was on his face as he tried to convince his family they would soon be reunited. While the children might have been fooled, Varina was not.

"He looked as though he was looking his last upon us," she remembered.

Davis pulled his raglan overcoat around him and then trudged alone back to the Executive Mansion, slipping and sliding up the flooding, clay streets.

What Davis did not learn until more than a month later when he rendezvoused with his family was that Varina's train had barely made it twelve miles before stopping for the night. The engine's steam power was so weak, probably from a combination of a leaking firebox and boiler and from the green wood, that it could not negotiate a slight grade in the driving rain. The engineer decided to wait until morning when he hoped the sun would dry the tracks so the engine could get enough traction to top the grade.

At some point, either immediately before leaving Richmond or on board the leaky baggage car, Varina wrote a letter to General John S. Preston, a friend who had suffered much public criticism because his duty was to enforce the 1863 conscription law that drafted thousands of men into the ranks who had not volunteered earlier in the war. The letter, apparently misdated either by accident or by design if Varina was trying to conceal the date she actually left Richmond, reveals a woman at once in fear for her country and for her husband's continued welfare now that she was no longer at home to care for him. It is also remarkable for its vagueness as to whom she is speaking about.

In the letter Varina mentions "Mr. Davis" only twice deep in the text, which she signed with a false name. Her use of a pseudonym in writing the letter was employed in the event she was captured on the way south. Varina hoped to keep her own identity secret, and if any Union officer actually read the letter, she hoped he would miss the passing references to her husband's name of Mr. Davis rather than President Davis. In the letter it is clear that while Varina's husband was publicly insisting the Confederacy could live on, his wife knew better than to hold on to an impossible dream.

Varina wrote:

My heart is sadder today than I can readily communicate to you at this distance. Affairs seem darker, the spirit of the people daily more depressed, women tremblingly come to me and beg me to say what I can to comfort them. All I can say is that my husband will never cry for quarter [mercy] and all we can hope for is that the spirit of the people may enable him to defend the women and children of our unhappy land. . . . Mr. Davis looks worn and exhausted, prays without ceasing and hopes for better than I can foresee arguing from the signs of the times.

She ended the letter on a sad note: "Excuse this scrawl; I am so depressed and uncertain of our future that I cannot successfully arrange my thoughts."

☆ ☆ ☆

THAT SAME NIGHT of March 30, 1865, back at the Executive Mansion, now empty of children's laughter, Davis sat down to write his own remarkable letter to one of his oldest friends, General Braxton Bragg. During the Mexican War Davis's regiment had saved Bragg's artillery battery from capture or annihilation at the Battle of Buena Vista in February 1847. The crucible of war in those few minutes of hot combat had made the two fast friends for life. He opened up to Bragg: "We both entered into this war at the beginning of it; we both staked everything on the issue, and lost all which either public or private enemies could take away," Davis wrote.

To a close friend—but not to the Confederacy's citizens—Davis had just admitted that the war was lost. Publicly, Davis took the opposite tack. Over the next month, the president would declare to everyone who would listen that the Confederacy could still—and would—win the war.

Davis apparently made no other plans in advance for his and the cabinet's own escape. For the next three days, he worked from his official office three blocks away or from his home office in the Confederate Executive Mansion. He was constantly checking reports from Lee and from distant battlefields in Alabama. Without Varina around to force him into a healthy schedule of work followed by relaxation, he ate little and slept little. She had undoubtedly forced him to make a promise to her that he would eat more, but when she was not around, he always broke that promise. Davis had never eaten much, but had never made any connection that his lifelong poor health and regular attacks of neuralgia may have been linked to his poor diet.

When the sun rose on April 2, 1865, he had no idea that by the end of the day he would be a president on the run. The end of the Confederacy was obvious to all who would look and listen, but Davis, true to form, had made no plans for running.

CHAPTER 4

"Not Abandon to the Enemy One Foot of Soil"

THE CONFEDERATE CABINET was in full flight on the night of April 2, 1865, but what a slow, pitiful flight it was. The cabinet's train was faring little better than Varina's as it pushed ahead through the night over the same poorly maintained tracks. The engine herked and jerked and wheezed down the rails toward Danville at a measly ten miles per hour, barely four times the pace a soldier could march and at half the pace a regiment of cavalry could have maintained—had President Jefferson Davis, Secretary of War John C. Breckinridge, or General Robert E. Lee ordered any cavalry to escort the fleeing government.

The assorted cabinet secretaries and their clerks did not complain about the noisy, smoky, amenity-bare passenger cars clattering along behind the second-rate engine. They knew enough about the poor conditions of the surviving Confederate locomotives to be thankful that there were any engines left in the capital city that could still pull cars. No one among the government elite dared ask the president of the railroad, who had wisely decided it was also time for him to leave the city, if the cars were overloaded. There was fear that even thinking such a thought would make the engine stop in its tracks. And if it stopped, the first people to find them would undoubtedly be a Union patrol.

H. W. Bruce, a Confederate congressman who took the opportunity to get aboard the train, even though its original intent was to evacuate only the cabinet and its assistants, noted the somber mood among the passengers:

I never knew so little conversation indulged by so large a number of acquaintances together, for we were nearly all acquainted with each other, and I may say, fellow fugitives driven by the same great calamity and wrong. Very few words were interchanged.

Secretary of the Navy Stephen Mallory sat in the rocking car pondering his future before the train even got out of sight of the station. Just the night before, he had heard the Confederate-instigated explosions that splintered the last of the James River Squadron ships he once commanded. It made little matter. Union ships would have done the same thing within a few days. Now the former U.S. senator who played the largest role in building up the United States Navy in the 1850s was without a job in the Confederate government. He must have marveled at the irony that the ships whose construction he had authorized while working in the U.S. capitol were poised to assist in the capture of the Confederate States capital.

Without any ships to command, Mallory had time to write down his thoughts.

Bored and unable to sleep as readily as his traveling companions who had liberally partaken of the apple brandy Secretary of the Treasury George Trenholm was passing around, Mallory started glancing around the train car. He realized that he and the other members of the cabinet were making history this night. He started writing down impressions in his diary of the things that were happening and of the people who would be with him until they escaped or they were captured. After four years of writing dry cabinet reports to a president who wanted and expected just that, Mallory must have welcomed the chance to spread his literary wings by inserting some visual imagery into his own diary.

"The train moved in gloomy silence over the James River. A commanding view of the city was thus afforded, and as the fugitives receded from the flickering lights, many and sad were the commentaries they made on the Confederate cause," Mallory wrote.

Mallory was aware of the danger the cabinet had placed itself in by escaping on a train without knowing where the enemy was.

Mallory noted:

All knew how the route to Danville approached the enemy's lines, all knew the activity of his large mounted force, and the chance between a safe passage of the Dan and a general gobble [capture] by Sheridan's cavalry seemed somewhat in favor of the gobble.

Mallory watched Postmaster General John Reagan, another man without a job since there was no need to move mail in and out of the fallen capital. Mallory noted that Reagan was "silent and somber, his eyes as bright and glistening as beads, but evidently seeing nothing around them, now whittling a stick down to the little end of nothing without ever reaching a satisfactory point."

Trenholm, a man of great wealth accumulated by owning blockade-running ships, did not seem as ill as he usually did, but then again, he was passing around what seemed like an inexhaustible supply of "Old Peach." Most everyone in the packed train car of twenty-nine men and one woman, Mrs. Trenholm, seemed to welcome the chance to drink some liquor to smooth the transition from government official to war refugee.

Benjamin, the secretary of state, continued to be unusually jolly for a man who was running from arrest on possible treason charges. Mallory wrote that Benjamin still had a smile on his face as he told tales of "other great national causes which had been redeemed from far gloomier reverses than ours."

Congressman Bruce awoke the next morning, April 3, as the train pulled into Burkeville Station, a stop below Amelia Court House, where Lee would be headed that same day. It was obvious to the people in that village that something had gone terribly wrong in Richmond:

We stopped at every station on the way, crowds thronging to the train at each to make inquiries, for the bad news in this case preserved its proverbial reputation for fast traveling. Everybody sought to see, shake hands with and speak to the President, who maintained all the way a bold front, gave no evidence by word or appearance of despair, but spoke all along encouragingly to the people.

Lieutenant John S. Wise, a son of former governor Henry Wise whom Davis had appointed a general early in the war, happened to be watching at one station when the train passed. He too focused on Davis. Wise was still appreciative of the president.

Mr. Davis sat at a car window. The crowd at the station cheered. He smiled and acknowledged their compliment, but his expression showed physical and mental exhaustion.

Wise, just 19 years old, had first seen combat just a year earlier as a Virginia Military Institute cadet at the Battle of New Market, Virginia, under the command of then general Breckinridge. While some historians question Wise's account, others credit him with having a keen sense of what he was observing:

I saw a government on wheels. It was the marvelous and incongruous debris of the wreck of the Confederate capital. There were very few women on these trains, but among the last in the long procession were trains bearing indiscriminate cargoes of men and things. In one car was a cage with an African parrot, and a box of tame squirrels and a hunchback! Everybody, not excepting the parrot, was wrought up to a pitch of intense excitement.

When no more trains came out of Richmond, Wise noted:

The cessation of all traffic gave our place a Sabbath stillness. Until now, there had been the constant rumble of trains on this main line of supplies to the army. After the intense excitement of Monday, when the whole Confederate government came rushing past at intervals of a few minutes, the unbroken silence reminded one of death after violent convulsions.

Davis himself seemed to have said little to anyone in the cars, but years later he would have to defend himself just for riding on the train. One of the controversies that erupted among the Confederacy's political and military leaders after the war was what happened to a request for food that Lee believed he had telegraphed on April 2 to the quartermasters in Richmond. Lee said he had asked for the supplies to be shipped by rail to Amelia Court House Station. When Lee arrived at the station on April 4, one day after the cabinet's train had passed, the general walked up to some box cars sitting on the siding, threw open the doors, and found it loaded with ammunition. None of the cars had the food Lee had requested.

One observer remembered:

> No face wore a heavier shadow than that of General Lee. The failure of the supply of rations completely paralyzed him. An anxious and haggard expression came to his face.

That same day an irritated Lee issued an open letter addressed to the citizens of Amelia County explaining that he had been "expecting to find plenty of provisions, which had been ordered to be placed here by the railroad several days since, but to my surprise and regret I find not a pound of subsistence for man or horse."

Whether Lee intended it as such, the pleading letter seemed like a dig at a government that had failed its army.

As early as 1866 some writers were claiming in newspaper articles that Davis and the cabinet had appropriated the trains that would normally have been loaded with the food Lee's men needed.

An indignant Davis, writing in his postwar book, *The Rise and Fall of the Confederate Government,* called the stories "fiction," and "manufactured without one fiber of truth." He claimed that the quartermaster department in Richmond never received a telegram from Lee requesting that food be sent to Amelia Court House (no such telegram appears in the *Official Records of the War of the Rebellion*). Had such a plea been forwarded to Davis before he left, "I would certainly have inquired as to the time of reaching that station and would have asked to have the train stopped so as to enable me to learn whether the supplies were in depot or not."

Lee always believed the delay at Amelia Station to gather food cost him the head start he had on Grant. Still, he did not directly accuse Davis of being responsible for the missing supplies.

A 140-mile train trip between Richmond and Danville should have taken no more than four to five hours. The train pulled into the Danville station in late afternoon, more than fifteen hours after it had left Richmond. The engineer had driven the train no faster than 10 to 15 miles per hour because he was fearful that rotted ties and pulled spikes would derail the engine and cars.

That such a disaster did not happen may have been lucky because maintenance of the railroads had fallen drastically in the last year. But even in this late stage of the war, bureaucrats were still thinking that the railroads could be of use in continuing the war. Just the previous month, an optimistic Breckinridge had sent notes to the presidents of the railroads asking them to standardize the width of their rails so engines from any line could run on the rails. It was common practice for the owners of railroads in prewar years to set their own railroad gauges. This forced cross-country shippers to change railroad companies, meaning the local railroads would collect freight charges from each leg of a cross-country shipment rather than set up some system where the originating shipper shared collected freight charges with the owners of the local railroads. It was a horribly inefficient and locally selfish means of running a network of railroads in wartime, but it was the system in place at the start of the war. When Breckinridge took office in February 1865, he was aghast to learn that no one in the Confederate cabinet had thought to order this simplest of all attempts to create a standard rail gauge that would have benefited the movement of troops and equipment.

Danville, a town of 6,000 located on the Dan River just above the North Carolina border in south central Virginia, had not experienced the heavy hand of war that had been visited on its distant neighbors. The residents had heard the stories about the shelling of large cities like Vicksburg, Charleston, and Petersburg 140 miles to the northeast, but the war had not struck them as yet. They had come close. The previous summer Danville residents had braced for an attack after Lexington, 110 miles away, and Lynchburg, 70 miles away, both to the northwest, had been attacked by Union major general David Hunter. In Lexington, the Virginia Military Institute's classrooms and library were burned to the ground, while Hunter was driven back at Lynchburg before he could penetrate further south toward Danville.

Danville residents were thankful. They believed Hunter would have targeted their town next because it was the location of several old tobacco barns that were being used to house 4,000 Union prisoners of war. They imagined Hunter freeing the prisoners and then burning the entire town in retaliation for the deaths of the sickest of the prisoners.

The town's residents welcomed the cabinet refugees, although Mallory found the cheers for the president "told as much of sorrow as of joy."

One of the reasons Mallory thought the town might have mixed emotions about their arrival was that a majority of Danville's residents had voted to remain in the Union early in 1861. It was not until President Lincoln issued orders for Virginia to supply several regiments of volunteer soldiers that Danville and surrounding Pittsylvania County cast their lot with the Confederacy and raised the Eighteenth Virginia Infantry and the Thirty-eighth Virginia, regiments which were fighting with Lee.

Davis himself felt very welcome in the town he had never before visited. He remembered years later that "nothing could have exceeded the kindness and hospitality of the patriotic citizens."

Major William T. Sutherlin invited Davis to stay in his large, ornate Italian villa-style home situated on four acres in the center of town. Sutherlin, the former Unionist mayor of the town, had made a fortune before the war processing tobacco. Now he was the town's Confederate quartermaster. Though he was just forty-four years old, Sutherlin had been too ill to take a field command. He considered it an honor to host Davis, Trenholm and his wife, Davis's aide Francis Lubbock, and Mallory. The other cabinet members found lodgings nearby.

Davis wasted no time in exploring what he considered the new Confederate capital city. The first order of business was to inspect the town's defenses because the unspoken fear was that Union cavalry would soon appear on the horizon. Davis probably embarrassed Danville's military commander, who had done little during the war other than guard prisoners, by promptly declaring that the trenches dug around the entire town were "as faulty in location as construction." The president of the country personally directed laborers to improve the town's defenses.

The war was not only on the president's mind, but he had already figured out how to win it. He wrote in *Rise and Fall of the Confederate Government* in 1881 that "as previously arranged with General Lee," he expected Lee to bring his army to Danville, form a new defensive line along the Dan and Roanoke Rivers, unite his army with General Joseph E. Johnston's in North Carolina, and then attack Union General William T. Sherman. Davis believed that "if successful," this Confederate victory in North Carolina would bring reinforcements back to the army. He then speculated that the combined armies of Lee and Johnston would be strong enough to frighten a pursuing Grant into turning around and retreating back north as he would be "far removed from his base of supplies."

Davis may have replayed this grand strategy in his head on the train ride from Richmond on April 2, but the last time Lee and his top generals had even discussed the possibility of linking up with Johnston had been more than three weeks earlier while at a strategy meeting in Davis's office. Davis now had no idea if Lee was even heading in the general direction of Danville, much less planning to move on to North Carolina. Davis was planning grand war strategy without knowing his main general's on-field tactical status.

The plans made at that month-old meeting had already proved hopelessly overoptimistic. If Lee's already exhausted army failed to hold onto a front of several hundred yards at Fort Stedman back in March, there was little reason for Davis to believe that Lee's army had suddenly grown stronger now that it had left the trenches of Petersburg in early April. Yet Davis imagined the Army of Northern Virginia and the Army of Tennessee, both losing at least one hundred men per day to desertion, could still force Sherman from the field. If such a battle in North Carolina were to take place, Sherman's single army would still outnumber Lee's and Johnston's combined armies by at least two to one.

Davis's confidence that Grant pursuing Lee into North Carolina would cause the Union general to outrun his supply lines had no merit. Davis was forgetting that while Grant's moving into the interior of Virginia might stretch his supply lines, Lee had no supply lines at all. Wilmington had been captured back in February and the Southside Railroad just a few days ago. While Grant's City Point beachhead supply base at the confluence of the Appomattox and James rivers was now fifty miles to the east, the Union Army had thousands of wagons that could easily keep food and ammunition flowing to Grant's army no matter how far away he roamed. The Union army also controlled supply lines in Beaufort, New Bern and Wilmington, North Carolina that could have been used to get supplies to Grant's army in pursuit of Lee.

If Davis had any doubt about the logistics power of the Union army, he could have asked his own generals about City Point, a supply depot at the confluence of the James and Appomattox Rivers near Petersburg. One of the most memorable smells the Confederate troops had of the Petersburg trenches was the aroma of piping hot bread being delivered to the Union troops in their trenches. Not only were the Union trains running from City Point to the front delivering ammunition, but also they were delivering bread baked in massive ovens constructed just for the purpose of keeping the soldiers supplied with fresh food. The Confederates, scrounging for anything they could eat, must have known the war was ending when they could smell the fresh bread of their enemies.

☆　☆　☆

ON THE MORNING OF APRIL 4, one day after arriving in Danville and while still unknowing of the location of the Army of Northern Virginia, Davis sat down to the first meeting of the cabinet in Danville. Mallory made no mention of the details of the cabinet meeting in his diary, nor did Davis. It is unknown if Davis even discussed with the cabinet that he wanted to issue a proclamation. But immediately after the meeting, Davis retired to a room in the Sutherlin house, sat down at a marble-topped table, and wrote one of the most remarkable documents of his presidency. It was also the last official proclamation he would make to the citizens of the Confederacy.

Davis started the document with the long, run-on sentences that were typical of the written communications and speeches of the politicians of the 1860s with the following observation:

> The general-in-chief of our army has found it necessary to make such movements of the troops as to uncover the capital and thus involve the withdrawal of the Government from the city of Richmond.

With that opening paragraph, Davis blamed Lee, not the advancing Federals, for the necessity of abandoning Richmond. Lee had only been given the rank of general in chief weeks earlier and only after Davis had demanded executive control over what the general could do. That Davis chose to use the phrase "general in chief" rather than name Lee may have been just his choice of bureaucratic words rather than an intentional slight. Still, the sentence is a pointed reference that it was Lee's "movements of troops" that created the situation that led to the "withdrawal of the Government from the city." Like most bureaucrats, Davis reasoned that the public would be more concerned about the "Government" than they would about their relatives serving in the army that was now in retreat.

Davis realized citizens would be insulted, maybe enraged if he tried to pretend totally that the loss of Richmond was not important to the conduct of the war.

> It would be unwise, even were it possible, to conceal the great moral as well as material injury to our cause that must result from the occupation of Richmond by the enemy.

But Davis also wanted to address his belief that the loss of Richmond did not mean that the war was over for the Confederacy. He was convinced this proclamation could rekindle the success of his February speech at the African Church in Richmond. In just a few minutes in front of a crowd, he had drawn rousing applause and favorable editorials from newspaper editors who normally hated him and his policies. Now he wanted to soothe the feelings of anyone who was uncertain the nation could survive. They had to be convinced that the dream of independence from the North was still possible—if only citizens believed it could happen.

> It is equally unwise and unworthy of us, as patriots engaged in a most sacred cause, to allow our energies to falter, our spirits to grow faint, or our efforts to become relaxed under reverses, however calamitous. While it has been to us a source of national pride that for four years of unequaled warfare we have been able, in close proximity to the center of the enemy's power, to maintain the seat of our chosen government free from the pollution of his presence; while the memories of the heroic dead who have freely given their lives to its defense must ever remain enshrined in our hearts; while the preservation of the capital, which is usually regarded as the evidence to mankind of separate national existence, was an object very dear to us, it is also true, and should not be forgotten, that the loss which we have suffered is not without compensation.

After opening the document with the statement that it had been Lee's fault that Richmond was captured, Davis now shifted focus to say that Lee's army was now free to fight Grant's army because it no longer had to defend the capital.

> For many months the largest and finest army of the Confederacy, under the command of a leader whose presence inspires equal confidence in the troops and the people, has been greatly trammeled by the necessity of keeping constant watch over the approaches to the capital, and has thus been forced to forego more than one opportunity for promising enterprise. The hopes and confidence of the enemy have been constantly excited by the be-

lief that their possession of Richmond would be the signal for our submission to their rule, and relieve them from the burden of war, as their failing resources admonish them it must be abandoned if not speedily brought to a successful close.

Davis now realized that his claims of losing the capital might be considered outrageous, so he shifted focus again to remind the citizens that the nation's morale depended on them keeping a positive attitude for the rest of the war.

It is for us, my countrymen, to show by our bearing under reverses how wretched has been the self-deception of those who have believed us less able to endure misfortune with fortitude than to encounter danger with courage. We have now entered upon a new phase of a struggle, the memory of which is to endure for all ages and to shed an increasing luster upon our country.

Davis told the citizens in the Confederacy that losing Richmond had really been a good thing. Now, he was about to go even further. He was going to tell the citizens that it was not necessary for any Southern city to remain uncaptured. In the next paragraph, he broadly suggested that the Confederacy could survive if its armies could roam freely throughout its own land. He came close but did not ask the citizens to join in this thinly veiled suggestion of hit-and-run guerilla insurgent tactics. Earlier in the war Davis had distanced himself from irregular guerillas like William Quantrill and Bill Anderson who had operated along the Kansas and Missouri borders practicing just the type of hit-and-run tactics he was about to describe might be necessary to continue and win the war.

Relieved from the necessity of guarding cities and particular points, important but not vital to our defense, with an army free to move from point to point and strike in detail the detachments and garrisons of the enemy, operating on the interior of our own country, where supplies are more accessible, and where the foe will be far removed from his own base and cut off from all succor in case of reverse, nothing is now needed to render our triumph certain but the exhibition of our own unquenchable resolve.

Davis then suggested the most amazing thing in the proclamation. If the Confederate citizenry just thought positively, all would be won.

Let us but will it, and we are free; and who, in the light of the past, dare doubt your purpose in the future?

Davis, without the apparent consent of the cabinet, then told the citizens that he and he alone had made the decision to continue fighting the war. Curiously, he only focused on the plight of the state of Virginia, while there were still Union armies advancing in other Confederate states like Alabama and North Carolina. His own state of Mississippi had been almost entirely occupied for nearly two years.

Animated by the confidence in your spirit and fortitude, which never yet has failed me, I announce to you, fellow-countrymen, that it is my purpose to maintain your cause with my whole heart and soul; that I will never consent to abandon to the enemy one foot of the soil of any one of the States of the Confederacy; that Virginia, noble State, whose ancient renown has been eclipsed by her still more glorious recent history; whose bosom has been bared to receive the main shock of this war; whose sons and daughters have exhibited heroism so sublime as to render her illustrious in all times to come; that Virginia with the help of her people, and by the blessing of Providence, shall be held and defended, and no peace ever be made with the infamous invaders of her homes by the sacrifice of any of her rights or territory.

Davis, then no more than a few miles from the North Carolina border, hinted that the escape south of the cabinet might soon begin again.

If by stress of numbers we should ever be compelled to a temporary withdrawal from her limits, or those of any other border State, again and again will we return, until the baffled and exhausted enemy shall abandon in despair his endless and impossible task of making slaves of a people resolved to be free.

Let us not, then, despond, my countrymen, but relying on the never-failing mercies and protecting care of our God, let us meet the foe with fresh defiance, with unconquered and unconquerable hearts.

Jeff'n Davis

Davis apparently did not see the irony in his use of the phrase "making slaves of a people resolved to be free." Ever since Lincoln's Emancipation Proclamation was issued on January 1, 1863, the North made the object of the war to free the slaves within the confines of the Confederacy. But at the same time, Lincoln had hinted to the Hampton Roads commissioners that the proclamation may be illegal and could be rescinded, but Davis had not believed him.

Ironically, while Lincoln was implying that his own Emancipation Proclamation might not mean much, Lee had convinced many Confederate leaders in early February that it was time to enroll slaves in the Confederate army with the promise that they would be emancipated in exchange for their service.

Davis handed the proclamation draft to Benjamin to deliver to the local newspaper so that it could be printed in the next edition and then distributed as a handbill. Davis next sent the proclamation by telegraph to other Confederate cities. Residents of Pittsylvania County read the document, but its distribution to most of the Confederacy's citizens seems doubtful as the once efficient mail system had broken down (Postmaster General Reagan was running with Davis), and Federals were cutting the telegraph lines in advance and behind the surviving armies. Couriers sent out from Danville by Davis were detailed to find Lee, not carry handbills.

If Davis hoped the written proclamation would set off a new burst of patriotism as happened after his February African Church speech, he failed. No one in Danville or Pittsylvania County rejoined the army or took to bushwhacking and guerilla war after reading the document.

Colonel Robert Withers, the town's commander and the one whose trench-digging skills had been criticized by Davis, asked several towns-people for their opinions on the document before concluding: "Evidently designed to neutralize the depressing effect of the surrender of the capital, I neither saw nor heard of anyone who was much enthused by the assurance."

THE MOST FAMOUS REFUGEE from Richmond to arrive in Danville after the cabinet was Admiral Raphael Semmes. He had commandeered a locomotive in Richmond, had chopped down a painted picket fence for fuel to raise steam in its firebox, and gathered the remaining complement of the James River Squadron of sailors. Semmes was irritated that the cabinet had left Richmond without him and his sailors, feeling that he had "been abandoned by the government and the army," but he also said he would "make no charges and utter no complaints."

Semmes was further irritated when some railroad officials tried to take back control of the train, which Semmes had essentially stolen. "We declined the offers of these good gentlemen and navigated to suit ourselves."

When Semmes met Davis in his makeshift office in the Sutherlin home, the admiral requested assignments for his sailors. At a loss for finding a suitable job for deep-water sailors now camped next to a shallow river, Davis ordered them to man the defenses of the town. Davis personally appointed Semmes a brigadier general, a lower rank than what the admiral believed he deserved, but Semmes agreed to take it. The appointment would never be made official because such promotions had to be approved by the Confederate Congress, which had also scattered as Union forces advanced on Richmond.

With creating a new brigadier general now cleared from his plate, Davis turned to finding general in chief Robert E. Lee. The president appropriated some of Withers' men and sent them out to find Lee's army. The last known location was around Amelia Court House, but since that time, one lone telegram had arrived that confirmed that the Yankees had taken Burkeville Station, which was south of Amelia Court House.

Davis had no idea where Lee was, but he felt confident the Army of Northern Virginia was on its way toward Danville. Sutherlin recalled after the war that Davis had expressed "great confidence he had in his [Lee's] ability as a commander, and his great admiration and love for him as a man."

With little else to do officially other than wait for some communication from Lee, Davis sat down to write to his wife, who he assumed was now in Charlotte, North Carolina.

He informed her about receiving Lee's telegram in church and the evacuation of the cabinet. Like any husband knowing that his wife would be concerned about the family furnishings, he told her that her favorite bust of him was in hiding, but that he had left the furniture in place. Most of the letter was remarkably mundane for a president on the run. The only hint of when he would see her again was at the end of the letter.

"I do not wish to leave Va., but cannot decide on my movements until those of the army are better developed." He then ended on a down note: "I weary of this sad recital and have nothing pleasant to tell. May God have you in his Holy keeping is the fervent prayer of your ever affectionate Husband."

Davis had just issued a proclamation to the citizens exhorting them to fight on and assuring them that the war could still be won, but he told his own wife that he had nothing pleasant to tell her.

The very next day, Davis received a letter from Varina, carried personally by Burton Harrison, the man he had assigned to make sure she got to Charlotte. It must have cheered Davis to read that at least one person in the Confederacy still believed he could do anything.

Varina wrote:

I who know that your strength when stirred up is great, and that you can do with a few what others have failed to do with many, am awaiting prayerfully the advent of the time when it is God's will to deliver us through his own appointed agent, I trust it will be you as I believe it is.

Varina had read "a digest" of the proclamation indicating that at least some of its content had reached Charlotte, but she confessed: "I could not make much of it except as encouraging exhortation, am anxious to see the whole thing."

☆　☆　☆

THERE WAS LITTLE TO DO in Danville other than wait on word from Lee. Mallory wrote in his diary that only Benjamin kept up a jolly mood pondering the fate of Lee saying: "No news is good news." Someone in the cabinet repeated a rumor claiming that Lee must be chasing Grant down and was too busy to alert Davis.

"The president was not deceived by these follies, but though he looked for disaster, he was wholly unprepared for Lee's capitulation," wrote Mallory.

Finally on the evening of April 8, Lieutenant Wise, the same keen observer who had called the cabinet's train "a government on wheels," arrived at the Sutherlin Mansion. Just hours earlier a telegram from Breckinridge had been received informing Davis of the reduced capacity of Lee's army. Now this young lieutenant personally confirmed what Breckinridge's short telegram had only hinted about.

Wise told Davis and the cabinet a shocking tale of how Lee had lost one third of his army and many generals at the Battle of Sayler's Creek on April 6. Wise, in a move bold for a teenaged officer, advised Davis that he personally saw no option for Lee but surrender. Davis, refusing to take the military estimation of a young lieutenant, gave him another set of letters and told him to find Lee and return with Lee's personal assessment of his situation. Young Wise did as he was told though he knew the effort was useless.

That same morning, Union cavalry under Major General George Stoneman fought a skirmish with 250 Confederate cavalry just thirty miles from Danville. Some Union prisoners taken during that battle told their captors that Stoneman was considering attacking Danville. He might have been, but it was not because the cabinet was in town. As Stoneman had been out of telegraph contact with his superiors for weeks, there was no way he could have known that Davis and the cabinet had even left Richmond. It was a lost opportunity for Stoneman to regain his reputation. He was within a day's ride of Danville where his 6,000 men could have easily overwhelmed any Confederate garrison Danville could muster, but he had no clue Davis was close.

While Stoneman never tried for Danville, the implied threat was enough to make Davis and the few hundred Confederate soldiers stationed in Danville nervous. Davis telegraphed General Pierre G. T. Beauregard in Greensboro for more troops to be moved to Danville.

Early on April 9, Davis sent an encoded message to Lee now that he knew the general location of the army. He suggested that Lee contact Johnston "before Sherman moves." As if somehow aware that Lee had exploded in anger when he discovered no food or clothing at Amelia Court House, Davis wrote: "We have here provisions and clothing for your Army and they are held for your use."

Lee would not see that message before he signed the surrender documents with Grant that afternoon at the home of Wilmer McLean in the quiet village of Appomattox Court House nearly ninety miles to the north. Lee was not able to act on his president's suggestions anyway. The Army of Northern Virginia was surrounded. It would have been suicide for Lee to have tried to fight a strong, well-equipped Union army that was at least four times his own size.

On the morning just hours before the surrender, about the same time that Davis was dictating the telegram, Lee was chatting with one of his young generals, Edward Porter Alexander, who as a colonel had directed the artillery barrage on the third day of the Battle of Gettysburg in July 1863. Lee asked Alexander what he would do now that the army was surrounded.

Alexander, flattered that the general of the army was asking the opinion of a lowly brigadier, answered:

We have only two alternatives to choose from. We must either surrender, or the army may be scattered into the woods and bushes either to rally upon Johnston in North Carolina, or make its way, each man to his own state, with his arms, and to report to his governor. This last course is the one which seems to me to offer us much the best chances. If there is any hope for the Confederacy, it is for delay.

Without knowing it, Alexander had essentially suggested the same thing that Davis had in his Danville Proclamation—dissolving the big Confederate armies into small guerilla units.

Lee did not hesitate before answering Alexander: "The men would have no rations and would be under no discipline. They are already demoralized by four years of war. The country would be full of lawless bands. And as for myself, while you young men might afford to go bushwhacking, the only proper and dignified course for me would be to surrender myself and take the consequences of my actions."

Alexander wrote in his memoirs: "I was so ashamed of having proposed to him such a foolish and wildcat scheme as my suggestion had been that I felt like begging him to forget that he had ever heard of it."

In one exchange with one subordinate, Lee rejected the very idea that Davis may have proposed to him had Lee been able to make it to Danville.

Official word of Lee's surrender arrived that afternoon from the line of couriers who finally had a secure means of taking messages from Lee to Davis. This time it was no rumor. The message was from one of the returning couriers who ran into Brigadier General Tom Rosser, a Confederate cavalry officer who had escaped rather than surrender with Lee.

Mallory wrote that the news "fell upon the ears of all like a fire bell in the night."

He said the cabinet members passed the message around, each reading it silently as if one's own interpretation of the news might be different from the others.

While there was no warning accompanying the news of Lee's surrender, Davis assumed that since the Army of Northern Virginia had been surrendered, the Union army's attention would soon focus on finding and capturing the Confederate cabinet. He ordered the cabinet to be packed and ready to leave for Greensboro, North Carolina, in four hours, less time than he had given them to leave Richmond.

Davis saw his only option was to head for the safety of the Army of Tennessee under General Joseph E. Johnston, an old enemy and antagonist. The animosity between the two men was obvious and well known to most high ranking officers in the Confederacy. Rumors placed the start of the lifelong feud back to West Point days when Davis, class of 1848, may have picked on Johnston, who was one year behind him. The bad blood accelerated early in 1861 when Johnston complained about the appointment of full generals in the Confederate army. When Confederate general appointments were made, Johnston was ranked fourth behind long-time Davis friend, 62-year-old Samuel Cooper, close Davis friend Albert Sidney Johnston, and Robert E. Lee. Both Albert Johnston and Lee had been colonels in the old U.S. army, while Joseph Johnston had been a brigadier general. In Joseph Johnston's mind, Davis had obviously insulted him and his abilities.

Joseph Johnston never got over what he considered an intentional slight early in the war, and he never accepted Davis's habit of putting him in command, complaining about his performance, relieving him, and reinstating him to command. Johnston had been replaced as commander of the Army of Tennessee by Davis the previous summer by General John Bell Hood. Hood's rashness on the battlefield had virtually destroyed the army Johnston had preserved during Sherman's spring and summer offensive toward Atlanta. When the army was a shadow of its former self, Davis fired Hood and brought back Johnston, as if the former commander could now work miracles with a depleted army.

One train-packing worry had been alleviated for Davis. The treasure train had stayed in Danville only three days before Davis sent it on to Charlotte where the gold was stored in the vaults of the former U.S. Mint. The train had left on April 6, three days before the cabinet would leave Danville.

Taking care of the Confederate treasury was beginning to wear on Lieutenant William H. Parker's nerves. He and his boys had been trained as sailors, not as nursemaids for gold. Before leaving for Charlotte, Parker went to Mallory and told him that the Treasury Department should be taking a more active role in guarding the Confederacy's money.

"It was not a time to be falling sick by the wayside, as some high officials were beginning to do," Parker said, a pointed reference to the continuing ailments of Trenholm, who still felt well enough to partake of peach brandy now and again.

☆　☆　☆

BEFORE LEAVING DANVILLE, Davis committed another in a long line of curious actions concerning his own safety. He did not order the 250 cavalrymen in Danville who had already clashed with Stoneman's raiders in Martinsville to ride along in advance and behind the train to Greensboro. Once again, Davis intentionally deprived himself and his cabinet of protection. Davis also left behind the much larger force of 3,000 infantrymen under General Henry Harrison Walker in Danville. Those men, who had been specifically ordered to Danville to bolster the defenses while the cabinet was in residence, could have started ahead or behind the train to continue their protective duties at Greensboro. Davis never gave the order, nor did he telegraph to Beauregard or Johnston asking for an escort.

Just as had been the case in Richmond, the inertia of evacuating was hard to overcome. Davis had ordered that the train be ready to pull out by 8:00 p.m., but that hour came and went as one cabinet minister and then another asked for more cars to be added to the train. And just as in Richmond, people who felt they were too important to be left behind lobbied to be added to the escaping party. One was Brigadier General Gabriel Rains, the inventor of the torpedo or land mine. Rains asked for a place for himself and his daughters. Rains mentioned to Burton Harrison, who was trying to organize the train loading, that he had some torpedoes with him, and they might prove valuable along the way. A nervous Harrison refused Rains passage, but the inventive general later persuaded his old friend Davis to find room for him. Rains presumably left his explosives at the train station.

It was nearly midnight before Davis, who had ordered the train ready to leave four hours earlier, arrived at the station. While eating one final meal with the Sutherlins, the topic of reaching the Trans-Mississippi by ship was brought up in conversation. Someone mentioned that the cabinet was virtually out of personal money, hinting that they should take some of the treasury funds in order to get passage on a ship. Davis had always refused to consider such a thing, insisting that the money was needed to pay troops. On hearing Davis say that he had given all his hard money to Varina, the Sutherlins offered him a sack of gold that they had been keeping for themselves for hard times. Davis refused.

Davis climbed into his car and discovered that his seatmate was one of the talkative daughters of Rains. The general did nothing to control his precocious child, who kept asking Davis question after question, apparently unaware of who he was and that he was her father's employer. Davis, used to the questions of children, never complained and never ordered the young girl away, although observers saw that he was clearly irritated.

Finally, more than five hours late, the train pulled out from the station, but it did not travel far before the old locomotive broke down from the strain of trying to pull so many heavily laden cars. More time was lost while the train was hauled back into Danville and the locomotive replaced. All the while the handful of armed guards that had been found for the train peered into the darkness looking for signs of Grant's cavalry coming from the north and Stoneman's cavalry coming from the south or west. They did not see them, but the Confederates knew that they must be on their way.

It was after Davis had left Danville that an officer in the town sent a telegram to Beauregard, then stopped in Greensboro: "The President started for Greensboro at 10 this evening. Are Greensboro and the road now safe?"

Davis was already on his way, riding on a very conspicuous train, moving blindly into the night without any knowledge of how close Stoneman was. He had no other choice.

Semmes, the old sea raider, remained behind in Danville, still not yet part of any obvious waterborne escape plan. Instead of sailing the ocean, the closest Semmes and his sailors got to the sea was wringing muddy water out of their socks that had soaked through their leather brogans while sitting in the trenches waiting for a cavalry attack that would never come. Semmes would follow Davis to Greensboro in a few days, giving the president another chance to look at him and perhaps think of how the old admiral's skills could be better used than commanding skilled sailors now reduced to mud-caked soldiers.

Sometime in the early morning of April 11, 1865, with a loquacious little girl beside him talking about anything and everything, Davis crossed the state line into North Carolina, breaking the intent if not the promise he had made just five days earlier to the Confederacy's citizens that he would not abandon Virginia. The month-old plan of combining Lee's Army of Northern Virginia with Johnston's Army of Tennessee was now shattered. The Army of Northern Virginia was now surrendered and captured. For all Davis knew, Lee himself may already be on his way to a Federal prison camp or to Washington to be put on display as a trophy of war.

Everyone with the exception of Davis could see that the end was near. Even peaceful Danville, which had not seen any fighting during the war, was being dragged into the war's aftermath. Captain John Dooley, a wounded and paroled former prisoner of the Federals, made his way into Danville just after Davis's train had left for Greensboro.

Dooley wrote:

> Danville is in a perfect uproar. The President and his Cabinet were here last night and hearing officially of Lee's surrender left these parts for Greensboro, N. C. . . . Large crowds of savage and blood thirsty looking stragglers parade the streets and appear awaiting an opportunity to do some ugly deed.

If Davis had seen the increasing flood of stragglers and deserters coming into Danville, he did not record his thoughts on them. He was thinking ahead to creating new armies, although he would have to depend on two men he detested: Generals Beauregard and Johnston. Johnston had recently named Beauregard to command over all remaining troops in western North Carolina who were not attached to the Army of Tennessee. Not only the future of the nation rested with Beauregard and Johnston, but so too the freedom of the cabinet. Davis's hopes of escaping farther south now lay with men whom he had always disliked and whom he had removed from responsibility on more than one occasion. Those grudges would not be put to rest now that the apparent end of the Confederacy had arrived.

☆   ☆   ☆

BACK IN WASHINGTON, President Lincoln celebrated the surrender of Lee's army by giving an impromptu speech to a crowd gathered outside the Executive Mansion. He would give another, more policy-oriented speech on another night. In the crowd would be one man who would be seeing Lincoln again before the week was out at Ford's Theater.

During both speeches, Lincoln made no references to placing blame for the war on Davis and the Confederate cabinet. Though Davis and the cabinet had been on the run for ten days, Lincoln had given no orders to chase them, nor did he intend to issue such orders.

On the morning of April 14, Good Friday, Lincoln held his regular cabinet meeting. Frederick Seward was invited to sit in for his father, Secretary of State William Seward, who had been seriously injured in a carriage accident and was now bedridden. Seward saw a content Lincoln with a "visible sign of relief" on his face. When some unidentified cabinet member brought up the subject of what should happen to the "heads of the rebel government," Seward said that "all those present thought that, for the sake of general amity and good will, it was desirable to have as few judicial proceedings as possible. Yet, would it be wise to let the leaders in treason go entirely unpunished?"

When Postmaster General William Dennison asked Lincoln if he would be sorry to see the Confederates escape the country, Lincoln replied, "I should not be sorry to have them leave the country; but I should be for following them up pretty close, to make sure of their going."

Hugh McCullouch, secretary of the Treasury, remembered that Lincoln told this story: "I am a good deal like the Irishman who had joined a temperance society, but thought he might take a drink now and then if he drank unbeknown to himself. A good many people thought that all the big Confederates ought to be arrested and tried as traitors. Perhaps they ought to be, but I should be right glad if they would get out of the country unbeknown to me."

To his cabinet and his top generals, Lincoln made it clear that he did not want Davis and the cabinet captured, imprisoned, or punished. He did not even want to know where they were.

CHAPTER 5

"Let Them Up Easy"

THE FAILING AND SOARING fortunes of the two combating governments was dramatically illustrated on April 4, two days after the cabinet had evacuated Richmond.

On that first morning in the temporary Confederate capital of Danville, the Confederate States president took it upon himself to give directions for redigging the trenches around the city. The commander in chief with no armies to direct was personally telling a few hundred men how to dig holes.

At about the same time 140 miles to the northeast in Richmond, the U.S. president slid into Davis's office chair. Not even two days after the Confederate capital had been abandoned by its cabinet, Lincoln personally occupied it.

While Lincoln was still sniffing the aroma of Davis's cigars hanging in the air in the Confederate Executive Mansion, elsewhere in Richmond the last representative of the Confederate government was writing out a note requesting an audience with Lincoln. Before the end of the day, this man would personally try to make peace between the United States and Virginia by pointedly leaving the president of the Confederacy out of negotiations. This man had no instructions from Davis, no permission from Davis, no authority at all to speak for the Confederacy, but he did have tacit approval from one member of the Confederate cabinet—his boss, Secretary of War John C. Breckinridge. Breckinridge had gone behind the president's back to seek peace, something that might have gotten him shot for treason if the

Confederate government had not been in flight and his moves had become known to Davis.

Lincoln would not only listen with interest to the man's proposals, but would assure him in conversation that the U.S. government, as represented by him, the president, had no interest in capturing, trying, or sentencing any Confederate leaders for any supposed crime of treason for seceding from the Union. Also tacitly implied by Lincoln were his plans for rebuilding a devastated South. Punishment of anyone was the furthest thing from his mind.

He wanted to make the most of his visit to Richmond. He believed its capture symbolized the war was almost over even if his generals were not yet confident of the outcome. When Lincoln arrived in Richmond, he was more than amenable to listening to anyone talking peace—even if it was someone who had no official capacity in the Confederate government.

THAT LINCOLN WOULD VISIT RICHMOND so soon after its surrender was a surprise not only to the citizens of Richmond but also to Lincoln's cabinet and family back in Washington. The president had been in Virginia since the last week of March keeping close tabs on Grant, making sure he was keeping up the pressure on Petersburg and Richmond. Too many times over the past four years Union generals such as George McClellan, John Pope, Ambrose Burnside, Joseph Hooker, and George Meade either had lost to General Robert E. Lee or had failed to annihilate him when they had the chance. Grant was no exception to Lincoln's impatience to end the war. While Lincoln had been impressed by General Ulysses S. Grant's western victories, Grant had spent almost a year failing to defeat Lee at The Wilderness, Spotsylvania Court House, North Anna River, and Cold Harbor. The best Grant had been able to do was encircle and besiege Lee in Petersburg and Richmond. While that was a better performance than any other of the men Lincoln appointed to lead his armies, the war still dragged on though its two remaining major cities in Virginia were under constant pressure. Lincoln wanted Grant to "press the thing" so that Lee would be forced to surrender, an act that Lincoln hoped would nudge other embattled generals around the South to follow suit.

Neither was Lincoln entirely happy with General William T. Sherman, whom he assumed was still down in North Carolina. While the general had devastated Georgia the previous summer and fall of 1864 and South Carolina in February and March, Sherman had allowed General Joseph E. Johnston's army to march away from Bentonville after being soundly defeated. Johnston's battered but still viable army of 20,000 men was now camped near Smithfield, about 140 miles south of Petersburg. Lincoln believed if Lee were to turn south and outrun Grant, he could hook up with Johnston and create a 50,000-man army that could be formidable to defeat. In Lincoln's mind, Sherman's reluctance to smash Johnston's army completely when he had the opportunity only set up the possibility for still more battles and bloodshed on both sides.

On March 27 Sherman arrived at Grant's headquarters at City Point, thinking the two of them would meet briefly to discuss strategy and he would soon be on his way back to Goldsboro, North Carolina, where he had left his resting army. Sherman was surprised when Grant ushered him into a room to meet the president. The only other time Lincoln had met Sherman was early in the war when an untested Colonel Sherman was lobbying the president for a general's appointment.

Almost immediately after exchanging pleasantries, Lincoln expressed concern about Sherman being away from his army in the event Johnston boldly attacked him. Sherman had been embarrassed at Shiloh, Tennessee, in April 1862 when he assured nervous colonels under his command that the Confederates were nowhere near their lines. Minutes later the Confederates attacked. Lincoln started asking about the readiness of Sherman's army to go on another forced march, a barely disguised hint that Lincoln believed Johnston had been resting and refitting for more than two weeks so that he was once again a strong military threat.

The next morning, March 28, Lincoln hosted a formal conference with Grant, Sherman, and Admiral David Porter. Secretary of War Edwin M. Stanton was still in Washington and not invited, although he would be expected to implement any war strategy changes Lincoln and the generals agreed on.

Lincoln may have personally enjoyed the symbolism of the location of the meeting, which was aboard the Union transport ship *River Queen*. In February on this same ship, negotiations with the Confederate peace commissioners broke down after Lincoln refused to acknowledge the existence of the Confederacy. If the Confederates were unwilling to submit to the Union peacefully in February aboard the *River Queen*, Lincoln would plan out the rest of the war aboard the same ship.

Lincoln opened the meeting once again by expressing concern that Johnston could slip away. He asked what would happen if Johnston were to head south and load his men on railroad cars. Sherman assured him that would not happen because his men had twisted the rails around trees so tightly that they would never be straightened. Lincoln heard, but he still worried that the end of the war was not in sight.

"Yes, Johnston will get away if he can, and you will never catch him until miles of travel and many bloody battles," Lincoln said.

Sherman had no answer for the president. It was true that he had allowed Johnston's army to leave the battlefield unmolested using the excuse that his own army was exhausted from months of campaigning.

What the Union leaders and even Davis did not know was that Johnston himself at this point considered his now greatly depleted army to be barely serviceable and no threat at all to Sherman. Johnston saw the Confederacy's only hope lying with Lee.

Johnston wrote a letter to Lee:

Sherman's force cannot be hindered by the small force I have. I can do no more than annoy him. I respectfully suggest that it is no longer a question whether you leave your present position; you have only to decide where to meet Sherman. I will be near him.

That letter was written before Lee lost more than a third of his effectives at the Battle of Sayler's Creek, Virginia, on April 6. After the battle, Lee's army was virtually as weak as Johnston's, a circumstance neither had contemplated in their meeting with Davis about linking up their two forces in North Carolina.

Grant and Sherman soberly told the president that they both concurred that the war would only be over with one more major battle. Grant said that one of the things he was afraid would happen was that he would arise one morning and discover that somehow Lee had slipped through his lines and that "the war would be prolonged for another year."

To their surprise, Lincoln, who had just demanded action from his two generals, turned somber at the mention of the need to bring both Lee and Johnston to combat.

"Must more blood be shed?" Lincoln asked. "Cannot this bloody battle be avoided? My God! Can't you spare more effusions of blood? We have had so much of it!" Lincoln said.

Sherman, ever blunt, even with the president, said that it was up to Davis and Lee to decide if there would be "one more desperate and bloody battle."

Lincoln was finally convinced that one more battle would be necessary and that both Grant and Sherman were prepared to fight it. Now with the war planning out of the way, Sherman decided to find out what a postwar United States would be like. Without getting Grant's approval to address the president directly, Sherman began asking Lincoln a series of questions:

I inquired of the President if he was all ready for the end of the war. What was to be done with the rebel armies when defeated? And what should be done with the political leaders, such as Jeff. Davis, etc. Should we allow them to escape, etc.?

At this point in late March, Lincoln had yet to discuss with his cabinet what to do with the South after the war was over. Still, the president had a ready answer for Sherman. Lincoln's answer indicated that he, as president, fully intended to direct any postwar efforts to rebuild the South. He was not going to leave those types of political decisions to a Congress dominated by Radical Republicans or even to the members of his own cabinet, some of whom also wanted to punish the South severely.

Sherman would remember:

> All he wanted of us was to defeat the opposing armies, and to get the men composing the Confederate armies back to their homes, at work on their farms and in their shops. As to Jeff. Davis, he was hardly at liberty to speak his mind fully, but intimated that he ought to clear out, "escape the country," only it would not do for him to say so openly.

Lincoln then told a story about how a man who had sworn off liquor discovered a way he could unknowingly enjoy his liquor if it was disguised as lemonade.

"I inferred that Mr. Lincoln wanted Davis to escape, 'unbeknown' to him," Sherman wrote.

The implication was clear to all the military leaders in the room. If there were no Confederate cabinet members captured, Lincoln would not have to deal with anyone in Congress or his own cabinet demanding that they be put on trial for treason.

Lincoln's choice of the story on March 28 to Sherman of the man drinking liquored lemonade matched so closely to the story he told his cabinet two weeks later of another drinking man imbibing "unbeknown" to himself that it seems as if Lincoln had already worked out a plan for allowing the Southern leaders to go free well before the war was over.

Sherman, impressed that Lincoln was already thinking about the postwar period of rebuilding the South, pressed the president on what specifically he should do in North Carolina. Lincoln suggested contacting Governor Zebulon Vance with the offer that if the armies in that state put down their arms, the state's people would have full rights restored as citizens of the United States. Sherman wrote that it appeared Lincoln had the deepest sympathy for the "whole people" including the South. It seemed Lincoln had taken to heart his own phrase from the second inaugural address that the nation had "charity for all, malice toward none."

Sherman wrote:

> In his mind he was all ready for the civil reorganization of affairs at the South as soon as the war was over. As soon as the rebel armies laid down their arms, and resumed their civil pursuits, they would at once be guaranteed all their rights as citizens of a common country; and that to avoid anarchy the State governments then in existence, with their civil functionaries, would be recognized by him as the government de facto until Congress could provide others.

In a conversation that lasted less than two hours, Lincoln shared with his two top generals and admiral what he had not discussed with his own cabinet or Congressional leaders. He did not want anyone in the South—including its cabinet members—to be punished for their roles in rebelling against the United States. He did not see any need for a period of time where the South would have to be rehabilitated or reconstructed back into the good graces of the United States.

ON APRIL 3, less than two weeks after his meeting with his military leaders—minus his secretary of war—Lincoln sent a telegram to Stanton casually announcing that he was visiting Petersburg and would soon be on his way to Richmond. Stanton exploded as best he could by telegraphed message: "Allow me to respectfully ask you to consider whether you ought to expose the nation to the consequences of any disaster to yourself in pursuit of a treacherous and dangerous enemy like the rebel army."

Lincoln, irritated himself at a cabinet member instructing him, answered with a curt: "I can take care of myself."

The next morning, April 4, Lincoln ordered Admiral David Dixon Porter to take him and his young son, Tad, up the James in a small ship, the *Malvern*. When downriver currents and obstacles became too much for the ship, the headstrong Lincoln climbed into a twelve-man rowboat, along with Porter and an escort of sailors, and made for the shore of the James River on the outskirts of the city.

Two days earlier the streets of Richmond had been filled with re-treating Confederate soldiers, drunken riffraff stealing from stores, and nervous black people pondering what would happen to them once the Confederate government finally collapsed. Guns were being fired at real or imagined enemies, fires were being started, and hoodlums were drinking whiskey from the street gutters. It had been bedlam, a dangerous situation for the Confederate cabinet to gather and then to leave from a train station that was increasingly attracting attention from the rabble.

Now the president of the United States, protected only by twelve very nervous seamen armed with short-barreled carbines that they had likely never even fired at another human being, started walking through the Confederate capital. Rocketts, the wharf where Lincoln landed, was the type of neighborhood that most of Richmond's citizens avoided. It was where the lower-class people who made their living from the river lived, a place that had frightened even Confederate generals as they made their way out of the city just two days earlier.

On this day, some sort of invisible telegraph alerted the city's freed slaves that the man who was responsible for their freedom was on his way to see his conquered city. A neighborhood that had frightened armed Confederate soldiers was welcoming the president of the United States.

Within minutes of Lincoln's landing, hundreds of spectators, black and white, were crowding the streets and hanging from trees and tele-graph poles to see the president. The only person who appeared un-aware that the president was visiting the city was Major General Godfrey Weitzel, the Union general whose troops had marched into the city one day earlier. The only protection Lincoln had for his first hour in Richmond as he trudged uphill from the river through in-creasing throngs of well-wishers were his seamen and his personal bodyguard, Colonel William Crook.

Crook grew concerned that the mixed-race crowd was so silent and intent on watching Lincoln walk up the hill from the river toward the center of town, a distance of about two miles. The silence was indicative of the shock the city was still experiencing. In February, Davis had assured the citizens that the war was still winnable. Two days ago the Confederate cabinet had fled the city. Just yesterday Negro soldiers had marched through the streets. Now, today, the man who had armed those Negroes was inspecting his prize of war.

"There was something oppressive in those thousands of watchers without a sound, either of welcome or hatred. I think we would have welcomed a yell of defiance," Crook remembered.

Crook glanced at Lincoln and saw that the silence was also playing on the nerves of the president. As they passed one house, Crook thought he saw a man aim a gun at the president from an upstairs window. He stepped in front of Lincoln, but no shot was fired.

"We were all so aware of the danger that our nerves were not steady," Crook wrote.

Even Lincoln's personal secretaries, John Hay and John Nicolay, who were not with him on this day, could not believe the poor judgment of Lincoln's impromptu visit to Richmond. In an admiring biography written by them, Hay and Nicolay said, "One cannot help but wonder at the manifest imprudence of both Mr. Lincoln and Admiral Porter in the whole proceeding."

Finally after walking for nearly an hour among Richmonders, Lincoln reached the Confederate Executive Mansion at about the same time as a hastily organized cavalry escort found his little party. Lincoln ignored the cavalrymen and walked into the house where Davis had lived for four years. Totally drained of energy, Lincoln flopped down in Davis's chair and quietly contemplated the symbolism of that simple gesture. One of Davis's servants gave him a glass of water. Reinvigorated, Lincoln took a quick tour of the house after being assured by a servant that Davis had left the house in good order for just such a visit by a Union dignitary.

Just as Lincoln returned to Davis's office, Weitzel, who had been out inspecting Richmond, arrived, and was totally shocked to see his commander in chief in a city that he did not consider yet fully secure. Satisfied that he had seen all of the Confederate White House that he wanted to see, Lincoln then asked for a tour of the city. Weitzel, unsure how to refuse, agreed and called up a carriage. The first one to be found was open topped. Lincoln did not hesitate to climb into a vehicle that elevated him several feet off the ground, making him even more of a visible target so that any die-hard Confederate citizen who wanted could take a shot at him.

As the flustered general was taking his calm commander in chief on a short tour of downtown Richmond, this time protected by a cavalry escort, Weitzel thought to ask Lincoln what his occupation policy should be toward the townspeople once they got used to the idea of having surrendered.

Lincoln replied that he could not put such a thought in a written order, but he said, "If I were in your place, I would let them up easy, let them up easy."

Twice in less than a week, Lincoln had said in the presence of three generals and an admiral that he did not wish the former citizens of the Confederacy to be treated harshly.

By this time Lincoln and Weitzel had spent at least an hour together, more than enough time for Weitzel to tell Lincoln that there was a very special woman in the city who union generals considered their secret weapon. She was Elizabeth Van Lew.

Van Lew was an often disheveled, gray-haired, 47-year-old spinster who had always hated the idea of slavery, so much so that when the war broke out in 1861 she organized a ring of spies operating in the Confederate capital. Her work was remarkable, and so effective that both Major General Benjamin Butler and Grant would come to depend on her regular communications. Varina Davis would regularly deny ever employing anyone like this, but historical rumors persist that Van Lew was able to put a black female maid who could read and who had a photographic memory on the Executive Mansion staff. It is known that Van Lew put one of her white agents on the staff at Libby prison, a Richmond prisoner-of-war camp for Union officers. The clever clerk regularly verbally abused the prisoners to keep up his image with his Confederate army bosses, but when prisoners escaped, that same man materialized out of the darkness to help them leave Richmond. Ben Butler kept in such close contact with Van Lew that he dubbed her his "secret collaborator."

Van Lew's ingenious efforts included having a trusted shoemaker make double-soled shoes with a hollow space between the soles. Her servants would stuff maps of Richmond's defenses and messages into the shoes and then walk out of the city carrying market baskets with the excuse that they were going to buy food from country farmers. The only farmers they were really interested in finding were Butler and Grant who would give the servants different shoes with return messages for Van Lew. The servants would walk right past Confederate pickets with baskets now filled with fresh produce supplied by the Union commissaries. The only searches ever conducted of her servants were their baskets, which always contained fresh food.

Van Lew's contributions to Grant's war plans were deeply appreciated by him, so much so that he ordered the first Union troops entering the city on the morning of April 3 to peel off and march directly to her house to protect her life and property should angry Richmonders take their revenge on a woman they had long suspected—but could never prove—was a spy in their midst. The unit was led by Lieutenant Colonel Ely S. Parker, Grant's personal aide, an indication that the top general not only knew who Van Lew was but realized her importance in capturing the city. As Parker's men turned up Van Lew's street, they easily figured out which house was hers. It was the one flying the huge U.S. flag. She had hidden it away for four years waiting for just this occasion.

Van Lew had to have known that Davis and the cabinet left on a train for Danville on the night of April 2. It was the talk of Richmond from the time churches let out at noon until the delayed midnight departure, nearly twelve hours from the time the evacuation intention was made known until the train actually left. That was plenty of time for any or all of Van Lew's contacts to have reached her home, just a few blocks from the train station itself.

While there is no historical record of Van Lew meeting with Weitzel or Lincoln to discuss what was arguably the most important piece of intelligence of the war at that time, the location of the Confederate cabinet, that same lack of confirmation might have been her intention. After the war Van Lew grew worried that her neighbors in Richmond would harm her if they discovered how much intelligence she had provided the Union army and how much her help had undermined the Confederacy. With the express approval of several top Union generals, Van Lew collected every piece of correspondence mentioning her name that was in the Federal archives in 1866. She destroyed scores, perhaps hundreds, of telegrams and reports before the *Official Records of the War of the Rebellion* were published starting in the 1880s. The most important Union spy during the war is barely mentioned in the greatest compilation of reports on the war.

But even if Van Lew did not meet with Weitzel and Lincoln to alert them that Davis had left Richmond on the Danville train, it was common knowledge to virtually all citizens in the city. All they would have had to do was invite a disgruntled citizen to tell them where Davis had gone. Had Lincoln set as a goal the capture of the Confederate cabinet, he could have ordered Weitzel to begin the chase as early as April 4 or 5, the two days he was in the occupied city. However, Lincoln issued no orders to chase down Davis.

Lincoln may have been thinking more about making peace than about capturing his counterpart. In fact, Lincoln thought it would be easier to make peace if his counterpart was on the run and unable to communicate with the tattered remnants of his dissolving government.

On Lincoln's first day in Richmond, April 4, the president answered a note and agreed to meet with one of the Confederacy's few officials remaining in the city. He had met the man in February 1865 when he was part of Stephens' peace mission. The man, who now represented—or at least proclaimed he represented—the Confederacy in Richmond was 54-year-old Confederate assistant secretary of war John A. Campbell.

Campbell had been one of Alabama's most respected lawyers when President Franklin Pierce appointed him to the United States Supreme Court in 1853 at the age of 42. It was during this time that he made the acquaintance of Secretary of War Jefferson Davis.

With the threat of war looming early in 1861 Justice Campbell, who opposed secession, tried to mediate the impending crisis by attending a series of meetings between Lincoln's newly installed Secretary of State William H. Seward and Secretary of War Simon Cameron. During those meetings, Campbell learned that while Seward was promising that Fort Sumter would not be reinforced and resupplied, Lincoln was outfitting a ship to do both. By the end of April 1861, Campbell had resigned from the United States Supreme Court, knowing that the war between North and South would not be settled other than by much bloodshed.

The following year Campbell agreed to be the Confederacy's assistant secretary of war. He served in the post for all of the war and initially opposed Secretary of War Breckinridge's appointment over him as secretary because he thought of the former vice president as a battlefield general rather than a potential good bureaucrat.

Campbell did not come unprepared to his meeting with Lincoln. He and Breckinridge had discussed weeks earlier what should happen on the day when the Federals occupied the city. Campbell, without ever having broached the subject with Davis and even without sending a telegram to Danville asking permission to speak for the Confederate government, suggested to Lincoln several strategies for ending the war.

Campbell even came prepared with a Shakespeare quote from *Henry V*: "For when lenity and cruelty play for a kingdom, the gentler gamester is the soonest winner."

That Campbell did not have the authority of the Confederacy was obvious to Lincoln, but both men were looking for some kind of common ground that would allow them to bypass the involvement of Davis. Campbell knew, and Lincoln could have known, that Davis was then in Danville, but neither man proposed contacting the Confederate president to discuss terms of a general Confederate surrender.

Campbell and Lincoln agreed to a second meeting the following day, April 5, with Lincoln inviting Campbell to bring other prominent secessionists to the meeting. There were no Confederate civilian government leaders left in the city, so Campbell returned with one prominent lawyer, George A. Myers.

The meeting ran quick and covered a variety of subjects with the principal object being how to end the war since Lee was still in the field with his army. Together, Lincoln and Campbell came up with the idea of calling a special session of the Virginia legislature to ask them to pull the state's remaining troops out of the Confederacy. Lincoln believed that if Virginia authorized such an action, the other states would follow suit. Some North Carolina politicians were already following similar tactics in trying to reach Sherman with a similar proposal.

Lincoln, always thinking of the political angles, realized that his own suggestion was potentially dangerous for him in Congress. He had always maintained that he would not meet or agree to deal with Confederate politicians seeking peace because he did not want to recognize the idea that the Confederacy existed as a separate nation. To Lincoln, the Confederacy was a collection of rebelling states that had never left the Union. Their stars were still on the U.S. flag. In his opinion, there had been no secession.

Yet, here he was breaking his own rules. If he officially went to the U.S. Congress with the plan he and Campbell were discussing to let Confederate Virginia back into the Union, Congress would gleefully point out he was violating his own oath of never recognizing the Confederacy. On the other hand, Lincoln reasoned, if he treated Virginia as a state government, not a Confederate government, the Radical Republicans in Congress would have no recourse but to let him try his idea of undermining the Confederate government from the inside.

To Lincoln, the status of Virginia's soldiers was the key to the life and death of the Confederacy. While neither Campbell nor Lincoln could know, it was the evening of April 4 that Lee discovered the food he expected to find at the railroad sidings at Amelia Court House had never left Richmond. It was the next day on April 5 that Lee issued his written plea for food from the area farmers. Even without being forced into battle, the Confederates were starving.

Lincoln seemed to have an open mind about what Campbell was suggesting. It was Lincoln's suggestion to allow the current Confederate-elected state legislators to remain in place so that they could vote on the idea of pulling their state troops out of Lee's army. Campbell assured Lincoln that Lee would do what the state legislature ordered him to do. Lee was, after all, a believer in states' rights.

Lincoln went on to make other concessions, including one not to embarrass former Confederate soldiers by requiring them to take oaths of allegiance to the United States. Just as he had hinted at the Hampton Roads Peace Conference back in February, Lincoln suggested that Congress might be persuaded to rescind the Emancipation Proclamation, although Lincoln himself would continue to support it publicly. Campbell told Lincoln that he thought slavery was a dead issue. Campbell also was surprised when Lincoln offered to return all property the Union had captured back to its owners if it had not already been sold at auction. That meant that the South's always thin manufacturing base, as well as its vast agricultural holdings, could quickly be put back into production, a key to healing the region's destroyed economy.

Campbell then edged into conversation that which would be of most interest to the Confederate cabinet if they were in a position to hear it—what would happen to them. Lincoln said that "scarcely anyone" would be denied a pardon, and he saw no reason why former Confederates would not be granted full citizenship back into the United States.

Campbell left the meeting emboldened by what Lincoln had told him might be accomplished. The president had made no promises, but if Lincoln could convince his cabinet and Congress to go along, the shooting war could be ended in Virginia within a matter of days. Assuming that the other Southern states would follow the Old Dominion's lead, the process of bringing all the Southern states back into the Union could be accomplished in a matter of weeks. Perhaps most important of all to put the Southern people at ease in their new role as defeated Americans was that the leaders of the Confederacy and the nation would not be arrested and tried for treason, a crime that carried the death sentence. If Lincoln could accomplish what he had talked about, the nation's wounds would begin to heal immediately.

There were problems on Campbell's end of the discussion. The judge had no idea how to let anyone in the Confederate cabinet know about his meeting with Lincoln. He had no way to reach them in Danville where he assumed they were because he had not heard that they were captured. Nor did he actually have any power at all to negotiate with the president of the United States. Campbell, now an unemployed assistant secretary of war, had essentially planned out the postwar South with the postwar president of the United States. Campbell decided to wait a few days before trying to reach Davis to be sure

Lincoln was following through on the ideas the two of them had discussed.

On April 5, having spent nearly two full days in Richmond, Lincoln sailed back down the James River for City Point aboard the *Malvern*, which had finally passed through the leftover Confederate obstructions in the James. On board the ship that night, the president pondered this new, unforeseen opportunity for peace that would not have been possible had he not taken the opportunity to visit Richmond himself. Lincoln wrote a letter to Grant detailing the plan to get the Virginia legislature back into session. It would be dropped off in City Point so that the letter could make its way to Grant who was now somewhere west of Petersburg chasing Lee's army.

"If they [Campbell and the lawyer in Richmond who had sat in on the meeting] attempt this, [you are] to permit and protect them, unless they attempt something hostile to the United States, in which case to give them notice and time to leave, and to arrest any remaining after such time," Lincoln told Grant.

Lincoln must have thought more about if his cabinet would accept the suggestions he and Campbell had discussed while he added that he was not sure if the idea would work, "but I thought it best to notify you so that if you should see signs you may understand them." Lincoln did not want Grant to arrest Campbell for trying to reorganize the Virginia legislature right under the noses of a Federal occupying force. At the same time, Lincoln did not want Grant to think that the president wanted the Union forces to pull back from attacking Lee while waiting for the Virginia legislature to reform.

"Nothing that I have done, or probably shall do, is to delay, hinder, or interfere with your work," Lincoln wrote.

By "work" Lincoln meant chasing down Lee's army. The president had decided to play both angles to see which one would lead to the end of the war first: the peace plan with Campbell or the war plan with Grant.

To show Campbell that he was following through, Lincoln sent a similar letter to Weitzel telling him to let Campbell read it, but not to make it public.

That night, Lincoln had a morbid dream that he shared with his bodyguard. He dreamed the Executive Mansion had caught fire in his absence. He was so shaken by the vibrancy of the vision that he telegraphed back to Washington to see if the dream had actually been a vision of something that had already occurred.

Lincoln, unwilling to head back to Washington when he could stay closer to the action, did not sail back to Washington until the evening of April 8. All he knew of Grant was that he was somewhere to the west, and he was closing in on Lee.

The next morning, April 9, the president and Mrs. Lincoln were standing on deck chatting with several prominent government officials including Senator Charles Sumner, a Republican from Massachusetts who had been continually telling Lincoln that the South needed a period of "reconstruction." To Sumner's surprise, Mrs. Lincoln turned to her husband and virtually shouted: "Do not allow him to escape the law! He must be hanged!" Three times, according to Sumner, Lincoln replied to suggestions that Davis must die for treason: "Judge not lest you be judged."

Once more Lincoln, always a master equivocator when it came to average political decisions, had not changed his tone or attitude on punishing the fleeing Confederate cabinet. He did not want them caught. As of April 9, he had not ordered Grant to pursue them now that they were gone from Richmond for a full week.

What Lincoln did not know was that his decision to let Grant pursue the war strategy had worked. That afternoon, Robert E. Lee would surrender the Army of Northern Virginia, about 28,000 men, down from a Gettysburg high of 80,000. That night Lincoln would celebrate the victory with a short, off-the-cuff speech. He asked a band that had led the crowd to the Executive Mansion to play "Dixie."

Lincoln shouted down to the crowd, a smile on his face:

I have always thought "Dixie" one of the best tunes I have ever heard. Our adversaries over the way attempted to appropriate it, but I insisted today that we fairly captured it. I presented the question to the attorney general, and he gave me his legal opin-

ion that it is our lawful prize. I now request the band to favor
me with its performance. It is good to show the rebels that with
us they will be free to hear it again.

Lincoln knew full well that "Dixie" had been the unofficial national
anthem of the Confederacy. With his last sentence, he was showing
once again that he believed the nation could and should be reunited
starting with listening to the same song that had been a prewar favorite among Northern audiences since the moment it was introduced
on a New York City stage.

Lincoln's cabinet and Congress were not willing to let playing "Dixie"
bind the nation back together. Men like Representative Thaddeus
Stevens of Pennsylvania and Senator Sumner were on record wanting
a harsh period of punishment for the South. Stevens was floating an
idea to confiscate all the land in the Southern states from white land
owners then turn it over to the freedmen. Stevens was also demanding full voting rights for freedmen in the South. Sumner was calling
for the South to be divided into military districts and occupied like a
foreign, conquered nation. Neither man intended to allow the South
back into the country as quickly and as easily as Lincoln imagined.

When Lincoln broached the idea of allowing the states to reform their
legislatures, his cabinet sided with the Congress. Stanton told Lincoln
in the next cabinet meeting that the idea to reform the Virginia legislature:

Would be giving away the scepter of the conqueror, that it would
transfer the result of our victory of our arms from the field to the
very legislature which four years before had said, "give us war,"
that it would put the Government in the hands of its enemies;
that it would surely bring trouble with Congress. Any effort to
reorganize the Government should be under Federal authority
solely, treating the rebel organizations and governments as absolutely null and void.

Lincoln, sensing that his idea of letting the South "up easy" would
not be accepted by a vengeful North, polled all his cabinet. None,

even Secretary of the Navy Gideon Welles, who could usually be counted on to rubber stamp anything the president suggested, agreed with Lincoln. Just as Lincoln had learned back in February when he sought to pass a resolution compensating slaveholders after the war, the cabinet was willing to reject the idea of a kinder and gentler reconstruction. In February, Lincoln had moaned, "You are all against me." Now he felt similarly rejected in April.

On April 12, three days after Lee had surrendered and two days after the Confederate cabinet had moved from Danville to Greensboro, Lincoln began trying to rebuild his relationship with his cabinet and the Congress by severing relations with Campbell. But Campbell had already placed a newspaper story in the Richmond papers announcing that the United States had agreed to let the Virginia legislature meet "as the first step toward the reinstatement of the Old Dominion in the Union."

Lincoln sent a telegram to Weitzel disavowing Campbell's idea that Lincoln had "called the insurgent Legislature of Virginia together." Lincoln went on to say that he only meant that "gentlemen" who had once served as legislators should be able to withdraw their troops from the Confederacy in exchange for getting their property back. Lincoln then went on to say that since Lee had already surrendered, any agreement that he had with Campbell was now "withdrawn or countermanded." He told Weitzel that the Virginia legislature should not be allowed to assemble, "but if any have come, allow them safe-return to their homes."

Lincoln was backtracking on just about everything he and Campbell had agreed to in their conversation just one week earlier. Though he rescinded his approval of the gathering of the Virginia legislature in Richmond, the damage to the president's image in Washington had been done. Radical Republicans in Congress were grumbling that Lincoln had overstepped his bounds by negotiating with former Confederates. In their view no single man could speak for the U.S. government, not even the president. Congress would demand a central role in planning the future of the South. Lincoln did not even have Vice President Andrew Johnson, the only Southern senator who did not resign his Tennessee seat in 1861, on his side. Johnson was telling everyone who would listen that the rebels had to be punished: "Treason is a crime and must be made odious."

Lincoln had nothing to worry about with his favorite general, Grant. The commanding general had become a Lincoln man who shared the president's sense that compassion would go a long way toward reconciliation between the warring regions. He had not humiliated Lee in the surrender negotiations, nor had he even considered putting him under arrest, although Lee had put on his dress uniform in anticipation of being taken into custody. At Lee's request, Grant had readily given 25,000 rations to the starving Army of Northern Virginia within hours of the surrender negotiations. He ordered the printing presses to begin turning out thousands of paroles so that Lee's men could start back for home as soon as their arms were stacked. Grant believed in Lincoln's vision of letting the South up easy.

Writing in his memoirs Grant said, "The great majority of the Northern people, and the soldiers unanimously, would have favored a speedy reconstruction on terms that would be the least humiliating to the people who had rebelled against their government." Grant went on to say that he did not think the defeated Confederates would make good citizens if they thought they had a yoke around their necks. He also agreed with Lincoln that the freed slaves should not be immediately given the right to vote, but over time they "could prepare themselves for the privileges of citizenship before the full right would be conferred."

Campbell was not surprised to hear from Weitzel that Lincoln had sent a formal letter denying the Virginia legislature permission to meet. He had been a politician in Washington and knew that the terms Lincoln was talking about in private with him were probably too generous to be acceptable to the Radicals in Congress. He also realized that life in occupied Richmond was about to change radically from Lincoln's "let them up easy" policy that Weitzel had been following. The Union general told Campbell of a letter he had received from Stanton demanding that each church pastor in Richmond include a prayer at every Sunday service for the president of the United States. Union officers would monitor each church service in the city. If those officers did not hear a prayer for the president, they were authorized to arrest the pastors who had failed to say the prayer.

The federal government, in direct violation of the First Amendment guaranteeing freedom of religion, was now dictating what Southern pastors could say in their prayers.

Weary and disappointed from trying to convince his own political party and his own cabinet to accept his ideas on ending the war, and feeling the need to celebrate, Lincoln decided to go see a comedy at Ford's Theater. If anyone needed a laugh on April 14, 1865, it was the president of the United States.

CHAPTER 6

"A Miss Is as Good as a Mile"

IT WOULD HAVE BEEN EASY to capture Davis in the first week that he fled Richmond.

Had President Lincoln or General Godfrey Weitzel followed through on any tip they received in Richmond that Davis was in Danville, they could have sent word to Grant in central Virginia or to a Union cavalry command that was already operating in southwestern Virginia and northwestern North Carolina, areas that were south of where Davis was fleeing. A determined effort by a concentrated Union cavalry force could have intercepted Davis at Danville, Greensboro, or along the railroad running between the two towns.

The 6,000-man raiding party, six times larger than any single cavalry unit still operating in General Robert E. Lee's Army of Northern Virginia, was commanded by Major General George Stoneman, a 42-year-old native of New York State. Stoneman, a tall, gaunt man with deep set, dark eyes that telegraphed his anger, had been a professional soldier since graduation from West Point in 1846. His roommate had been a man who gained much more fame and success on the battlefield—Thomas "Stonewall" Jackson, commander of the Confederate Second Corps until his death in May 1863.

Stoneman's performance in the Union army to date had been spotty. He had been praised early in the war for refusing to surrender his United States Army command in Texas after that state seceded. But then he was virtually ignored by his first commander, Union general George McClellan, who relegated cavalry to scouting missions for the infantry. One of McClellan's successors, Joe Hooker, liked Stoneman and assigned him the task of drawing off Lee's cavalry at the Battle of Chancellorsville, Virginia, in May 1863. Lee did not take the bait and kept his cavalry with him while Stoneman rode aimlessly in Lee's rear before returning to Hooker.

Transferred west to General William T. Sherman's theater of operations, Stoneman tried to lead his men on a rescue mission to free the Union prisoners at Camp Sumter at Andersonville, Georgia, in the summer of 1864 during Sherman's Atlanta campaign. Had Stoneman succeeded, he would have been the nation's most beloved hero. Instead, the general was captured by Confederate cavalry. As Sherman's cavalry corps commander, Stoneman was the highest-ranking Union general captured during the war.

Itching to restore his image with his superiors, Stoneman continually volunteered to lead cavalry raids such as one in December 1864 to destroy salt works in southwestern Virginia. He had hardly rested from his return from that successful foray when he proposed a March–April 1865 raid through western North Carolina and southwestern Virginia. Stoneman's goals were to strike at the region's civilian breadbasket and to free the Union prisoners at Salisbury, North Carolina. Swooping into central North Carolina and capturing Salisbury would be justice achieved for his failure to get close to Andersonville the previous summer.

What Stoneman did not know was that his superiors had already given up on him. Just before leaving on the raid, his commanding general received a letter recommending Stoneman's dismissal from the army, but the sympathetic general put the discharge in a drawer. He wanted Stoneman to have one more chance to redeem himself.

On March 23, 1865, Stoneman rode out of eastern Tennessee with nine regiments totaling 6,000 men. Some were battle-hardened Northern veterans like the Fifteenth Pennsylvania. Others were Southerners who had joined the Union army rather than the Confederate army. Three regiments were made up of men from Tennessee and western North Carolina, so used to riding and fighting that Stoneman fondly called them "my Cossacks." Stoneman also had three regiments of Kentuckians who had fought with him in other raids.

The raiders moved rapidly through the Blue Ridge Mountains of North Carolina, finding little military opposition, but many small factories to burn. Chancing that no organized opposition could be mounted against him, Stoneman broke up the force into several parts so that they could cover more ground and destroy more targets.

On April 4, the same day Lincoln was visiting Richmond, one unit captured Christiansburg, Virginia, at the southern end of the Shenandoah Valley. The Federals, mindful that telegraph operators recognized each other's tapping signatures, forced the Christiansburg telegraph operator to contact his counterpart in Lynchburg, Virginia, to learn war news. The Lynchburg operator willingly volunteered the news that Lee had abandoned Petersburg and Richmond. The questions kept coming until the Lynchburg operator finally tapped out: "I'm talking to Yankees, aren't I?"

On April 9, the same day Lee surrendered at Appomattox Court House, Stoneman's entire 6,000-man force reentered North Carolina. On April 10, the same day the cabinet left Danville bound for Greensboro, Colonel William J. Palmer of the Fifteenth Pennsylvania Cavalry captured the small town of Salem (now Winston-Salem), North Carolina.

The residents of Salem, nervous after hearing so many stories of how Sherman's men had burned cities and towns in Georgia and South Carolina, were surprised at how well behaved Stoneman's men were. One resident remembered:

In very great comparative silence about 3,000 cavalry passed through our town. Had it not been for the noise their horses and swords made, it would have hardly been noticed that so large a number of troops were passing through our streets.

Stoneman's men would not rest long. The larger town of Greensboro, thirty miles to the east of Salem, interested them. Had they taken a more intense interest in it, they could have written a piece of history for themselves.

☆　　☆　　☆

THE THREAT OF STONEMAN through the end of March and into April was not a secret to the residents of northwestern North Carolina and southwestern Virginia or to the leadership in Richmond. Davis had known about Stoneman's raid almost from its inception. On March 30, the day he sent Varina Davis and the children from Richmond, Davis asked Secretary of War John C. Breckinridge by letter if he knew where Stoneman was at that time:

Have you heard any information of the reported arrival of Stoneman on the R.R. near Salisbury? My family is about to leave and I am anxious to learn the truth of that and other reports.

Varina would have to pass through Salisbury on her way to Charlotte, North Carolina.

The report Davis heard was false. On March 30 the raiders were around Elkin, North Carolina, more than sixty miles to the northwest of Salisbury and still heading northwest to strike at targets in Virginia. Still, Davis had reason to worry. If Stoneman suddenly changed directions, a cavalry force could leisurely reach Salisbury in two days.

Greensboro itself had been on edge for days because citizens were regularly getting sketchy reports of what Stoneman was doing as he moved east along the spine of the mountains in western North Carolina.

Athos, an anonymous writer for the *Greensboro Patriot* newspaper reported in a postwar edition that a quick-thinking telegraph operator in early April might have helped spare the town from attack before the cabinet arrived. At the same time that Stoneman's telegrapher had been trying to fool the Lynchburg telegrapher that he was Christiansburg's operator, he tried the same thing on the fellow manning the keys in Greensboro. If Athos's story was true, the Greensboro telegraph operator also discovered the ruse and saved the president from danger. Furthermore, and more important, if Athos's story was true, Stoneman had at least some inkling that Davis was in the area.

Stoneman's telegrapher impersonator asked the Greensboro telegrapher if

President Davis was in town and if there were enough troops to defend the place. Our operator knowing, by some peculiarity, that if [sic] was the enemy, replied that Davis was not in town and Johnston with a large force was present. All the reverse was true, as Johnston's army had not arrived then and Jefferson Davis had. But at the time we did not care to risk an attack. This turned him away from us and sent him galloping to Salisbury.

It was early in the morning of April 11 when the cabinet train pulled to a stop in downtown Greensboro, a town of a few thousand that grew up just south of the Revolutionary War battlefield of Guilford Courthouse. It was here in March 1781 that British General Lord Cornwallis had unwittingly begun the end of that war when he won a bloody victory over Patriot forces, but was so crippled himself that he had to retreat back into South Carolina to refit and rest his battered army. Just months later, the victor of this battle would become the loser of the war when Cornwallis would surrender at Yorktown, Virginia.

Davis was not thinking of the irony of stopping in a town where a barely won victory led to ultimate defeat. He was here to meet two generals and convince them to inspire their men to defeat both Sherman and Ulysses S. Grant.

As Davis was surveying downtown Greensboro, a town that he had never visited, someone told him he had just had a close call. Not long after his train had passed over the Reedy Creek Bridge to the north of the city, a force of Union cavalry had burned it. No one knew for sure at that time that it was Stoneman's raiders, but the suspicion was strong.

"A miss is as good as a mile," Davis dryly replied.

There was no crowd of admiring civilians cheering the arrival of the cabinet as there had been in Danville. Like Danville, Greensboro had been a reluctant participant in secession. The town itself had voted against secession back in February 1861, but when North Carolina seceded after the firing on Fort Sumter, Guilford County had contributed thousands of young men to the war effort. Most of them did not return home the whole men they were when they left. Now word of

Lee's surrender arrived at almost the same time the threat of Stoneman's raiders was announced almost hourly. Greensboro's citizens were not anxious to embrace the fleeing cabinet members. Welcoming them, even housing them, would only endanger the town with the inevitable visit from Union soldiers.

Secretary of the Navy Stephen Mallory complained that "Greensboro had been a flourishing town, and there were many commodious and well-furnished residences in and about, but their doors were closed and their latch-strings pulled in against the members of a retreating government." Obviously irritated at the cool reception, Mallory continued later in his account that "offhand, generous hospitality has ever been regarded as characteristic of the South and had such a scene as this been predicted of any of its people, it would have encountered a universal unbelief."

When Mallory's postwar article about the cabinet's flight appeared in *Century Magazine* in the 1880s, Greensboro residents were furious. Some wrote their own articles explaining that Davis was offered several houses, all of which he turned down out of fear that following Federals would burn them down for harboring him. Of all the cabinet officers, only Secretary of the Treasury George Trenholm stayed in a home, that of former governor John Motley Morehead. The rest stayed in the train cars in which they had arrived . . . though Davis spent some time in a house rented by Wood.

THAT UNION FORCE that almost nabbed Davis at the Reedy Creek Bridge before reaching Greensboro was a one hundred-man detachment from the Fifteenth Pennsylvania Cavalry, commanded by Major Abraham Garner. Garner's men had ridden from Salem specifically to find and burn this last railroad bridge from Danville before reaching Greensboro. As the railroad line itself was new, so was the bridge. It took the cavalrymen considerable time before they could soak the green wood in enough turpentine so that it would burn. While some men were working on the bridge, others were cautiously scouting toward Greensboro. These Union troopers captured some Confederate soldiers who told them exciting news that confirmed the Confederate end of the story—that Davis's train passed over that same bridge not more than an hour before the raiders arrived.

The Fifteenth Pennsylvania's second in command, Lieutenant Colonel Charles Betts, also probed Greensboro's defenses on the northern side of the town. Betts and his seventy-five-man detachment attacked the camp of the Third South Carolina Cavalry while the unaware Confederates were having breakfast. Most of the Confederates scattered, allowing Betts to later burn the wagon bridge over Buffalo Creek and capture at least another one hundred men including the lieutenant colonel commanding the regiment. Betts' performance in attacking a greater force so impressed his superiors they nominated him for a Congressional Medal of Honor, which he finally received in 1892. Just as Garner heard that Davis was in Greensboro, prisoners taken by Betts told him the same thing, adding that Davis was inside a railroad car parked on a siding less than two miles from the burning bridge.

While presumably both Garner and Betts reported the Davis stories to Palmer, commander of the Fifteenth Pennsylvania Cavalry, there was no attempt by the rest of the regiment to probe farther into Greensboro to see how many troops were defending the city in general and the Confederate president in particular.

Palmer's decision not to investigate the presence of Davis with fewer than 200 troops may have been prudent. On April 1, Confederate general Pierre Beauregard ordered three brigades of infantry to Greensboro to construct light earthworks in anticipation of an attack by Stoneman. These troops were not part of General Joseph E. Johnston's Army of Tennessee then east of Raleigh, but were "returned troops," units that were being transferred from one command to another or groups of men who had been wounded, sick, or otherwise on furlough from their units that were scattered around the South. They likely numbered 2,500 men, more than Palmer had in the immediate vicinity, but probably not as high in quality if judged by the artillery crews in Greensboro. The only guns Beauregard could find to defend Greensboro did not have horses to pull them anywhere. They were brought in by train and pulled into place by their crews.

Had Stoneman, then personally some 50 miles to the west and intent on capturing the prison camp at Salisbury, heard the rumors and decided to act on them without specific orders from Washington City, and had he concentrated all his forces to probe Greensboro looking for Davis, he would have outnumbered the Confederates by more than two to one. Stoneman's entire command still numbered 6,000 men, compared to fewer than 3,000 exhausted Confederates then in Greensboro. Stoneman, using his entire command, could probably have captured Greensboro, Davis, and the cabinet had he known of Davis's presence and had he shown the initiative that his superiors always suspected as lacking in him.

But from Stoneman's perspective, he had been ordered to move fast and not report in by telegraph to his superiors lest his own communications lines be tapped by Confederates. Just as Sherman remained out of contact with Grant when marching to the sea in the fall of 1864, Stoneman in the spring of 1865 sought to duplicate the boldness and success of Sherman. Just as Sherman ignored opportunities to send couriers back to Union lines with word of his progress, so did Stoneman, who only occasionally sent reports back to his headquarters in Knoxville. Stoneman knew where he was and what he was supposed to do, destroy Confederate property in North Carolina. Nothing else mattered to him.

There is no definitive historical evidence that Garner, Betts, or Palmer passed along to Stoneman any rumors that Davis was in Greensboro. If they did pass along the rumors, Stoneman may have felt he had no orders to act on them. No *Official Records* or reports at the time of the action around Greensboro mention the rumors. The rumors were first mentioned in print in a post-war history of the Fifteenth Regiment of Pennsylvania Cavalry.

☆   ☆   ☆

CONFEDERATE GENERAL BEAUREGARD did not look forward to any meeting with Davis. The two men despised each other.

The 47-year-old native of Louisiana had been the center of attention at Fort Sumter, First Battle of Manassas, Shiloh, and the siege of Charleston and performed well in most of his assignments. It could even be said that he had saved the day for the South on more than one occasion. Beauregard was the one who had rushed reinforcements to Petersburg when Lee did not believe the Federals were really attacking the previous summer. If not for Beauregard, Petersburg would have fallen nearly a year ago.

Beauregard had repeatedly saved the Confederacy from disaster for more than four years, but Davis had never liked the little man who regularly received a shipment of hair dye delivered to him by blockade-runners. The bad blood dated back to July 1861 (Battle of Bull Run) when Beauregard insisted he could have captured Washington City after the First Battle of Manassas if only Davis had given the word and the necessary food and ammunition.

The general had planned to meet Davis in Danville when he received a telegram informing him that Davis was now on his way to Greensboro. Beauregard decided to wait for his president in Greensboro. When the general awoke in his train car office the next morning, he found that Davis's train had arrived in the city while he was sleeping.

Steeling himself for what he suspected would be a cold greeting, Beauregard entered the president's car. After a few minutes of small talk, Beauregard told Davis that the situation was hopeless. He ticked off the bad news: Sherman was less than one hundred miles to the east with 91,000 men facing Johnston's 20,000 effectives; northern Alabama and south central Georgia were virtually captured; and Mobile was about to be captured. Beauregard said he would not conceal "the truth so the president would have a clear knowledge of the situation and be prepared for the inevitable."

To Beauregard's startled surprise, Davis told him the war was not over, that it could still be won if all the troops not yet captured in the east crossed the Mississippi and joined with Brigadier General Edmund Kirby Smith's army in Texas, which Davis estimated at 60,000 men. Beauregard was aghast. The last he heard, Kirby Smith was near Galveston, Texas, a distance of more than 1,200 miles and a march of more than two months. Davis was dreaming if he thought the Army of Tennessee would follow him that far.

Dismissing Beauregard, Davis sent a telegram to Johnston, order-

Jefferson Davis in 1861. (Library of Congress)

Varina Davis in 1861, formal portrait. (Library of Congress)

The Davis children in
Montreal, 1865.
(*left to right*) Jefferson Jr.,
Maggie, Varina Anne (Pie
Cake), and William.
(Museum of the Confederacy)

Jim Limber Davis, the
foster son or ward of the
Davis family, 1864.
(Museum of the Confederacy)

Flight of Davis in Georgia, drawn by Frank Vizetelly, an artist for the
Illustrated London News, who accompanied Davis on part of the escape.
(Library of Congress)

"End of the Rebellion." A fanciful illustration showing President Andrew
Johnson and a black soldier on the left, with a conspirator whispering into
John Wilkes Booth's ear on the right. Booth hides a pistol and a knife. Davis
lurks behind Booth clutching a bag of money. (Library of Congress)

Composite photo of members of the First Wisconsin Cavalry, who fired into
the Fourth Michigan Cavalry. (Wisconsin Historical Society)

Lt. Col. Benjamin Pritchard,
commander of the unit
that captured Davis.
(Archives of Michigan)

Lt. Julian Dickinson, of the Fourth
Michigan, who perpetuated the
story of Davis in women's clothes
twenty years after the capture.
(Archives of Michigan)

Maj. Gen. James H. Wilson,
who treated the Davis family
to a dinner in Macon.
(Library of Congress)

THE ARCH CONSPIRATOR
JEFFERSON DAVIS,
As he appeared when captured by the Michigan Cavalry.
Copyright secured. Published 56 Chestnut St., Philadelphia.

A realistic image of Davis in women's clothes and clutching a Bowie knife. This is one of the most realistic of the cartoons demeaning Davis. (Archives of Michigan)

"Jeff's Last Shift." Published in Boston, the cartoon shows inaccurate depictions of rifles and pistols. (Library of Congress)

"The Last Groans of the Confederacy," depicting Mrs. Davis trying to pass off her husband as her mother. (Library of Congress)

"Jeff's Race for the Last Ditch!" This cover of a music sheet incorrectly lists Pritchard as commander of the *Fifth* Michigan Cavalry. (Library of Congress)

"A Proper Family Re-union," depicting Jefferson Davis in a dress in hell with Revolutionary War traitor Benedict Arnold. The cauldron is labeled "treason toddy." (Library of Congress)

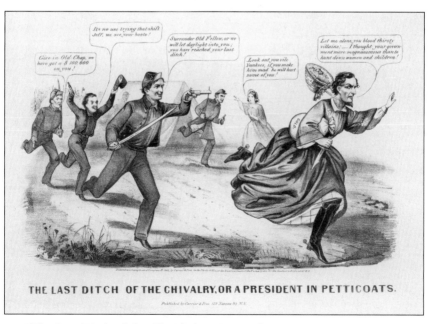

"The Last Ditch of the Chivalry, or A President in Petticoats." Davis is shown saying, "I thought your government more magnanimous than to hunt down women and children!" (Library of Congress)

A smiling Jefferson Davis posing in the gray suit of clothes he was wearing when he was captured. He had the photo taken in 1867, after his release. (Wisconsin Historical Society)

"Finale of the Jeff Davis Die-nasty." Davis, in a dress, has already been hanged. Waiting in line are Lee, Breckinridge, Benjamin, and Senators Yancy, Toombs, and Wigfall. The last in line is John Wilkes Booth. In the upper right corner, Lincoln is with the angels. (Library of Congress)

FREEDOM'S IMMORTAL TRIUMPH!

FINALE of the "JEFF DAVIS DIE-NASTY."
"Last Scene of all, that ends this strange eventful History."

Charles O'Conor, Jefferson Davis's New York lawyer.
(Library of Congress)

Clement C. Clay, alleged Lincoln assassination conspirator, who was imprisoned at Fortress Monroe with Davis.
(Library of Congress)

Gen. Nelson Miles, whose career
was derailed for a time after
carrying out the cruel orders of
Stanton to shackle Davis.
(Library of Congress)

Secretary of War Edwin Stanton,
who ordered Davis to be shackled.
(Library of Congress)

Judge John Underwood,
who presided over Davis's trial.
(Library of Congress)

Chief Justice Salmon Chase,
who released Davis on bail and
never called him back for trial.
(Library of Congress)

Newspaper editor Horace Greeley,
who recruited other Northerners to
raise bail for Davis.
(Library of Congress)

"John Brown
Exhibiting His
Hangman," drawn by
Oscar Harpel in 1865
in Cincinnati, Ohio.
(Library of Congress)

Currier & Ives print
slamming Horace
Greeley for paying
Davis's bond, which
led to his release
from prison.
(Library of Congress)

JEFF. D_ HUNG ON A "SOUR APPLE TREE", OR TREASON MADE ODIOUS.

Davis in prison, drawn by Alfred Waud, an artist for the
Illustrated London News. (Library of Congress)

Scene on May 13, 1867, when Jefferson Davis was brought into court in
Richmond to be released, from *Frank Leslie's Illustrated Newspaper.*
(Library of Congress)

Jefferson and Varina Davis in 1867, after his release from Fortress Monroe.
No wartime photos of them together exist. (Museum of the Confederacy)

ing him to Greensboro for his assessment of the situation. Davis also dashed off a telegram to North Carolina governor Zebulon Vance telling him that:

We must redouble our efforts to meet present disaster. An army holding its position with determination to fight on, and manifest ability to maintain the struggle, will attract all the scattered soldiers and daily rapidly gather strength. Moral influence is wanting, and I am sure you can do much more now to revive the spirit and hope of the people.

Vance, who had been the colonel of the Twenty-sixth North Carolina Infantry Regiment before being elected governor and who knew that 40,000 of the 125,000 men who fought for his state had already been killed, had just been accused by the Confederate president of not doing enough "to revive the spirit and hope of the people."

Johnston arrived in Greensboro on April 12 to meet with Davis, Secretary of State Judah Benjamin, Mallory, and Postmaster General John Reagan. Davis's telegram had suggested that he wanted to hear from Johnston on how best to deal with the declining situation. Johnston walked into the room expecting to give his grim assessment and to gain permission to ask for terms of surrender from Sherman.

To Johnston's surprise, Davis did not ask for a detailed analysis of the fighting ability of the Army of Tennessee. Instead, Davis launched into the same explanation he had given Beauregard of how the Confederacy would still keep on fighting. Davis had no knowledge of the condition of Johnston's army, but he knew without asking that the Confederacy could still fight on no matter how ill prepared or how unwilling its armies were to continue combat.

Johnston wrote in his postwar memoirs:

The President's object seemed to be to give, not to obtain information; for addressing the party, he said that in two or three weeks he would have a large army in the field by bringing back into the ranks those who abandoned them in less desperate circumstances, and by calling out the enrolled men whom the

conscript bureau was unable to bring into the army. It was remarked, by the military officers, that men who left the army
when our cause was not desperate, and those who, under the
same circumstances, could not be forced into it, would scarcely,
in the present desperate condition of our affairs, enter the service upon mere invitation.

A stunned Johnston left the audience without ever having told the
president of the hopelessness of his situation. Mallory followed Johnston out of the room and into Beauregard's office. There the three
men conferred on what to do to convince Davis that the war was lost.
Mallory told Johnston it was his duty to tell Davis that "further resistance with the means at our command would not only be useless,
but unjustifiable."

That night Breckinridge arrived from Danville. The entire cabinet
met again with the purpose of hearing from both Beauregard and
Johnston. Davis opened the meeting again with the assertion that the
war could still be won.

Davis said:

Our late disasters are terrible; but I do not think we should regard them as fatal. I think we can whip the enemy yet, if our
people will turn out. We must look at matters calmly, however,
and see what is left for us to do. Whatever can be done must
be done at once. We have not a day to lose.

He then asked Johnston for his opinion.

Johnston, never a man for small talk, particularly with a president
he hated, launched into his dire assessment:

Our people are tired of war, feel themselves whipped and will
not fight. Our country is overrun, its military resources greatly
diminished, while the enemy's military power and resources were
never greater and may be increased to the extent desired. . . . If
I march out of North Carolina, her people will leave my ranks.
It will be the same as I proceed through South Carolina and

Georgia, and I shall expect to retain no man beyond the by-road or cow path that leads to his home. My small force is melting away like snow before the sun, and I am hopeless of recruiting it.

While Mallory did not remember the use of such words in his postwar article detailing the conference, Johnston in his postwar book recalled that he had said to Davis that it "would be the greatest of human crimes for us to continue the war," and it would lead to "the complete devastation of our country and the ruin of its people."

According to Mallory, the room was silent for two to three minutes as everyone watched Davis silently folding and unfolding a piece of paper. Finally, Davis quietly asked Beauregard for his assessment.

"I concur in all General Johnston said," was all that Beauregard said.

Davis then polled the cabinet. All but Benjamin were in favor of surrendering. Davis asked Johnston what he proposed since it was Union policy not to talk to Confederate political leaders. Johnston said he would send a note to Sherman to "obtain terms."

Davis agreed to the idea but dictated the letter himself with Mallory, a noted good penman, writing the actual document. Johnston, the man who proposed the letter, was reduced to watching and waiting so he could hand it off to a courier to send to Sherman whose headquarters were in Raleigh. Just as he had done back in February when he insisted the peace commissioners carry a letter detailing how the Union must acknowledge the existence of the Confederacy, Davis put terms in the letter that Sherman, Grant, and Lincoln would not accept. In the letter Davis asked for a "suspension of active operations" by the Union armies "to permit the civil authorities to enter into the needful arrangements to terminate the existing war."

The cabinet shook their heads in silence and frustration with this all-but-expected stubborn reaction of the man the fire-eaters had appointed as leader of the Confederacy. The fleeing president of a shattered country was asking his enemies, whose combined armies numbered nearly 200,000, not to advance on his remaining army of fewer than 20,000 effectives until he figured out what to do. Though Davis knew from experience and from Lincoln's public statements that he would not be recognized by the United States as a real president, Davis still insisted on being the public face of the Confederacy and its armies in the field.

The letter left Greensboro on April 13, the same day Johnston left to return to his army. He would not see Davis again. He did not ever want to see the man again. Within a few days, Johnston would act as the de facto leader of the Confederacy in defiance of Davis.

☆ ☆ ☆

IT WAS NOT LONG after the meeting ended that Davis received a long telegram from Lee that began with the ominous sentence: "It is with pain that I announce to you Excy. The surrender of the army of A. N.V. [Army of Northern Virginia]."

In the telegram, dated April 12, the same day that his men stacked their arms at Appomattox Court House and three days after the formal surrender with Grant, Lee listed the missing food supplies at Amelia Court House as the main reason for his army's surrender. He explained that looking for food had delayed his retreat march by twenty-four hours.

"The delay was fatal and could not be retrieved," Lee wrote.

The rest of the lengthy telegram detailed how Lee's army had surrendered and how at the end he had less than 8,000 infantry under arms. Lee underestimated the strength of the Union army by saying he was outnumbered by five times. If Lee had only 8,000 armed men, the Union army actually outnumbered him by more than ten times.

For years, Davis's critics used Lee's explanation in this telegram as evidence that had Davis's bureaucracy done its job in the hours before the cabinet retreated and had supplied the Army of Northern Virginia with train cars loaded with food, Lee's army might have successfully escaped.

With that day's head start on Grant lost to looking for food, Lee could see no other course other than surrender on April 9, 1865.

Lee concluded:

If we could have forced our way one day longer, it would have been at a great sacrifice of life; at its end, I did not see how a surrender could have been avoided. We had no sustenance for man or horse, and it could not have been gathered in the country. The supplies ordered to Pamplin's Station from Lynchburg could not reach us, and the men deprived of food and sleep for many days, were worn out and exhausted.

In one of war's ironies, one of the people watching Davis read the official notice from General Robert E. Lee detailing his surrender to Grant was Private Robert E. Lee, Jr., a 22-year-old artilleryman who had escaped his father's surrender in order to join up with Johnston's army. Lee, Jr., said that Davis wept while reading the telegram.

After the meeting, while Davis himself was still absorbing the disaster of Lee's telegram, his aides once again brought up the idea of escaping by sea. Davis's aide John Taylor Wood introduced Davis to a fellow 1853 United States Naval Academy graduate, Lieutenant Colonel Charles E. Thorburn. Little seems to be known about Thorburn's military career, particularly how a former United States Navy officer was granted a commission as a lieutenant colonel in the Confederate army. History does record Thorburn spent some of the war as a blockade-runner and as a secret courier between the Confederacy and England.

Being a secret agent was a job for which Thorburn was not well suited. While his ship, the CSS *Cornubia*, was being chased by a Union warship in November 1863, Thorburn tossed some secret documents overboard without bothering to weigh them down so that they would sink to the bottom of the ocean. The chasing Union vessel scooped up the bag floating on the ocean's surface and discovered a wealth of information about the Confederacy's European political contacts and contracts for vessels in France. Among the vital information the United States learned from Thorburn's lack of scientific knowledge that a bag of paper floats was that France and England still had no interest in helping the Confederacy.

Thorburn also had a reputation for being a blowhard. While acting as a harbormaster in Wilmington, he once refused permission for North Carolina governor Vance to disembark from an arrived blockade-runner that the governor had boarded to inspect. Thorburn insisted that the ship be quarantined for yellow fever for up to six weeks, and he did not care how short a time Vance had been aboard. Vance had to be restrained from killing the pompous officer.

Just how well the famous and competent aide Wood knew about the seemingly self-important and perhaps incompetent Thorburn's ocean-navigating skills is unknown. What is apparent is Wood believed the story Thorburn told of having hidden a boat on the Indian River on Florida's east coast that could be used to get Davis to Texas. Curiously, no other cabinet member mentions Thorburn's plan in his memoirs, not even Mallory who seemed to record the smiles and frowns of everyone he saw on his escape south. Only Burton Harrison, Davis's personal secretary, would later discuss Thorburn in his memories of the escape south.

One skilled ship captain who could have helped Davis escape by sea made a point to end his oceangoing career on land in Greensboro. That was Admiral Raphael Semmes who transferred his little command of 250 former sailors turned artillerymen from Danville to Greensboro after Davis and the cabinet had left for Charlotte. While Semmes spoke glowingly of Davis in his postwar memoirs, the admiral seemed to stay clear of his president in Danville for the week that they were in the same city. Semmes requested and took a general's commission and stayed in the trenches with his men, claiming that he was needed there to deal with the "raiding parties [that] were careening around us in various directions, robbing and maltreating the inhabitants, but none of the thieves ventured within reach of our guns."

Semmes was apparently referring to Stoneman's raid, which never came close to Danville. Just like all seamen, Semmes enjoyed embellishing a good story, particularly when he could make himself into the hero.

Semmes willingly put himself under the command of Johnston as he spent the last days of the war trying to establish himself as a ground general. He knew from newspaper accounts that the Northeastern states' merchants were still furious at the loss of their ships to a man they considered a pirate. Semmes realized that if he helped Davis escape by sea and if they were caught on the open ocean, those charges of piracy would be easier to prove. The admiral did not want piracy tacked on top of charges of treason to his nation.

The crafty sea captain knew how to put distance between himself and his former raiding days.

When Semmes formally surrendered on May 1, 1865, about three weeks after he last saw Davis in Danville, he refused the suggestion of the Union general in charge of the surrender to let Union clerks fill in the names of his sailor/artillerymen later on the then blank surrender documents. Instead, Semmes stayed in the room with the clerk writing in the name of each man in Semmes' Confederate artillery command. He then had the Union general sign the parole documents. Semmes never left the room. When the Northern newspapers found out about his surrender as a soldier, many of them charged that the Union general had been duped and that he had not recognized the famous captain of the CSS *Alabama* who had signed his name as an artillery general.

☆   ☆   ☆

AT SOME POINT while in Greensboro, whether in conference with the mysterious Thorburn or with others, Davis was convinced by unknown people that Abbeville, South Carolina, should be a stopping point on his escape route. On April 14, while still in Greensboro, he wrote Varina a letter telling her: "I will come to you if I can. Everything is dark. . . . If you can go to Abbeville it seems best as I am now advised."

Who advised Davis to head toward Abbeville and why is unknown. Abbeville is more than 240 miles to the southwest of Greensboro in the far western part of South Carolina. It is close to the foothills, not a direct route south toward Florida or the Atlantic coast if he was intending to escape by sea. Setting Abbeville as a destination and then heading for Florida adds at least a couple of hundred miles, more than a week of travel, to any trip by wagon or horseback, hardly the plan of a cabinet that lived in fear of seeing a Union cavalry force appear on the horizon.

Still, moving into the backwoods of South Carolina and then Georgia and Florida might have been the strategy decided on by Breckinridge who seems to have taken over the planning of the escape from a lackadaisical Davis. Breckinridge may have decided to travel quietly toward an area where Union troops had not yet penetrated rather than risk striking south through a region that Sherman's vast army had visited and that might still have scattered patrols. One other factor that may have pointed toward Abbeville was that Davis had a friend living there, former United States senator Armistead Burt who was senator when freshman congressman Davis came to the House of Representatives in 1846. Burt's wife was also the niece of Davis's political hero, John C. Calhoun, who had laid the groundwork for Southern secession in the 1830s.

Another mystery about the escape plan is why the initial route chosen to leave Greensboro was directly south, following the railroad line toward Charlotte. Taking a train was out of the question. The line was torn up by Stoneman's raiders south of Greensboro in several places while Davis and the cabinet were still in town. Rather than wait for the rails to be repaired, the party chose to move on in wagons and on horseback while still following the rail lines. While traveling in wagons would slow the escape, the more dangerous aspect of the plan was its direction toward Salisbury. Stoneman's raiders captured the town on April 12 and attacked the railroad bridge over the Yadkin River just north of Salisbury on April 13.

A strong command of 6,000 cavalrymen were now less than forty-five miles, or a day's cavalry ride south from the Confederate cabinet's location in Greensboro. Even if the track below Greensboro was repaired and a train taken farther south to save the slow trek of wagons, a strong Union force was now in front of the cabinet holding both the railroad line and the major town on the line.

Luckily for the Confederates, Stoneman was still out of telegraph contact with his commanders both in Washington and in Knoxville. Even if he heard the rumors line officers Palmer, Betts, and Garner collected from prisoners that Davis was in Greensboro, Stoneman's orders to tear up property had not changed. Stoneman was nothing if not single-minded—not unlike Davis himself. The Union general's focus was to redeem the reputation he lost at Chancellorsville under Hooker and on the aborted ride to Andersonville prison camp under Sherman. Nothing else mattered to him.

When Stoneman captured the town of Salisbury on April 13, he thought he would totally redeem himself with the freeing of the Union prisoners held there. That would not happen. Less than a month earlier, most of the prisoners were evacuated from the prison camp and put on trains for Wilmington in anticipation of their being exchanged for the fast-coming end of the war. Stoneman had to be satisfied with burning what was left of the prison. On the evening of April 13, while Davis was still in Greensboro to the north, Stoneman and his men rode southwest out of Salisbury toward the town of Statesville. Though couriers from Stoneman could have reached Sherman's lines within two days to check on how his mission was being received by his superiors, he did not send them to Sherman. He was in occasional contact with his superiors back in Knoxville, a trip of a week.

Thanks to Stoneman's ride out of Salisbury, Davis's way south was suddenly wide open, but no one on his staff knew that. Rather than wait for word on the situation in Salisbury, the party started moving on the afternoon of April 15. For all Davis and the cabinet knew, Stoneman's men could be on the outskirts of Salisbury waiting for them to ride into their blue-coated arms.

Breckinridge might have felt confident about heading toward the last known position of Stoneman because for the first time the cabinet had a military escort. Two brigades of cavalry made up of Tennesseans and Kentuckians under newly promoted general George G. Dibrell had been reassigned from the Army of Tennessee to Greensboro. While he may not have known it, or even knew enough to ask because of his seeming depression about the turn of events, Davis had his old enemy Johnston to thank for the cavalry protection. Johnston had ordered Dibrell and his men to Greensboro on his own accord without asking permission from either Davis or Breckinridge.

Those two brigades, numbering about 1,300 men, were augmented by two smaller units of cavalry, one commanded by Breckinridge's cousin, William P. Breckinridge, and another unit of Mississippians who refused to surrender with Lee. The total number of cavalry now protecting

Davis numbered around 2,400 men, enough that Breckinridge must have felt confident they could properly defend against any attack.

While the wagons were being loaded with records, Greensboro became overrun with unruly soldiers, some paroled from Lee and others deserted from Johnston. Powerless to do much about the rising unrest, Davis, seemingly in his own depressed world, simply watched as the men raided government stores and even threatened his own aides as they were trying to gather government records.

Joining the party for the first time was Thorburn, the man with the hidden boat in Florida in which he had faith he could negotiate both the Atlantic and the Gulf of Mexico to reach Texas. Also joining the entourage was a 34-year-old Englishman named Frank Vizetelly. Vizetelly was a newspaper artist for the *Illustrated London News* who had become a Southern sympathizer. Davis had been savaged by newspapermen during his entire term of office, but he probably liked the colorful, theatrical Vizetelly who drew sketches of the cabinet's journey south for the next three weeks.

It was raining so hard that day that the wagon train barely made ten miles. At one point the wagon carrying Secretary of State Benjamin and General Samuel Cooper became lodged in the mud. Men who were once the most powerful men in the South were reduced to pushing and pulling on a mud-soaked wagon wheel as if they were common teamsters.

As Jefferson Davis pressed on southward in a driving rainstorm on the late afternoon of April 15, he had no idea that Abraham Lincoln had died early that morning.

CHAPTER 7

~~~~~~~~~~~~~~~~~~~~~~~~~~~~

"Disastrous for Our People"

No ONE IN OFFICIAL WASHINGTON wanted to celebrate the end of the war with the president of the United States by attending the play *Our American Cousin* at Ford's Theater on the evening of Friday, April 14. Feeling in a celebratory mood now that General Robert E. Lee had surrendered, and it appeared that General Joseph E. Johnston would be forced to surrender, Lincoln spent the rest of the day after his regular Friday cabinet meeting doing little more than asking all his close friends and associates if they would celebrate with him that evening. His first choices were the two men who Lincoln felt helped end the war: General Ulysses S. Grant said no as did Secretary of War Stanton. Both men claimed they wanted to spend time with their families, although Grant's family was often in his camp throughout the war, and Stanton went home to his family every night in Washington.

Lincoln asked a dozen people to go to the play with him and Mrs. Lincoln that night. All of them said no. But Lincoln wanted to laugh. He wanted to clap. He wanted to hear music. He wanted to hear cheering and applause. He wanted his friends to share in the joy that was the end of the war.

He must have been curious about his sudden pariah-like treatment from the men he worked with every day. On most days Lincoln could not keep cabinet members out of his office. Someone was always seeking favors like giving some cousin a job or granting some constituent's son a commutation of a death sentence for cowardice.

But, today, no one wanted to be seen with the president of the United States.

Lincoln finally convinced Clara Harris, the daughter of a politician he knew to accompany him and Mrs. Lincoln to the theater. Her fiancé, a skinny major the president barely knew, Henry Rathbone, was delighted to take the president up on his offer. Presumably, Lincoln did not check into the couple's background before asking them to the play. Rathbone and Harris were not letting the fact that they were stepbrother and stepsister get in the way of their impending marriage.

The choice of the sick-looking Rathbone as a guest is even more dramatic when his physique is compared to the two men Lincoln would have liked to have accompanied him to Ford's Theater that night. Both of them were close friends of the president, loyal to him as opposed to his cabinet members, and most important of all—they were large, strong, and quick-thinking men who could have made short work of the thin, weak John Wilkes Booth when he barged his way into the presidential box.

The absence of these two men from Ford's Theater on the night Lincoln was shot remains a historical curiosity.

Stanton had ordered Ward Lamon, Lincoln's closest friend from Springfield, to Richmond to oversee Richmond's surrender even though the city had fallen more than two weeks earlier. Lamon was no military man, no diplomat, and no expert in rebuilding burned-out cities. He was simply Lincoln's very large friend who never went anywhere without being armed and who had protected Lincoln every day for the previous four years. For some reason, Stanton wanted Lamon in Richmond and away from Lincoln in the days after the Confederate collapse. The president could not have asked his best friend Lamon to go to the play since he was one hundred miles away.

Another man Lincoln wanted to ask to the play was Major Thomas Eckert, the supervisor of the War Department telegraph office. Eckert was a close confidant of the president and another large, well-muscled man who bent iron pokers over his forearm to demonstrate his strength to admirers. Stanton refused permission for Eckert to attend the play with Lincoln. In fact, when Lincoln told Stanton he would ask Eckert to the play, Stanton told Lincoln that Eckert was detailed on an important mission that night. In reality, Eckert spent the evening at home with his wife wondering why his boss Stanton would refuse him some private time with Lincoln.

Stanton lied. Lincoln died.

After avoiding Lincoln all day on April 14, the president's supposed friends gathered around his deathbed after midnight on April 15. They crowded into the tiny bedroom across from the theater where the president had been carried off to die. So many of his friends shoved themselves into the room that they pushed Mary Todd Lincoln into the hallway where she had to beg for news of her husband. No one would bring news to her. As much as they said they loved President Lincoln, his friends hated Mrs. Lincoln.

More than a dozen cabinet members, senators, and congressmen wanted to be there for the moment the president expired. None of them had wanted to celebrate the end of the war with the president who had won the war, but all of them wanted to be in on this bit of history, the first American president to be assassinated in office. Stanton even had scripted the perfect phrase and had it ready for when Lincoln finally took his last breath on Saturday morning: "Now he belongs to the ages."

☆ ☆ ☆

THOUGH DAVIS'S COLUMN finally had military protection on the third leg of its trek leaving Greensboro on the afternoon of April 15, Secretary of the Navy Stephen Mallory remembered in his postwar writing:

The cabinet left Greensboro to proceed further south, with plans unformed, clinging to the hope that Johnston and Sherman could secure peace and the quiet of the country, but still doubtful as to the result and still more doubtful as to the consequences of failure. It was evident to every dispassionate mind that no further military stand could be made, and that Mr. Davis should secure his safety by leaving the country in the event of the failure of these negotiations; and hence it was deemed expedient that he should place himself further south, to be ready to cross the Mississippi and get into Mexico, or to leave the coast of Florida for the Bahamas or Cuba. But it was no less evident that Mr. Davis was extremely reluctant to quit the country at all, and he would make no effort to leave it so long as he could find an organized body of troops, however small, in the field. He shrank from the idea of abandoning any body of men who might still be found willing to strike for the cause, and gave little attention to the question of his own safety.

Though Davis seemed blissfully oblivious, he and his cabinet were now in more danger than they were since evacuating Richmond.

On April 17, Davis was in Salisbury, North Carolina, which still smelled of the smoke from the empty prison camp that General George Stoneman's men had put to the torch. That same morning, Union general William T. Sherman met for the first time with his counterpart Confederate general Johnston at a farmhouse near Durham Station, North Carolina. The farmhouse was less than twenty miles from Sherman's headquarters in Raleigh and one hundred miles northeast of Salisbury.

Stoneman probably knew Sherman was within riding distance somewhere between Smithfield and Raleigh when he vacated Salisbury since Sherman had defeated Johnston at Bentonville four days before his own raiders had mounted their horses in Tennessee on March 25. Certainly, Stoneman would have heard reports from residents of towns like Salem and Salisbury of Sherman being just east of him, easily within reach of teams of well-armed couriers. Had Stoneman sent couriers to find Sherman with word that some of his regimental commanders had heard rumors that Davis was in the area, Sherman could have detached some of the 6,000 cavalry he had under his command to send a reconnaissance party toward Stoneman's position. With Stoneman to the southwest of Salisbury and Sherman to the northeast, the two generals would have caught the Confederate cabinet in Salisbury within two weeks of the evacuation of Richmond.

On that Monday, April 17, Sherman had barely shaken hands with Johnston when he thrust into his opponent's hands a telegram that had been received in Raleigh just a few hours earlier. Johnston was only the third man in all of North Carolina to read the telegram, counting the telegraph operator who Sherman had sworn to secrecy.

Sherman closely watched Johnston's reaction to the telegram, remarking in his memoirs that "the perspiration came out in large drops on his forehead and he did not try to conceal his distress."

For unknown reasons, Stanton had waited a full two days before informing Sherman of the news that President Abraham Lincoln had been shot on Friday night, April 14, and died the next morning, April 15.

Johnston's reaction was immediately to tell Sherman that Lincoln's assassination "was the greatest possible calamity" for the South. He wisely followed that comment with another that he hoped Sherman did not think the murder was part of a plot to end the war.

Sherman replied,

I could not believe that he or General Lee, or the officers of the Confederate army, could possibly be privy to acts of assassination; but I would not say as much for Jeff. Davis, George Sanders [a Confederate secret agent in Canada], and men of that stripe.

Johnston, ignoring the chance that Union telegraphers might be tapping the Confederate lines, left the meeting and immediately sent a telegram to Lexington, North Carolina, along the route that he expected the cabinet to take. He addressed the note to Secretary of War John C. Breckinridge rather than Davis knowing that Sherman would not deal directly with Davis as a Confederate government official, but Sherman might deal with the secretary of war who also held a major general's commission. Johnston's telegram asked for Breckinridge to come back immediately to Greensboro so he could sit in on a second round of negotiations with Sherman. Johnston made no mention in the telegram of Lincoln's assassination, perhaps out of fear that the receiving telegrapher would spread the word throughout the South, and there might be demonstrations of joy before Sherman could reveal the sobering news to his own army.

After arriving in Lexington and finding the telegram waiting for Breckinridge, Davis agreed to let the Secretary of War return to join Johnston. His only condition was that Postmaster General John Reagan also attend any meeting with Sherman. Davis might have suspected that Johnston and Breckinridge had been talking about surrender behind his back. Sending the trusted Reagan as a third party to the talks would protect what Davis thought was the Confederacy's civilian interests from being surrendered by its military men.

Starting on April 17 and continuing on April 18, Davis seemed to shake off his depression, according to his secretary, Burton Harrison. Nothing happened to make the Confederate president any happier; no word had been received back from Johnston's and Breckinridge's negotiations with Sherman. Still, Davis was uncommonly jolly in public. His jocularity puzzled everyone in the group.

Harrison wrote of the event:

> Mr. Davis was singularly equable and cheerful; he seemed to have had a great load taken from his mind, to feel relieved of responsibilities, and his conversation was bright and agreeable. He talked of men and of books, particularly of Walter Scott and Byron, of horses and dogs and sports, of the woods and fields, of trees and many plants, of roads, and how to make them, of the habits of birds, and of a variety of other topics.

Why Davis seemed to have a load lifted from his mind is left unstated by Harrison, but it seems likely that the president expected Johnston and Breckinridge to come to some good terms with Sherman.

While Johnston, Davis, and Breckinridge were dancing around the issues of who was authorized to do what on behalf of the Confederacy without giving much thought to their own immediate futures, Sherman and his top generals were discussing how they could evacuate Davis out of the United States. Without checking with the suddenly installed new president Johnson, Sherman was operating under the assumption that Johnson endorsed Lincoln's wishes that the Confederate cabinet be allowed to escape.

"Either Logan or Blair insisted that if asked for, we should even provide a vessel to carry them to Nassau from Charleston," Sherman wrote in his postwar memoirs.

Logan was Major General John "Black Jack" Logan, commander of the Union Fifteenth Corps, which had set fire to Columbia, but who was now amenable to ending the war as quickly and as bloodlessly as possible. Blair was Major General Francis Preston Blair, Jr., son of Lincoln advisor Frances Preston Blair, who had initiated the peace mission to the Confederacy in February.

When Sherman met with Johnston and Breckinridge two days later on April 19 at the same farmhouse, the Union general told Breckinridge to his face that he should "get away" since it was he, as vice president in 1861, who had formally announced the results of the Electoral College vote that Lincoln had been elected. Sherman believed the nation would be angrier with former vice president Breckinridge than it would with former senator Davis.

"I may have also advised him that Mr. Davis, too, should get abroad as soon as possible," Sherman wrote.

If Breckinridge appreciated Sherman's advice, he still left the meeting an angry man. While contemplating terms inside the farmhouse, Sherman absently poured himself a glass of whiskey without offering any to Johnston or Breckinridge. That inadvertent slight resulted in the aristocratic Breckinridge proclaiming to Johnston that the commoner Sherman was nothing more than a "hog."

Davis and party arrived in Charlotte, North Carolina, on Wednesday, April 19, four days after the Lincoln assassination, which was still unknown to everyone in the South but Johnston and Breckinridge. Davis had expected to find Varina Davis here waiting on him, but he learned that she had left town in a wagon train along with Lieutenant William H. Parker and his intrepid band of teenagers guarding the Confederate treasury. Rumors had reached the town of 3,000 that Stoneman's raiders knew about both the First Lady and the gold, so Varina evacuated the city while she had something that would count as an armed guard.

Just as Varina found the city's residents less than willing to put her up when she arrived in Charlotte on April 6, so, too, did Davis when he arrived nearly two weeks later. Though Charlotte had developed a reputation for rebelliousness during the American Revolution when British General Lord Cornwallis called it a "hornets' nest" of patriots, and even though the city had enthusiastically embraced secession, Charlotte's citizens were now wary of anything that smacked of supporting the Confederacy. Towns people imagined what harboring the Confederate cabinet could mean if the Union army followed them— destruction of their homes and their own arrests.

Only one man volunteered to put Davis up in his home, and the president should have been suspicious of that man's supposed generosity.

He was Lewis Bates, a native of Massachusetts who inexplicably stayed in the South after the war started to manage an express company. Harrison was suspicious of Bates' "convivial habits," particularly since he lived alone but kept "open house." Men seemed to come and go from Bates' house, which made Harrison suspicious of the man's morals.

"It was not at all a seemly place for Mr. Davis," Harrison said, but he had no choice as no other man in Charlotte offered his residence to Davis. The rest of the cabinet had received housing offers, but no one but Bates wanted to chance hosting the Confederate president.

Davis did not immediately enter Bates' house. Bates had gone to the train station to greet the president, not realizing that the party was arriving by wagon and horseback. Bates had not yet arrived back at his house to welcome Davis who was standing on the front porch when a telegraph operator rushed up and thrust a sheet of paper into Davis's hand. The telegram was from Breckinridge, as Davis had hoped and expected, but the telegram's contents were very unexpected.

HIS EXCELLENCY PRESIDENT DAVIS

PRESIDENT LINCOLN WAS ASSASSINATED IN THE THEATRE IN WASH-

INGTON ON THE NIGHT OF THE 11TH INST [meaning the current month of April] SEWARD'S HOUSE WAS ENTERED ON THE SAME NIGHT AND HE WAS REPEATEDLY STABBED AND IS PROBABLY MORTALLY WOUNDED.

Breckinridge had two facts wrong, apparently from getting his information from Johnston who did not keep a copy of the telegram Sherman had showed him. Lincoln had not died in the theatre, and the day he was shot was April 14, not the eleventh, but the gravity of the new political climate in the nation was obvious.

Davis read the short note, looked up in confusion, and then read it again. He passed the note to a local businessman saying: "Here is a very extraordinary communication. It is sad news."

Davis stood frozen in his steps from the startling news. Before the businessman who held the telegram could read it to the now curious crowd, a detail of Kentucky cavalrymen under Brigadier General Basil Duke rode up to the house's front porch. Unaware of Davis's now somber mood, the Kentuckians cheered their native son and asked for a speech. Davis stammered out a few words thanking the cavalrymen for their service. Just as he had done repeatedly with his own cabinet, he urged them to continue fighting. Davis personally said nothing to the cavalrymen about Lincoln's assassination.

After Davis had finished his short talk, the Charlotte resident read the telegram to the curious crowd who had seen Davis's face fall when he read it. One of the cavalrymen shouted in joy, but Davis raised his hand to quiet the man. This was not a time for cheering.

At this time, Bates came puffing up to his house to shake hands with Davis and to unlock his front door. Witnesses would clearly remember that Bates was not on the scene when Davis received the news about Lincoln, spoke to the crowd, and made his remark about the "sad news."

According to Mallory's memory, once inside the house, Davis wondered aloud if the story was a "canard," or false story, that Breckinridge had unwittingly passed along. Davis pondered his own question for a moment and then said that "events no less startling were constantly occurring."

Mallory remembered that he expressed his own deep regret for Lincoln's death, particularly since the cabinet was aware of his "moderation and sense of justice," and then the naval secretary spoke what others must have been thinking: "My apprehension that the South would be accused of instigating his death."

According to Mallory, Davis immediately replied:

I certainly have no special regard for Mr. Lincoln, but there are a great many men of whose end I would much rather have heard of than his. I fear it will be disastrous for our people, and I regret it deeply.

Several weeks later Bates, clearly enjoying an unexpected national celebrity, would remember the exchanges between the cabinet members differently.

What Davis considered a disaster was the succession to the presidency of Andrew Johnson. As mentioned earlier, it was Johnson, a former tailor, who Davis unwittingly insulted in 1847. Davis had suggested during a House debate that professionally trained officers made better army leaders than former tailors and blacksmiths.

However, at 57, just one year younger than Davis, Johnson had an entirely different view of the world. Having grown up poor and illiterate himself, he identified with the yeoman farmers who made up most of the population of the nation. He once advocated a homestead act that would give the poor free farms. He hated the educated aristocracy, which included men like Davis, who controlled most elections. He totally rejected the idea of states' rights prevailing over a centralized government, making him the only Southern senator not to resign his seat in 1861 and leave Washington for the Confederacy.

By being a very visible Southern-born "war Democrat," Johnson presented Lincoln with a way to help with his 1864 reelection campaign. To disrupt the Democrats' chances of electing Major General George McClellan president, Lincoln crossed party lines and drafted Johnson as his vice president, never dreaming that the man rumored to be an alcoholic would ever be in any decision-making capacity. To

Lincoln's horror, the rumors proved true when Johnson showed up drunk for his own inauguration and launched into an embarrassing, incomprehensible acceptance speech.

Now Davis's own horror had come true. The worst enemy he had ever made while serving in the U.S. Congress was now the nation's president. Davis had no illusions that Johnson would have any sympathy for him or the South.

Years later, while writing *The Rise and Fall of the Confederate Government* and lamenting in print over the assassination of Lincoln, Davis compared Lincoln to Johnson with:

> He [Lincoln] had power over the Northern people, and was without personal malignity towards the people of the South; his successor [Johnson] was without power in the North, and was the embodiment of malignity toward the Southern people.

There was little for Davis and the rest of the cabinet to do in Charlotte other than wait for Breckinridge to bring word of negotiations with Sherman. Finally, on the morning of April 22, Breckinridge and Reagan arrived in Charlotte. They were gone four days and did not communicate with the president other than to send the short telegram about Lincoln's assassination. Davis had no idea what his two ministers, Johnston, and Sherman had discussed.

When the cabinet met that night at 10:00 p.m., few could believe the good fortune they had experienced in dealing with a man like Sherman who had shown no mercy on Southern civilians in Mississippi, Tennessee, Georgia, and South Carolina. Indeed, at one point in the negotiations, Sherman had joked that it seemed like he was surrendering to the Confederates rather than the other way around.

Under the agreement drawn up by Sherman, the United States would essentially allow the Southern states back into the Union in exchange for the Confederate army disbanding and returning its weapons to the state armories—from where many of them were captured in 1861. Sherman, believing he was following the wishes of Lincoln expressed in February, promised not to punish the South. About the only issues

not addressed in the documents agreed to between Sherman, Breckinridge, and Johnston were what to do with the political leaders of the
Confederacy.

Without discussing the detailed document that night, Davis handed
each cabinet member a copy of the terms, asking him to write out a
report on his impressions that would be delivered the next day at another cabinet meeting.

One man who did not like the terms was Davis.

Davis did not write his own report as he had asked his cabinet to
write, but he did express his thoughts in a letter to his wife, who he
knew was somewhere on her way to Abbeville, South Carolina.

Instead of writing to his wife about the incredibly fair way Sherman
was willing to treat his defeated enemy, the lengthy letter, the longest
he had written to her since leaving Richmond, disparaged the average
if dejected Confederate soldier: "If the men who had straggled, say thirty
to forty thousand in number, had come back with their arms and with
a disposition to fight, we might have repaired the damage."

Not surprisingly, the letter also disparaged generals Johnston and
Beauregard saying, "Their only idea was retreat."

Davis, showing that the depression had not left him despite his
jolly appearances to others, also displayed some self-pity: "I have sac-
rificed so much for the cause of the Confederacy that I can measure
my ability to make any further sacrifice required."

He did not share in his cabinet's enthusiasm for the terms. He believed the terms "may be rejected by the Yankee Government." He
predicted that there would be "the long night of oppression which
will follow the return of our people to the Union."

Once again his thoughts turned to the safety of Varina who he had
now told at various times to be prepared to defend herself, kill herself, or escape to Florida. Now he suggested she make for Mississippi
first, and then to Mobile [Davis still believed it was in Confederate
hands, although it had actually surrendered on April 12, ten days ear-
lier] to board a ship for a foreign port. If Mobile was unreachable,
he told her to cross the Mississippi River and head to Texas.

Davis hinted that he might not follow her:

For myself, it may be that a devoted band of cavalry will cling to me, and I can force my way across the Mississippi, and if nothing can be done there which it will be proper to do, then I can go to Mexico, and have the world from which to choose a location.

Perhaps Davis was covering for himself should the letter fall into Union hands, as he made no mention in the letter about any plans to make for Florida and Thorburn's hidden boat.

While waiting for the cabinet meeting to start to discuss Sherman's offer, North Carolina's governor Zebulon Vance made an appearance in the room. Vance did not say if he had read the scolding telegram Davis had sent him while still in Greensboro, which included an accusation that "moral influence is wanting, and I am sure you can do much more now to revive the spirit and hope of the people."

Instead of filling Vance in on Sherman's generous terms, Davis took the opportunity to pitch the governor on the idea of gathering all the North Carolina troops and heading for the Trans-Mississippi.

Vance listened in stunned silence. Just reaching the Mississippi River was a journey of nearly seven hundred miles to the west. Kirby Smith's army was then in coastal Texas, several hundred miles to the southwest of the river. Under the best of conditions without Yankees harassing them, it would take a thrown-together Confederate army until mid-summer to march to the Trans-Mississippi Department.

The cabinet stared at Davis. Johnston's pitiful little force was just miles from Sherman's massive army that everyone knew could obliterate the remaining Confederates in a one-day battle. Yet, the stubborn president still refused to admit defeat. It took Breckinridge to break the embarrassing silence to tell Vance that it was his responsibility to stay in North Carolina.

If Davis expected his cabinet to back him in rejecting Sherman's terms for surrender, he was disappointed. Even Benjamin, who always nodded in acquiescence to whatever Davis proposed in the past, finally turned against him.

In his lengthy letter outlining the dim military circumstances, Benjamin concluded:

The Confederacy is, in a word, unable to continue the war by armies in the field, and the struggle can no longer be maintained in any other manner than by a guerrilla or partisan warfare. Such a warfare is not, in my opinion, desirable, nor does it promise any useful result. It would entail far more suffering on our own people than it would cause damage to the enemy; and the people have been such heavy sufferers by the calamities of the war for the last four years that it is at least questionable whether they would be willing to engage in such a contest unless forced to endure its horrors in preference to dishonor and degradation. The terms of the convention imply no dishonor, impose no degradation, exact only what the victor always requires, the relinquishment by his foe of the object for which the struggle was commenced. Seeing no reasonable hope of our ability to conquer our independence, admitting the undeniable fact that we have been vanquished in the war, it is my opinion that these terms should be accepted, being as favorable as any that we, as the defeated belligerent, have reason to expect or can hope to secure.

Attorney General George Davis concurred and directed Davis as to what he should do:

The chief duty left for you to perform, is to provide as far as possible, for the speedy delivery of the people from the horrors of war and anarchy by approving the convention [proposal by Sherman], issuing a proclamation saying why terms were accepted, disbanding armies, resigning as president, and recommending the states carry the agreement into effect.

Reagan also agreed that Davis had to surrender, but he also included some digs at the United States government:

I do not conceal from myself nor would I withhold from your Excellency the danger of trusting the people who drove us to war by their unconstitutional and unjust aggression, and who will now add the consciousness of power to their love of domination and greed of gain.

Mallory said:

The Confederacy is conquered. Its days are numbered. People expect you not to stand upon constitutional limitations, but to assume and exercise all powers which to you may seem necessary and proper to shield them from useless war.

Davis finally, however, reluctantly agreed to endorse the terms Breckinridge and Johnston had worked out with Sherman. That telegram of acceptance had barely left the telegrapher's keys in Charlotte when Johnston in Greensboro sent another telegram that was received in Charlotte late on April 24.

It was another stunning message. Not only had Stanton who was back in Washington entirely rejected Sherman's written terms to the Confederates at Durham Station, he also ordered Sherman to annihilate Johnston's army if it did not surrender under the same unconditional terms Lee had signed at Appomattox Court House on April 9. General Grant himself rushed down from Washington to deliver the news personally to Sherman.

Stanton's refusal of Sherman's terms coupled with the knowledge that his old enemy Johnson was now president seemed to harden Davis's resolve to fight it out until the end. He was greatly emboldened by a letter arriving from Lieutenant General Wade Hampton, the South Carolina multimillionaire who now commanded Johnston's cavalry. Hampton made it clear that he did not intend to surrender to anyone. He apparently did not ask permission of Johnston to write the letter.

Hampton's attitude seemed a copy of Davis's own belief that there were tens of thousands of Southerners willing to continue fighting. Hampton believed if they could gather 50,000 men on the east side of the Mississippi and another 50,000 men on the other side, such a large force would convince Europe to come into the war on the side of the South.

Hampton was ignoring reality. England and France had long ago rejected any idea to come into the war on the Southern side. Both nations had stockpiled prewar Southern cotton and had found other national sources for it. Neither country was about to come out in favor of a nation that still held slaves.

Still, Hampton could not imagine any circumstances that could be worse than coming back into the Union:

No suffering which can be inflicted by the passage over our country of the Yankee armies can equal what would fall on us if we return to the Union [Hampton wrote in a letter to Davis dated April 19 and received on April 24]. We shall have to pay the debt incurred by the U.S. in this war, and we shall live under a base and vulgar tyranny. No sacrifice would be too great to escape this train of horrors, and I think it far better for us to fight to the extreme limit of our country, rather than to reconstruct the Union upon any terms.

Hampton's plan to continue the war was more detailed than anything the cabinet or even Davis considered. He suggested disbanding all the infantry regiments, putting them on horses, and then heading for the Mississippi. Once there, they would reequip and then come back over to the eastern shore of the Mississippi to do battle with the occupying Yankees. Where Hampton intended getting the horses is unknown. Beauregard had sent several artillery batteries to Greensboro by train and told their crews to dig in behind trenches because there were no horses to keep them mobile.

Hampton was nothing if not confident in his abilities to lead men against overwhelming forces.

Hampton wrote:

If I had 20,000 mounted men here I could force Sherman to retreat in 20 days. Give me a good force of cavalry and I will take them safely across the Mississippi and if you desire to go in that direction, it will give me great pleasure to escort you. My own mind is made up. As to my course, I shall fight as long as my government remains in existence, when that ceases to live I shall seek some other country, for I shall never take the oath of allegiance.

Hampton added that his officers are "not subdued, nor do they despair" and he ended the long letter pledging to bring "men who will fight to Texas and will seek refuge in Mexico rather than in the Union."

Two days later Hampton arrived in Greensboro, thinking he would find Davis there. When he did not, Hampton wrote Davis another letter. Hampton must have thought that the first letter could have fallen into enemy hands, so in his second letter he used much the same language as he had in the first, warning that returning to the United States "would bring all the horrors of war coupled with all the degradation that can be inflicted on a conquered people." Once again he offered to escort Davis to Texas.

Hampton's letter was like an elixir to Davis who had just listened to his cabinet and his top general agree to surrender.

Mallory wrote:

It was evident that he was greatly affected by the constancy and spirit of these men [referring to cavalry commanders Hampton, Duke, Dibbrell, and General Samuel Ferguson], and he became indifferent to his own safety, thinking only of gathering together a body of troops to make head against the foe and so arouse the people to arms.

Harrison, remarking on Davis's cheerfulness, said Davis turned to him and said, "I cannot feel like a beaten man!"

After conferring with Johnston, Hampton went to Charlotte to talk about his plan to escort Davis to Mississippi. While Hampton was still in Charlotte, Stanton rejected Sherman's peace plans, but neither Hampton nor Davis knew of this before they agreed on their own course of action—raising that dreamed of army of cavalrymen.

Johnston wrote in his postwar memoirs that on April 25 he received a message from Davis asking him to continue negotiations with Sherman, but to "bring off" the cavalry and to equip any infantry willing to fight on with mounts. If such a telegram from Davis was received, Johnston realized what Davis was suggesting—creating Hampton's force to make a dash for the Mississippi.

Instead of following Davis's orders, Johnston then did something he had been thinking of doing for weeks—ignore Davis. Without asking permission from Davis or Breckinridge, Johnston sent a note to Sherman asking for a third meeting. At his third meeting with Sherman, Johnston said he would surrender his army under whatever conditions Washington demanded.

Johnston made no mention to Sherman of Hampton's plans to escape and escort Davis to the Mississippi.

Johnston said in his postwar memoirs that he rejected the president's request to "bring off" the cavalry because it would have provided too heavy an escort for the cabinet, and it would have done nothing to protect the civilians and the rest of the army from further combat. He said he sent a telegram to Davis suggesting that he and the cabinet flee while they could.

Upon learning of Johnston's complete and unconditional surrender to Sherman, Hampton decided that organizing a 20,000-man cavalry force after Johnston had formally surrendered the entire army would be dishonorable.

In a letter to Johnston, Hampton wrote:

By your advice I went to consult with the President, the armistice having been annulled. After full conference with him, a plan was agreed on to enable him to leave the country. He charged me with the execution of this plan, and he is now moving in accordance with it. On my return here I find myself not only powerless to assist him, but placed in a position of great delicacy. I must either leave him to his fate, without an effort to avert it, or subject myself to possible censure by not accepting the terms of the convention you have made. If I do not accompany him I shall never cease to reproach myself, and if I go with him I may go under the ban of outlawry. I choose the latter, because I believe it to be my duty to do so. But I leave my command to abide the terms, as I shall not ask a man to go with me. Should any join me, they will be stragglers like myself and, like myself, willing to sacrifice everything for the cause and for our Government.

Davis never gave Johnston the benefit of the doubt when evaluating the military situation he faced in April 1865. In a note to himself about the discussions he and Johnston had in Greensboro about the possibility of surrendering, Davis wrote:

Had I known the surrender of the army was in General Johnston's mind predetermined, it would have given me no embarrassment to find a successor who would have had different ideas of the duty of a soldier to the government whose commission he bore, and who would not have failed to remember the obligations he avowed when that commission was accepted.

It made no difference to Davis that Johnston was outnumbered by at least four to one and that his larger army at the time had been easily whipped by Sherman in March at Bentonville, North Carolina. That Johnston even thought about surrendering before bringing Sherman to battle at least one more time was something that Davis could not abide.

On April 26, Davis and the cabinet were ready to leave Charlotte, minus one official. Attorney General George Davis resigned, telling Davis that as a widower he had no choice but to stay in North Carolina and care for his children. He would be leaving for Wilmington and awaiting his fate. Davis did not protest the decision.

The other cabinet members must have seen Attorney General Davis's departure as opening the opportunity for more of them to leave when they felt the time had come. Up until hearing the demands of the Washington politicians for unconditional surrender of all Confederate armies, all of them had been steadfastly behind Davis. He was the president. He was the leader.

Now that Johnston was forced to surrender or face annihilation of his army, things had changed. The cabinet abandoned Davis as their spiritual and political leader and agreed with Johnston that all hope for the Confederacy was lost. Once Davis had been commander in chief of more than one million men from Texas to northern Virginia. Now Davis commanded no more than a few thousand exhausted cavalrymen made up of Tennesseans, Kentuckians, and Mississippians riding woe-begotten horses. There were no more ammunition stockpiles, no more food warehouses, and no more sources of fresh horses. What they had on them was all they could expect to have.

The strange cheerfulness that Davis had exuded over the last several days was now replaced with a more familiar aloofness, maybe depression. Just before leaving Charlotte, North Carolina, Davis penned another letter to Varina. Though he knew Hampton had already bowed out of his earlier plan to raise a huge cavalry force and lead the president to the Mississippi, Davis lied to his wife:

I will organize what force of Cavalry can be had. Hampton offers to lead this and he thinks he can force his way across the Mississippi. The route will be too rough and perilous for you and children to go with me. . . . Will try to see you soon.

Davis could not know it, but his three-week-long escape south with leisurely stopovers in Danville, Greensboro, and Charlotte was about to cost him and his cabinet their freedoms. Losing those freedoms may have been his fault.

Davis could have abandoned Richmond on April 2 and then moved to Danville just as he did to avoid Grant's army moving west from Petersburg to stop Lee's army. Then, while Grant was occupied with Lee, Davis and the cabinet could have moved directly southeast toward the coast of North or South Carolina rather than south and southwest toward the foothills of South Carolina as they eventually did.

Had they moved to the coast, the Confederate government may have made it out of the country and to safety.

The Carolina coast is more than six hundred miles long, with scores of rivers and creeks that could hide boats and ships of all sizes. While the large blockade-running ports like Wilmington were shut down, more than three quarters of the South's blockade-runners were successful in avoiding capture during four years of war. A single small, fast ship carrying only passengers without a heavy cargo of cotton could have outrun most Union warships had it even been sighted on the high seas. Captain John Taylor Wood, a skilled blockade-runner, would have known how to handle such a ship and could have easily raised a crew from the leftover sailors from the James River Squadron who traveled with the cabinet when it first left Richmond.

Even if the cabinet's ship was run down, the ship was boarded, and the passengers were identified, the Union commanders would have to come to shore to wire the War Department and Lincoln about what they should do with their famous fugitives. If Lincoln was willing to carry through with what he had said to Admiral David Dixon Porter in the conference with Grant and Sherman, the president would have ordered the Union navy to escort the Confederates' escape ship to whatever foreign destination the passengers wanted. The only unknown would have been what would have happened if a stubborn Davis told the Union commanders that he intended sailing for Texas. Under those circumstances Lincoln would probably have ordered the arrest of the cabinet.

That two-week window of opportunity for the Confederate cabinet to have fled the country with Lincoln's blessing closed on the night of April 14 when John Wilkes Booth fired a .44 caliber lead ball into the president's head.

☆　☆　☆

IN LINCOLN'S MIND the end of the war was a joyous occasion, cause for celebration and forgiveness. He wanted to "let the South up easy." He wanted the Confederate leaders to leave the country. He wanted a quick restoration of the Union.

His death on Saturday morning, April 15, changed everything.

The president's assassination presented an excellent opportunity to the Radical Republicans in his own cabinet and in the United States Senate and House. Lincoln could be made into a martyr at the same time the punishment and plundering of the South could be written into law.

To start that process, Davis had to be captured. Later he could be charged, tried, imprisoned, and executed, but right now he had to be found.

On April 27, a month after Lincoln said he wanted Davis to be able to flee the country, twenty-five days after Davis had evacuated Richmond, and less than two weeks after Lincoln's death, Stanton had General Henry Halleck send a telegram to General George Thomas in Tennessee. Thomas was the commanding general over Stoneman, who Stanton believed was still in North Carolina and who Stanton believed was probably closer to Davis than any other Union forces.

> The bankers have information to-day that Jeff. Davis' specie is moving south from Goldsborough [this mention is either a typographical error on the part of the telegrapher or incorrect intelligence; Davis was never in Goldsboro, a town 130 miles east of Greensboro where Davis was] in wagons as fast as possible. I suggest that commanders be telegraphed through General Thomas that Wilson obey no orders from Sherman, and notifying him and Canby, and commanders on the Mississippi, to take measures to intercept the rebel chiefs and their plunder. The specie is estimated at $6,000,000 to $13,000,000.

It was the first time that Stanton had expressed any public interest in capturing Davis, but curiously, Davis himself did not seem to be the prime interest of the federal government. Stanton wanted the Confederacy's money. Where Stanton got his wildly inflated figures of the Confederate treasury is unknown. By its own actual inventory, the Confederate cabinet was carrying no more than $500,000–$600,000 in gold and silver.

Stanton's reference to "obey no orders from Sherman" was an indication of how quickly Sherman had fallen out of favor now that Lincoln was dead. Stanton viewed Sherman's attempts at making a sweeping peace with the Confederacy as virtual treason on Sherman's part. Rumors began circulating in Washington that Sherman's peace terms to Johnston showed that he had finally lost his mind and that he was planning to march on Washington and set himself up as a military dictator.

When Stoneman received the telegram from Stanton, he ordered his generals to "follow him [Davis] to the ends of the earth, if possible, and never give him up."

For the first time since fleeing Richmond more than three weeks earlier, Davis and the Confederate cabinet were being sought by the United States government. The cabinet knew they would be charged with treason if they were caught. They did not know that they would also be charged with the murder of Abraham Lincoln.

CHAPTER 8

"We Are Falling to Pieces"

"WE ARE FALLING TO PIECES," wrote Captain John Taylor Wood in his diary. "I feel the spirit of the people is broken."

The cabinet had reached that conclusion after abandoning Richmond three weeks earlier. Generals Joseph E. Johnston and Pierre Beauregard shared the same opinion when they looked at their ranks of exhausted men who had not yet deserted and gone home.

Only Jefferson Davis refused to acknowledge that the Confederacy was dead, and his major concern should be for his own escape.

Though he was an excellent horseman, Davis refused to use his sturdy mounts to ride ahead of the slow-moving wagon train. He would not abandon the weaker members of the cabinet such as Secretary of the Treasury Trenholm who was so sickly he had to lie in the bottom of an ambulance, and elderly General Samuel Cooper who no longer could ride a horse. Davis's black and white view of governance had not changed. If the cabinet train moved at a slow pace because of the poor health of some members, then that was the pace that would be shared by all.

"The idea of personal safety, when the country's condition was before his eyes, was an unpleasant one to him, and he was ever ready to defer its consideration," said Secretary of the Navy Stephen Mallory.

The cabinet barely made fifteen miles after leaving Charlotte, North Carolina, before stopping in Fort Mill, South Carolina, just north of the Catawba River. There Davis held another cabinet meeting where weary, neuralgic Trenholm finally admitted to himself and Davis that he could not go any farther. He resigned and Davis asked John Reagan to take over treasurer duties. When Reagan protested that he was still postmaster general and he knew nothing about being a treasurer, Davis made one of his rare jokes.

"There really is not much for the Treasury Secretary to do anymore [meaning there was not much money in the treasury]," Davis said with one of his rare smiles and a touch on Reagan's shoulder.

Reagan reluctantly agreed and listened as Trenholm gasped out that he thought there was about $80,000 in gold and silver with them. This was not counting the bulk of the Confederate treasury that was somewhere in South Carolina. At some point in front of them was the intrepid band of teenaged midshipmen commanded by Lieutenant William H. Parker, who was growing increasingly frustrated at his unwanted duty as bank guard.

For the next several days after leaving Fort Mill, the column, finally with a cavalry escort, rode south toward Abbeville, South Carolina. Davis often rode at the head of the column, oblivious to military protocol that should have put him in the middle of the column for his protection. Sometimes he rode among the cavalrymen, speaking to them as equals rather than their commander in chief. Whether they realized it or not, Davis was trying to keep up their morale. He had heard the mumblings among the men that traveling with so many wagons and ambulances made the column an easily tracked target for Union cavalry.

At one roadside cabin, a woman came out bearing a child. She asked Davis if he was the Confederate president. When Davis nodded, the woman held up her baby and said, "He is named for you." Davis reached into his pocket and handed the woman a gold coin, telling her to give it to her son as a memento of his passing. As Davis rode away, he remarked to an aide that it was the last coin in his pockets. As he had repeatedly done during the trip, Davis refused any issue from the coins that were in the following wagons. He insisted that the money was to pay the soldiers.

Brigadier General Basil Duke was the most storied of the men protecting Davis. Just 27 years old, he was the brother-in-law of cavalryman

Brigadier General John Hunt Morgan who had raided Indiana and Ohio in the summer of 1863. Duke took over the brigade after Morgan's death and had won his own level of fame as a brave cavalryman. He and his Kentuckians were willing to do whatever Davis and Secretary of War John C. Breckinridge asked them to do.

Duke and his expert horsemen, men used to cavalry charges rather than plodding along in wagon ruts, were particularly frustrated at the slowness of the march. To entertain themselves they speculated on the chances of each of the cabinet members actually getting away.

"It was the general opinion that Mr. Davis could escape if he really wished to do so, but we feared that his pride would prevent his making the attempt," Duke wrote in his post-war memoirs. Duke also believed fellow Kentuckian Breckinridge and Tennessee-born Reagan, who had spent time surveying Texas, could get away on horseback if discovered.

Duke's men were unanimous in their opinion that soft, fat, city lawyer Judah P. Benjamin would never even be able to mount a horse.

On May 1, the party rode into Cokesbury, South Carolina. There to the joy of Davis was General Braxton Bragg. Davis walked up to Bragg, fully expecting him to offer new words of encouragement that would outweigh all the negativity he was hearing from his cabinet. Bragg, hat in hand out of respect for his friend of twenty years, quietly told Davis that the cabinet was right. The nation was lost.

Crushed yet again by his military and political advisors, Davis took comfort in a letter from Varina that was waiting for him. She was still ahead of him and still moving.

In a letter dated three days earlier on April 28 from Abbeville, just twenty miles to the southwest, Varina told her husband not to seek her out in favor of saving himself. She sought to soothe his feelings that he had sent her on this overland journey fraught with danger.

Varina wrote:

You must remember that you did not invite me to a Hero's home, but to that of a humble farmer. I have shared all your triumphs, been the only beneficiary of them, now I am but claiming the privilege for the first time of being all to you now these pleasures have past for me.

In the letter, Varina suggests that she shall head for Florida and then to Bermuda or Nassau and then to England to set the children up in school. She then promises to meet her husband in Texas "once more to suffer with you if need be."

What neither Varina nor Jefferson knew was that one option for action that Davis thought was open to him was now past. Ever since Lieutenant General Richard Taylor had roundly defeated a 25,000-man Union invasion of Texas during the Red River Campaign in the spring of 1864 with a tiny force of 8,000 Confederates, Davis had thought his former brother-in-law to be invincible. Men like generals Stonewall Jackson in the eastern theater and Nathan Bedford Forrest in the western theater had praised Taylor's skills so highly while he was fighting for them that Davis believed the son of General Zachary Taylor was every bit as good as those storied commanders.

At one time that might have been true, but Davis himself played a role in crippling the ability of Taylor to accomplish much of anything.

Davis forgot that in January 1865 he approved the transfer of most of Taylor's troops from Alabama to Johnston in the Carolinas so that Johnston could fight Sherman's advance into North Carolina. Taylor now had fewer than 12,000 men scattered across three states. The general who had routed Union forces from the Shenandoah Valley in Virginia to the Red River in Texas and Louisiana was now unable to stop even one cavalry raid through the heart of Alabama. Taylor could not prevent the capture of all the land around Mobile itself, another fact of which Davis was unaware. Even if Davis found a boat and got close to Mobile, there would be no safe place for him to land to find Taylor's army.

On April 30, just before an unaware Davis reached Abbeville, Taylor agreed to a truce with Union forces in anticipation of his surrender within a few days. Taylor would agree to the same terms offered General Robert E. Lee and Johnston—unconditional surrender.

Taylor would later remember that he "shared the fortunes of the Confederacy, having sat by its cradle and followed its hearse."

Davis was still not willing to let the nation he led die a natural death.

The party rode into Abbeville on the morning of May 2. His old friend Armistead Burt welcomed Davis into his home, telling him that Varina had left just three days earlier on her way to Washington, Georgia.

Also waiting for Davis in Abbeville were Parker, his midshipmen, and the gold and silver that had been entrusted to them back in Richmond on April 2. Parker had taken the heavy cargo all the way to Augusta, Georgia, before bringing it back to Abbeville in hopes that Davis would pass that way. On several occasions Parker heard rumors that straggling Confederate soldiers planned to attack his guard and steal the money. Each time he urged his teens to be ready to fight and kill anyone who would try to steal the treasure. Each time nothing came of the rumors.

Now, finally, here was Davis in Abbeville, creating the perfect time for Parker to give up his unpleasant duty of bank guard. Parker was so tired of guarding the money that on the way back from Augusta to Abbeville he briefly contemplated dumping the gold and silver in the Savannah River so that no one, Union cavalry or Confederate stragglers, would get at it and he could be free of his responsibilities.

The men riding into town were not the same dignified cabinet officers Parker had last seen in Danville.

"It reminded me of scenes I had witnessed in Central American Revolutions!" Parker wrote. He apparently meant that the cabinet now looked like a ragged crew of revolutionaries.

Parker had his doubts about Davis's cavalry escorts, none of whom he had previously seen since they joined the retreat in Greensboro and Charlotte, long after Parker had left Danville with the treasury train.

Parker said:

Many of the men were traveling with him, I believe, to get their rations. Some of them were throwing away or selling their arms, as they looked upon the war as over. There were many noble spirits among them who were ready, and anxious, to follow and defend the president to the death; but taken as an organization they were demoralized.

Parker said all the cabinet officers but Breckinridge were depressed while the secretary of war "presented his usual bold cavalier manner."

Parker had two private meetings with Davis on the afternoon of May 2, 1865. His observations of Davis's behavior, which he had not experienced for nearly a month, confirmed what the cabinet had been observing about the president every day for that same month.

When Parker told Davis that he had disbanded his company of midshipmen, Davis seemed shocked. He repeatedly said several times, "I am very sorry to hear that," as if Davis were expecting to include the boys in his army moving toward Texas.

Parker was peeved at his president for even thinking that the boys, some as young as 14, could be incorporated into a new army that was expected to fight an unwinnable war. When writing his memoirs of meeting Davis, Parker would insert another dig at the president's cavalry escort by writing: "After seeing the escort, I realized Mr. Davis's regret," implying that his uniformed midshipmen looked more like soldiers than the ragged cavalrymen.

Parker was bolder in talking to Davis than anyone in his closest circle had been up to that point. The naval officer bluntly told the president that his capture was "inevitable" if he prolonged his stay "in Abbeville."

Parker said of Davis:

He replied that he would never desert the Southern people; that he had been elected by them to the office he held; and would stand by them. He gave me to understand that he would not take any step which might be construed into an inglorious flight. He was most impressive on this point. The mere idea that he might be looked upon as fleeing, seemed to arouse him.

While it seems unlikely that Parker knew of the waterborne escape plans of John Taylor Wood and Charles Thorburn, Parker came up with a plan almost identical to the one they proposed to Davis in

Greensboro. Parker suggested that he and three other unnamed naval officers leave immediately for the east coast of Florida where they would "seize a vessel of some kind and get to Cuba or the Bahamas, but this was rejected."

With that rejection, a frustrated Parker ended his service to the Confederacy. He would wait in Abbeville several days until he heard that a Union cavalry force was in Washington, Georgia. He would then ride to that town to surrender formally.

On the same night Davis thanked Parker for his service, the president called in the five brigadier generals who commanded the cavalrymen acting as his escort. Davis said he wanted their honest opinions about the condition of their men and their morale as far as continuing the war. It was the same question he had asked of Johnston and Beauregard. He had not liked their answers. He would not like the answers of these lesser generals.

To a man, each brigadier frankly told the president that the men were tired of fighting. None believed they could make it to the Mississippi River. Their horses were too tired, their ammunition was too scarce, and their belief that they could win was at an ebb. Samuel Ferguson, the general who Johnston had counted as his least reliable and whose ranks were often depleted by deserters, ironically seemed the most eloquent. Ferguson insisted that the cavalry force, then in Abbeville, was too small to defeat any Union cavalry sent to pursue them and too large to evade detection. Ferguson said his men were soldiers, not guerrillas who would be forced to steal from the civilian population to survive. If they could not fight as soldiers, they wanted to disband.

When Davis asked the generals why they were still in the field if they felt the cause was lost, the brigadiers answered that they were protecting him. Repeatedly, Davis tried to win these men over, drawing on his oratorical skills that had won over his opponents while serving in the U.S. Congress. The generals, all of whom had been too minor for Davis to have much to deal with before this trip south, responded with only silence. They respected him too much to argue with him, but they knew that he was wrong. The war was over for them and their cavalrymen.

Duke summed up his fellow generals' opinion of Davis with the following: "The very ardor of his resolution prevented him from properly estimating the resources at his command."

Davis finally lost his temper and lashed out at the brigadiers saying that if "all the friends of the South were prepared to consent to her degradation," then he could do nothing more himself. He left the room, seemingly staggered by the rejection of the last few generals who had stood by him for more than two weeks. Some men would later remember that some aide to Davis had to support him on his arm as he left the room. As Davis had probably fallen into his old habits of not eating regular, filling meals, his need for support could have been true. If so, it could have been a sign that his body was shutting down from lack of nourishment.

From that moment, Breckinridge took over the column, telling the brigadiers that they could tell their men and officers that they could take discharges from service. No one would be ordered to stay in the column. Breckinridge made it clear that the objective of the march was no longer to reach the Mississippi to continue the war, but to protect President Davis from capture. Breckinridge did not ask the president for permission about changing the column's goals. He was no longer asking the president's permission for anything.

It was after midnight on May 3 when Davis and the dwindling column finally began moving out of Abbeville. The last official meeting of the Confederate government had taken place. There would be one more meeting to come, but no opinions but Davis's would be offered.

☆ ☆ ☆

EVEN BEFORE PRESIDENT LINCOLN'S ASSASSINATION, many influential men in the North did not intend to listen to any suggestions by Lincoln that the South be allowed back into the Union without punishment.

One of those was Judge Joseph Holt, judge advocate general of the United States Army and head of the Bureau of Military Justice. Like Davis and Lincoln, Holt was also a native of Kentucky, and just one year older than Davis and two years older than Lincoln. Holt was a professional politician, having served as secretary of war in the Buchanan administration where he met that president's then attorney general Edwin Stanton. Though born a Southerner, Holt became a staunch Unionist at the start of the war. Lincoln appointed him judge advocate general in September 1862, knowing that his friend would not impede any of the president's orders to arrest civilians and have them tried in front of military tribunals if those civilians were deemed to be harming the war effort.

On April 14, 1865, while watching the U.S. flag being raised over Fort Sumter on the fourth anniversary of the day it was hauled down by Confederates in 1861, Holt said in a speech that the leaders of the Confederacy were "miscreants, the Iscariots of the human race. May God in His eternal justice forbid that they should ever be shown mercy or forbearance." That same night Lincoln would go to the theater.

By April 24, just ten days after Lincoln had been mortally wounded and two days before John Wilkes Booth would be cornered and killed, Holt had finished collecting all the evidence he thought he needed to charge Confederate leaders with Lincoln's murder. Having faith in Holt, Stanton sent a telegram to General Major John Dix in New York City reading: "This Department has information that the President's murder was organized in Canada and approved at Richmond. One of the assassins now in prison, who attempted to kill Mr. Seward, is believed to be one of the Saint Albans raiders." [Stanton believed Holt's flawed intelligence. The raider was Lewis Powell, who was not one of the Confederates who robbed several banks in St. Albans, Vermont, on October 19, 1864.]

Before finding, arresting, and questioning Booth, the man who killed Lincoln, the United States government was already charging that Booth was part of a Confederacy conspiracy to assassinate the president, vice president, and secretary of state.

It would be another three days, April 27, before Stanton would send out the first telegram calling for General George Stoneman to launch the pursuit of Davis. In that April 27 telegram concentrating on the "plunder" Davis was supposed to have with him, there was no mention of Davis being a suspect in Lincoln's assassination, though Holt had virtually named him a co-conspirator three days earlier. Stanton knew from Holt that Davis was an assassination suspect, but he failed to insert that fact into the telegram urging thousands of Union soldiers to track down the fleeing Confederate president.

Stoneman, exhausted by the month-long raid he had conceived, would not get the chance personally to share in the glory of the chase for Davis. He was already back in Knoxville, nursing his sore backside, unable even to mount a horse. All Stoneman could do was order three brigades of cavalry still in North Carolina to move southwest from Asheville, North Carolina, along the Saluda River into South Carolina to intercept the Confederate cabinet's wagon train before it reached the Savannah River dividing Georgia and South Carolina. Stoneman sent out couriers to find his most veteran officer, Colonel William J. Palmer, commander of the Fifteenth Pennsylvania Cavalry whose detachments had probed Greensboro when Davis was in town.

When the couriers reached Palmer, the cavalry veteran assessed the situation and proceeded to move on Spartanburg, South Carolina, in anticipation of catching Davis in a vice with the other brigades moving down from Asheville. Not finding Davis in Spartanburg, Palmer concentrated on searching the larger towns in the region. He looked in Anderson, South Carolina, and Athens, Georgia, where he took credence in a rumor that Davis would try to board a train to Atlanta. When Davis was not found, Palmer's men moved on to Madison, Georgia, but did not find him there either.

Palmer, who had not reacted to or may not have heard the true rumors that Davis was in Greensboro on April 11, now found himself one step behind the elusive president. While he could not bag the focus of his search, Palmer was finding prominent Confederates. His men overran one column believed to harbor Davis, but instead they found the famed Confederate cavalry leader Major General Joe Wheeler. Another column captured General Braxton Bragg.

Davis soon learned of Palmer's pursuit. The cabinet's strategy now changed to one where they would ride harder and farther into the night to lessen the chances that their trail would be found.

Davis must have known it, but was too stubborn to admit it. It was already too late to ride hard. The Federal cavalry was now behind them and beside them. The only way still open was to the south.

It was only a matter of time before that escape direction also closed.

Secretary of War Edwin Stanton finally realized that Palmer's brigades might be too far behind Davis if the Confederate column was moving fast. To cut Davis off from reaching points farther south than he was known to have passed, Stanton wired a warning to Union Major general James H. Wilson, then in Macon, Georgia, 160 miles, or four days of average riding, to the southwest of Abbeville.

Wilson responded to the telegram by blanketing the entire southeast with cavalry. He ordered patrols to ride as far north as Atlanta and as far south as Tallahassee, Florida. All the major fords of the rivers were covered. Wilson was not going to let Davis slip through his lines. Capturing and being the first to interrogate the Confederate president formally would be a feather in his cap.

On May 2, the first attempt to tie Davis both formally and publicly to Lincoln's murder was made. President Andrew Johnson, at the urging of Stanton, issued a national proclamation:

Whereas it appears, from evidence in the bureau of military justice, that the atrocious murder of the late President Abraham Lincoln, and the attempted assassination of the Honorable William H. Seward, Secretary of State, were incited, concerted, and procured by and between Jefferson Davis, late of Richmond, Virginia, and Jacob Thompson and Clement C. Clay, Beverley Tucker, George N. Sanders, William C. Cleary, and other rebels and traitors against the government of the United States, harbored in Canada: Now, therefore, to the end of that justice may be done, I do offer and promise for the arrest of said persons, or either of them, so that they can be brought to trial, the following rewards: $100,000 for Davis, $25,000 for Clay, Thompson, Sanders, and Tucker, and $10,000 for Cleary.

When Wilson got his copy of the proclamation, he had posters printed with the reward amounts in hopes that they would entice not-so-loyal Southerners to alert him if they saw any strangers riding past their houses.

Clement C. Clay (who had left the Davis party back in Danville when he realized how slowly it would move); Jacob Thompson; Beverly Tucker; George N. Sanders; and William C. Cleary, a clerk for Thompson, were all Confederates operating in Canada. While it was true they were Confederate Secret Service agents, they were not very good at it. All of them were well known to Union spies who kept them under constant surveillance. The fact that the men's actions in Canada were well known would work against the United States government when it tried to make the men appear to be master spies who had the ability to plan the assassination of the president of the United States.

The federal government would eventually come to regret printing the posters and going public with such serious charges. ·

IT WAS A DARK, drizzly night on May 2 when Mallory, who was acting as a lookout at the head of the column, lost sight of his traveling companion. Nervous that he might be lost, he was relieved to see a light in a house by the side of the road. As he rode up, he could dimly make out another rider, who he mistook to be General Duke since the man wore a hat that had gold lace on it. Mallory was about to speak when the man asked, "What troops are these coming up?" Mallory had parked himself next to a Union cavalry officer who was out on his own patrol looking for the Confederate cabinet. Mallory coolly explained that they were just a column of paroled Confederate soldiers on their way home. The Yankee accepted that story. He did not recognize the Confederate president as Davis rode past, still oblivious to the danger now closing in around him.

On May 3 the party crossed the Savannah River and into the state of Georgia with a goal of reaching the nearby town of Washington.

Secretary of State Judah P. Benjamin took the opportunity to leave the party here, not even bothering to resign his post formally, probably out of fear that if the party were captured, a Yankee examination of the papers would indicate that he was nearby. When asked where he would go, Benjamin called out with a grin: "To the furthest place away from the United States, if it takes me to China!" When someone pointed out that his trunk bore his initials of J. P. B., Benjamin had a ready cover story. There was a Frenchman traveling in the United States who had those same initials, and he knew enough French to affect an accent while speaking made-up broken English.

The cavalrymen waved and bid him good luck. They liked Benjamin. He was one cabinet member who always had a jolly continence compared to the dour and sober president. Still, as the carriage bearing Benjamin and his aide rolled out of sight, the cavalrymen continued to take bets that Benjamin would not escape.

They would not know it for months, but those men betting against Benjamin would lose their money.

MONEY WAS ON THE MINDS of most of the Confederate cavalrymen still in the column. As they reached the Savannah River, many of the cavalrymen who rode the two hundred miles from Charlotte over the past two weeks were ready to head home. More threw away their weapons as others had done in Abbeville so that the expected Union cavalry would not mistake them for an armed threat. Some cavalrymen held onto their weapons and edged toward the money wagons, demanding to be paid.

Breckinridge tried to reason with the increasingly rowdy crowd, appealing to their pride as Southerners. But the horsemen's patriotism had slowly seeped out of them over four years. They wanted to be paid and to go home. Reluctantly, but necessarily, Breckinridge created a two-hundred-man guard drawn from all the brigades so as to break up the chance of friends talking themselves into trying to steal the treasury for themselves instead of guarding it. Over the course of several hours, Breckinridge, without getting permission from either acting secretary of the treasury Reagan or Davis, counted out and paid out more than $100,000 in silver coin to the impatient troopers.

The payout at least gave Breckinridge an accurate count of how many men were in the column; some 4,100 payouts of $25.25 were issued. Breckinridge fully expected most of those men to melt away into the woods. The only cavalrymen he knew he could count on were his own few hundred Kentuckians under Basil Duke who had promised Breckinridge many times that they would follow him as long as he commanded them.

On May 3, Davis and the cabinet rode into Washington, a town of about 2,000 people who had not seen a Yankee in four years of warfare. The town had felt threatened. Augusta, just forty miles away, was the site of the Confederate Powder Works, where the Confederacy had manufactured nearly three million pounds of black powder. Augusta was one of the key infrastructure cities in the South, but Sherman had steered away from that vital manufactory to concentrate on attacking South Carolina's state capital of Columbia.

Observers were happy to see their president in what they described as a suit of "Confederate gray." Some noticed something curious on his wide-brimmed hat: a wide band of black cloth. It looked like a mourning cloth that would normally be worn around a man's left coat sleeve in memory of a comrade who had fallen in battle. No one asked Davis about his strange-looking hatband, and no other citizens along the trip south left any mention of it in their writings of their encounters with Davis. Perhaps the president was making a silent protest about what he judged to be his soldiers' abandonment of the Confederacy when he was still willing and ready to fight for it.

Now that he was in a city rather than the woods, Mallory decided that he too was through traveling with the cabinet. Taking his cue from Benjamin, the naval secretary resigned from the cabinet once the president had awakened from the deep sleep he fell into as soon as the town's banker welcomed him. Mallory told the president that he was willing to help him get to Florida, but if that was not the president's destination, then he would head for Atlanta. Davis still refused to commit to Florida. Mallory would not even stay around for the meeting Davis had called. He boarded a train and left for Atlanta where he would later surrender himself.

Remarkably, also in town were two of Davis's oldest political enemies: Robert Toombs and Louis Wigfall. Toombs was the former U.S. senator from Georgia whose excessive drinking cost him the Confederate presidential nomination back in 1861. Wigfall was the former senator from Texas, who promoted states' rights over Davis's pragmatic appeal to create a central Confederacy that would revert to states' rights once the war was won.

Davis would not invite either of the two men to the meeting he had called in Washington, Georgia. The president did not have much control left over the Confederacy, but he could still dictate who was invited to meetings of his inner circle.

Davis was still his vindictive self, but Toombs was willing to forgive and forget. With the end of the war in sight, Toombs put aside all his old bad feelings about Davis and told Reagan that he would do all he could to help supply Davis and help him get away. When Toombs asked Reagan if Davis had a good horse, Reagan replied that Lee had sent him Traveller (Lee's prized horse) by way of Robert E. Lee, Jr., when the cabinet was still in Greensboro.

How Reagan made such a mistake in misidentifying the most famous horse in the Confederacy is lost to history. It seems doubtful that Lee, Jr., would have lied as to the identity of the gray horse he must have given Davis in Greensboro, just as it is doubtful that Davis would not have recognized that the gray horse he received was not Traveller. Lee rode away from Appomattox on Traveller on April 12 heading toward Richmond. Reagan apparently never knew he was mistaken in his belief that Lee had given up his favorite horse to Davis because his account was written after the war.

When Reagan went to a now-awake Davis and told the president of Toombs' concern for his safety, Davis thawed his personality somewhat and replied that Toombs was always a "whole-souled man." Davis told Reagan that he forgave Toombs for all those legislative fights, although the two apparently did not meet while both of them were in Washington, Georgia. Being formally kind to each other in absentia was one thing. Seeing old enemies in person was something else again.

Oddly, Davis did not hold up the meeting for Breckinridge, the man technically responsible for the planning of war strategy. Breckinridge was still back at the Savannah River, nervously counting out the last of the silver coins to increasingly tense soldiers.

The last meeting of the Confederate government was attended by the only remaining cabinet member who had not cut out on Davis—Reagan. The brigade commanders who had accompanied Davis from Charlotte were not present, but his old friend and woeful advisor, Braxton Bragg, was. Also, there were Wood and Thorburn, the sailors with that ever-ready but very distant boat waiting in Florida to sail Davis to Texas or the Bahamas. Also horning in on the meeting was a man Davis might not have even recognized, Brigadier General Felix Robertson of Texas, who had served most of the war in the western theater.

Davis conducted what amounted to the last unofficial meeting of the Confederate government almost like a monologue, without asking questions or advice. The last time he asked anyone's opinion was in Abbeville where his brigadiers told him that they were tired of the war and would not fight any more battles. Davis would not be embarrassed again like that in front of these few remaining officers.

During his talk Davis told the same tale he had been telling for weeks—that he believed that the Confederacy could still live if it raised an army of cavalrymen and moved beyond the Mississippi. If anyone in the room had heard the news that Davis's brother-in-law Taylor had already surrendered the remnants of the army Davis had been counting on to form the nucleus of the force he would take to Texas, they did not speak up. All Davis wanted to talk about was reaching Texas.

"This seemed to be a fixed hope in the mind of Mr. Davis," wrote Mrs. M. E. Robertson, wife of the town banker who allowed Davis to meet in his bank. "He was perfectly unconscious of his own danger, while his friends, realizing his own situation, were in eager haste and excitement to get him on his journey." Mrs. Robertson, as a civilian woman, was almost certainly not at the meeting, but her husband, being the building's owner, probably was. Her detailed postwar article would have been based on notes taken down by her husband.

Davis continued talking about his plans to continue the war, ignoring the fact that most of his own escort were melting away, were demanding back pay, or were threatening to take all that remained of the Confederate treasury by force. As Davis and the rest left the building, one officer turned to his aide and said, "The Confederate government is dissolved."

After more than a month of leisurely riding horses behind ambulances and wagons leaden with elderly generals, out-of-shape cabinet members, and now useless government records, Davis finally seemed to be in a hurry. What probably spurred his interest was word that Varina and his children were no more than a half a day's ride south of him. For weeks he had been thinking that he should intentionally avoid his family. He feared that he would endanger them if the approaching Union cavalry attacked his column without realizing that it contained women and children.

Now so close to reuniting with Varina, Davis changed his mind. Instead of trying to convince a number of cavalrymen to go with him, as he had been doing since leaving Charlotte, he freed most of his escort, asking only that twenty volunteers follow him south.

Since his own column was reduced to only a handful of men, Davis now felt he had to reach Varina as quickly as possible to protect her from the same advancing Federals who were looking for him. He did not wait for Breckinridge to arrive in Washington, Georgia. Davis knew that if the secretary of war accompanied him, so too would Duke's Kentucky cavalry, who were still with Breckinridge at the Savannah River.

Davis now wanted to ride hard, fast, and light so that he could catch up with his family. If he had a small party, they might escape notice of the Federals—exactly the same thing his cabinet and brigadiers had been telling him for the past month. Now that the cabinet was no longer around to give advice, he was willing to do what they had told him all along. Davis was still being Davis. He was still taking only his own counsel.

As Davis mounted his horse to head south, the local minister came up to bless him. Davis shook the man's hand and responded with a Bible quote of his own: "Though he slay me, I will trust in him."

According to witnesses, Davis only told the preacher that single line, which constitutes the first part of Job 13, 15. Davis left off the rest of line 15, which reads: "But I will maintain mine own ways before him."

Even before God, Jefferson Davis was going to go his own way, following only his own advice.

CHAPTER 9

"Success Depended on Instantaneous Action"

THE CONFEDERATE GOVERNMENT COLUMN that left Charlotte, North Carolina, on April 26, 1865, numbered more than 4,000 men, a brigade-sized cavalry force that was larger than the cavalry command of Major General J.E.B. Stuart during the July 3, 1863, cavalry battle at Gettysburg. On that day, for the first time in the flight south, Davis had substantial protection from Union attack. Had any of Major General George Stoneman's individual regiments looking for Davis stumbled onto Davis's column on its flight into South Carolina, they would have turned away, knowing they were outnumbered.

Now, on the morning of May 4, 1865, as Davis rode east out of Washington, Georgia, his protective escort had dwindled to fewer than twenty troopers, all adventurous volunteers from Kentucky and Mississippi who wanted to see how the game would play out. All the Confederate cabinet members except Postmaster General John Reagan had left the party. Of all the top government officials who fled Richmond with the president only his loyal aides, Joseph Johnston (son of Confederate General Albert Sidney Johnston who had been killed at Shiloh, Tennessee, in April 1862), Francis Lubbock, and John Taylor Wood remained. Also still with the column was Wood's friend, the mysterious Colonel Charles Thorburn.

Secretary of War John C. Breckinridge, who was detained at the Savannah River to supervise the paying of the departing cavalrymen, did not intentionally abandon his president as the other cabinet members had done all along the way since leaving Charlotte. He arrived

in Washington, Georgia, after Davis had left town. The still-loyal secretary of war, now knowing that Davis was moving south with only
a tiny bodyguard, split up the remaining volunteer troopers who were
with him into columns and intentionally ordered them to ride away
from the direction Davis was moving. Breckinridge thought if any pursuing Union cavalry heard about columns of Confederate cavalrymen
moving to the east, they would follow them rather than any small
party heading directly south. Breckinridge was guessing that Union officers would assume Davis would be in the middle of a protective cavalry force.

The plan worked, but not for long. The next day strong Union
columns spotted the two decoy Confederate columns. Both columns
surrendered without firing a shot. Breckinridge himself slipped away
unnoticed with the half-formed notion that he could catch up with
Davis's party, which was heading directly south.

Luckily for him, Breckinridge would not find the Davis party.

Davis would not know that Breckinridge's decoy cavalry column
had bought him some time until years later. Davis's newest choice in
cabinet members had proved the most help and the most loyal in the
escape south.

For the first time since leaving Richmond, Davis was on his own.
He had spent the past month slowly, leisurely, lackadaisically heading
in a southwesterly direction, and stopping for a week in Danville to
see if General Robert E. Lee would catch up to him. He stopped for
another few days in Greensboro to see if General Joseph E. Johnston
could stop Sherman. Davis stopped again for another few days in
Charlotte to complain about Johnston's surrender to Sherman. Leaving Charlotte, Davis stopped for still more cabinet meetings or for
when one cabinet member or another wanted to rest due to illness or
exhaustion.

Realizing that his wife and family could not be more than a day
or two ahead of him, Davis now changed his mind about his slow,
methodical move to the Mississippi. He now wanted to move quickly
to join Varina and the children so that he could protect them, both
from former Confederates no longer under discipline and from Union
soldiers looking for him.

Paradoxically, Davis now no longer had the manpower to protect his family and its wagon train. All of the 4,000 Kentuckians, Tennesseans, and Mississippians who left Charlotte with Davis were all heading home. They would have followed him to the ends of the earth to guard him if only he had abandoned his wagon train and mounted his horse. That cabinet wagon train that started from Greensboro never contained anything more valuable than personal baggage and government records that no longer seemed to matter to the life of the Confederacy. Davis could have been in Florida by now had he only mounted his horse and abandoned the wagons.

Davis had no way of knowing of the irony of his present situation. Just as he was riding away from Washington, Georgia, on the morning of May 4, the site of the last meeting of the Confederate government he would ever call, the body of Abraham Lincoln was also beginning its final journey some 730 miles to the north in Springfield, Illinois. Lincoln's body was being escorted in a funeral parade through that town that would end at his tomb. In both small towns, Washington and Springfield, tears were on the faces of the people standing on the sidewalks watching their respective sad parades. The people in Washington watched as the president they had never seen in person rode out of their town to an unknown fate. In Springfield, the citizens watched as the small-town lawyer they had sent away as president four years earlier returned as a martyr to the war that he had fought during his stay away from them.

Lincoln would be buried in his customary suit of black. Davis would ride away from Washington wearing his customary suit of gray. On top of his head was a gray hat with the brim turned up in a jaunty-looking tilt to the left. Just as Lincoln favored wearing the same color and type of suit day in and day out, so did Davis.

What Davis wore on his way south would become a historical issue for the rest of his life.

After a month of refusing to believe his country was dead and ignoring his friends' and aides' entreaties to save himself, Davis finally became engaged in planning his own escape. His military training came back to him. Instead of riding out of town the way he intended to go, south, he rode east out of Washington, Georgia. In the event some

Federal patrol came looking for Davis, the citizens would be able to say honestly that they saw him riding toward the Georgia coast. Once out of sight of curious citizens, the party turned due south, toward northern Florida.

As Davis and the cavalrymen rode past the continuous stream of defeated Confederate soldiers trudging along the same road, they began to hear rumors of a wagon train heading in the same direction. The description sounded like Varina and the children. But Davis also heard darker warnings from the Confederate parolees that bands of marauders had also discovered the wagon train and were planning to take what supplies it might be carrying.

Davis pressed on, riding so hard and fast that the twenty cavalrymen riding with him exhausted their horses and fell behind his pace. Davis ignored their pleas for him to slow down. Soon the fugitive president, the most wanted man in the nation now that John Wilkes Booth was dead, was riding into the moonlit night with only his aides to protect him. If they were armed at all, each man would have carried nothing more than a six-shot revolver. They would be no match for either robbers or Federals.

Soon, the party came upon a camp with four wagons. A voice boomed from the night asking who they were. Davis must have smiled. A month ago he had assigned his personal secretary, Burton Harrison, the duty of taking his wife and children out of Richmond with no more definite destination than Charlotte. From that city his wife had sent him a note that she and Harrison were heading to Abbeville. From Abbeville, she wrote that she might try for Florida. Her personal escape could have taken her down any number of roads from Abbeville, South Carolina.

Harrison had chosen this one road. It was his voice that challenged Davis.

For the next three days, Davis, reunited with his family, rode south. Davis, who had been so insistent after leaving Washington that his party must move fast, reverted to his old form. Just as had been the complaint of the cavalry since leaving Greensboro, the new column made up of Varina's wagons slowed the party so much that they were barely making twenty miles a day, one third of the distance that could be covered by a cavalry regiment looking for just such a wagon train. The president's aides tried arguing with Davis that he should ride ahead on his horse and separate himself from the wagon train. The aides insistently told Davis that he was recognizable to any Union officer, but Mrs. Davis was not. They suggested that she could pass herself off as a war refugee being escorted to safety by kindhearted paroled soldiers and fellow refugees.

Once again, the mysterious Thorburn reminded the president of that fabled boat hidden along the Indian River in Florida, just waiting for someone important like Davis to board it for Texas. Once again Davis listened to Thorburn's tale of the boat, unaware that General Richard Taylor had already surrendered in Alabama and Kirby Smith was planning a similar surrender in Texas. The two armies that Davis intended joining when he reached Texas no longer existed.

Davis was torn between his duty to his family and to his country. He knew his aides were correct that the wagons slowed the pace. If he stayed with the wagons, he stood a higher chance of being captured than if he rode ahead by himself. His methodical mind told him that if he could ride alone, he still had a chance of reaching Texas. If he found Taylor and Kirby Smith, then the Confederacy still lived.

But the wagons were also the only way Davis's family could escape. The children were small, too young to ride fast horses. They had no choice but to ride in the slow wagons: leaving deep ruts cut into the mud, an obvious trail that anyone could follow with ease. He had heard the stories that unsavory characters wanted those wagons: Confederates hungry for food and Federals hungry to bag the president of the Confederacy.

The mind of Davis, the family man, now battled with the mind of Davis, the man who had sworn to serve the Confederacy.

What kind of father would abandon his children to an unknown fate just to save himself from capture? What kind of husband would leave his wife armed with a pistol to protect her children while he ran away? But what kind of president would put the safety of his family above the needs of the entire Confederate nation?

Still, if he left the armed guard with the wagons, allowing them to pose as well-meaning protectors of this refugee family, Varina and the children would be as safe as he could hope to make them. Marauders would probably think carefully before attacking a wagon train protected by more than a dozen rifles. Federals might look at the wagon train, but if they did not find anyone matching Davis's description, they might allow it to pass. The Federals were looking for him, not his wife and children. As far as Davis knew, the government did not even know that his wife and children were anywhere near him.

Davis had not worked out exactly what he would do when he went to sleep on the night of May 9. He would make his decision the next day. Three things he did do were to stay dressed in his suit, to keep his horse saddled, and to put his pistols loaded in the holsters that were attached to his saddle.

BY MAY 1865 the war in the Deep South states of Alabama and Georgia was over too, thanks not only to Sherman's swath of destruction the previous summer and fall but also to the lightning cavalry raids by Union major general James H. Wilson's forces that spring.

Wilson, a 27-year-old native of Illinois, did not start his army career as a cavalryman. He graduated sixth in his 1860 West Point class, a ranking that first put him in faraway Oregon serving as a topographic engineer when the war started. He was soon transferred to the action, helping aim the Union rifled cannon (better than smoothbore guns) that reduced Confederate-held Fort Pulaski, Georgia, to rubble within a few hours of shelling in March 1862. Wilson served much of the war as a staff officer for General Ulysses S. Grant, but he chafed under the routine paperwork. He wanted to fight. Grant finally approved his appointment as a cavalry leader in 1864. Learning from one early defeat at the Battle of Staunton River Bridge in Virginia, Wilson transferred to General William T. Sherman's army in Tennessee where he trained the cavalry Sherman would take with him for the March to the Sea.

While serving in Tennessee, Wilson attracted attention from his superiors by repulsing a flank attack by Confederate major general Nathan Bedford Forrest at the Battle of Franklin in November 1864.

He followed that victory with another at Nashville. He then led a raid into Alabama and Georgia where he once again outmaneuvered the depleted forces of Forrest to capture several cities in Alabama before marching all the way to Macon just weeks before.

In a month-long raid, Wilson had destroyed numerous Confederate military installations, inflicted 1,200 casualties on the Confederates while capturing another 6,800, and lost fewer than 800 of his own men. Wilson accomplished all this without resorting to the rampant and wonton destruction Sherman had chosen to inflict on the Southern civilian population in the summer and fall of 1864.

On April 29, two days after General Joseph E. Johnston had surrendered his army and while Davis was in Yorkville, South Carolina, Wilson received word that Davis "under escort of a considerable force of cavalry, and with a large amount of treasure in wagons, was marching south from Charlotte, with the intention of going west of the Mississippi River."

Wilson's information was remarkably accurate and only three days old as Davis had only left Charlotte, North Carolina, on April 26. Only one detail was distorted. The treasure train had left Charlotte days earlier with Varina Davis.

The most remarkable fact that Wilson knew from the report was that Davis intended to strike out for the Trans-Mississippi. Davis had not made any public speeches or given any newspaper interviews describing that goal.

It was not until two years after the war that Wilson revealed just how he knew of Davis's plans. Some of Confederate general George Dibrell's column of supposed Confederate cavalry from Tennessee were actually Yankees from Ohio and Iowa.

On April 28, Union general Andrew J. Alexander approached Wilson with a bold idea—infiltrate Davis's column, which was known to be in Charlotte and soon to be heading south to some unknown destination. Wilson agreed, and a young, long-haired lieutenant with a swarthy complexion named Joseph A. O. Yeoman of the First Ohio Cavalry volunteered along with twenty other troopers from Alexander's Second Cavalry Brigade to be part of the plan. Yeoman, who was told that he looked like a Confederate with his dark skin and long hair, was outfitted in a Confederate major's uniform, and his men were dressed in other captured Confederate uniforms. Yeoman and his band of spies found Davis's party, which then numbered around 4,000, somewhere in South Carolina. The little band of Yankee spies simply slipped into the Confederate column, and no one asked who they were. It was easy, said Wilson in his postwar article about the brazen maneuver.

Wilson wrote:

The country was full of disbanded Confederate soldiers, all more or less demoralized and going home. Discipline was at an end, and every man of them was looking out for himself. This condition of affairs facilitated the operations of Yeoman, and encouraged him to believe that he might carry off the rebel chief; but the vigilance of devotion of the escort rendered it impossible to put this daring plan into effect, though it did not prevent his sending couriers into the nearest Federal picket post to report the movements of the party he was with.

Yeoman and his couriers gave Wilson precise information, including correctly naming four of the commanders of the cavalry brigades (Basil Duke, Samuel Ferguson, George Dibrell, and John Vaughn) escorting Davis, although Yeoman seems to have been off by about 1,000 of the brigades' total strength (2,000–3,000 according to Yeoman rather than the 4,000 estimated by Confederate sources).

More importantly, Wilson learned through Yeoman's spying that Davis was no longer heading to Mississippi, but was now heading south. Still, Wilson had to be sure that Davis did not slip through the net he was spreading. While cavalrymen are often bold and impulsive, not given to a lot of planning when they could be riding toward the action, Wilson used his engineering background and his mind for details—and a 15,000-man cavalry corps—to seal off virtually the entire southeast from Davis. Commanders from Atlanta to Tallahassee, a distance of nearly three hundred miles, were telegraphed to send troops to fords and bridges. Just to be positive Davis could not slip away,

Wilson sent detachments of men to monitor the passengers at railway stations in Georgia in case Davis somehow slipped through the cordon of cavalry.

Wilson also realized the power of incentive. On May 6, 1865, Wilson printed posters with huge headlines proclaiming: "$100,000 REWARD in Gold will be paid to any person or persons who will apprehend and deliver Jefferson Davis to any of the military authorities of the United States."

Curiously, in much smaller type, the poster also announced that "several million dollars in specie reported to be with him will become the property of the captors." The captors of Davis would get $100,000 in official reward, but the true value of the capture would be getting the gold and silver coins the United States government claimed Davis was hauling. Perhaps Wilson did not believe the reports of the millions of dollars Davis was carrying and put the information in lower type to deemphasize the rumor. What Wilson and Stanton in Washington did not know was that the Confederate treasure train had only $500,000 in gold and silver when it left Richmond. The bankers in Richmond, who Stanton said gave him the estimate, had given the Yankees wildly inflated financial figures.

Though Wilson had spies inside Davis's column, they were too small in number as a unit actually to capture Davis. If they even acted too interested in getting close to the Confederate president, they could be found out and killed. Yeoman stuck to the plan of continually sending messages back to Wilson until the general knew for sure that Davis's column had shrunk so much that it could be taken without a major battle.

Two of Wilson's best cavalry units were destined to capture Davis.

The First Wisconsin Cavalry Regiment, formed in the cities of Ripon and Kenosha, had immediate success early in the war against scattered Confederate forces in Missouri. They captured several small camps, even a steamship loaded with supplies. The regiment's colonel, Edward Daniels, was bold, too bold. Without orders confining him to a specific area of operations, Daniels and the First Wisconsin crossed into Arkansas where the regiment raided for several weeks, defeating all resistance. Though the regiment met with great success, Daniels' superiors took a dim view of a colonel acting without orders. He was relieved of command.

Daniels's superiors should have thought twice about relieving an officer who had been so successful. While the regiment, without Daniels, was being relocated back to Missouri, a Confederate column attacked its wagon train. Fifteen members of the regiment were killed and fifty-seven were captured. All the wagons, including two loaded with ammunition, were captured by the Confederates.

For the rest of the war, the First Wisconsin Cavalry conducted mostly small raids and foraging operations. On March 22, 1865, they were part of Wilson's raid into Alabama. The First Wisconsin, on April 12, was among the first troops to enter and occupy Montgomery, the state capital of Alabama. Wilson did not let them rest. He then sent the regiment against Fort Tyler at West Point, Georgia. On April 21 the regiment reached the large southeast Georgia town of Macon, expecting that they would soon be mustered out of service.

It had been a tough three years for the regiment. Some 3,700 men had served in the regiment at some time over the preceding three years. Three hundred and sixty-six had died with most of those deaths coming from diseases. Another 634 were discharged, mostly for sickness. Another 91 had deserted, unable to take the rigors of living in the open for nearly three years. The war took a particularly hard toll on the regiment's officers. In one skirmish, both the lieutenant colonel and the major in the regiment were killed.

One tough man who was still around was 42-year-old Lieutenant Colonel Henry Harnden of Ripon, Wisconsin, who had enlisted as a private in the regiment when he was aged 39 years, nearly twice the age of the average volunteer. Harnden, a man who had sailed the oceans and who had fought in the Mexican War, must have impressed his fellow soldiers because they soon began electing him to officer positions within the regiment. Within one year he was a captain, and within three years he was lieutenant colonel. He took over command of the regiment when the previous colonel was killed.

Harnden and the First Wisconsin were resting in Macon less than two weeks when Wilson put them in the field again in response to the reports he was getting from Yeoman as to the specific direction Davis was heading.

Wilson wanted to be sure that Davis would be caught, so he also assigned a second veteran regiment to the same task. That was the Fourth Michigan Regiment of Cavalry, under Colonel Robert H. Minty. The Fourth Michigan was formed in Detroit in August 1862 with so many volunteers from around the state that the regiment left Michigan with 223 more members than the standard 1,000-man regimental status.

Like the First Wisconsin, the Fourth Michigan had served exclusively in the western theater. They were engaged in scouting and skirmishing almost daily during Sherman's spring 1864 campaign to take Atlanta. In one year from summer 1863 through summer 1864, the regiment rode more than 2,500 miles before retiring for a short time to Nashville to reequip. Once rested, the regiment participated in Wilson's raid through Alabama and Georgia. By May 1865 the regiment had lost 47 dead to combat and 328 to disease, almost the same number as lost by the First Wisconsin. The men were tired, saddle sore, and ready to go home.

They would have one more mission to accomplish, one that would win them fame for the rest of their lives.

On May 6, a day when Davis was near Sandersville, Georgia, sixty miles, or one day's hard ride from Macon, Wilson heard from Yeoman that Davis had paid off his escort in gold at the Savannah River. That told Wilson that Davis's force was now greatly reduced and no military threat to anyone. Wilson ordered elements of First Wisconsin Cavalry to leave Macon on May 6. The next day a detachment from the Fourth Michigan Cavalry left Macon. Both headed east, anticipating that they would run into Davis head-on.

For some personal reason, Minty of the Fourth Michigan chose not to pursue Davis himself. Instead, he sent his second-in-command, Lieutenant Colonel Benjamin Pritchard, with 439 men and officers to picket the Ocmulgee River about sixty miles south of Harnden's destination of Dublin, Georgia. In Minty's official report filed on May 18, 1865, he wrote an order that "if he [Pritchard] found that Davis had already crossed the Ocmulgee to follow and capture or kill him."

Minty may have been reading too much into his orders from Wilson unless Wilson said something verbally that went unrecorded. In the *Official Records of the War of the Rebellion,* there is no order from Wilson or any other Federal officer or government official giving permission to Minty, Harnden, Yeoman, or anyone to try to kill Davis. In fact, Sherman, Wilson's commander at the time, was trying to ease the violence. In an April 27 order, Sherman wrote to Wilson:

I regard the war as over, but it is well to be prudent and cautious, as there is much danger of some of the discharged soldiers of both armies infesting the country as robbers. If you encounter any of these either punish them with extreme severity or carry them where the civil authorities of an organized State can try and punish.

Pritchard, 30, was a lawyer in Michigan before joining the Fourth Michigan as a captain. He proved popular with the men and rose through the ranks to lieutenant colonel. He fought with the regiment the entire war, only taking time off in 1864 to get married.

As a lawyer, Pritchard knew something about creating drama in the court of public opinion. He would soon get his chance.

For all the careful planning and spreading out of his cavalry command, Wilson did not see fit to send very large units in pursuit of Davis. Apparently trusting that Yeoman's information was accurate, the First Wisconsin left with just 150 horsemen. The Fourth Michigan detachment left Macon with a more reasonable number if they encountered trouble—400 riders.

Remarkably, Wilson apparently did not give colonels Harnden and Pritchard joint orders to operate with each other or to keep in close contact with each other. They may have even left Macon without knowing that each other's regiments were in the field looking for the same man—Davis.

On May 7 Harnden of the First Wisconsin arrived near Dublin, Georgia, where he discovered a clue to Davis's proximity. He talked to "some Negroes" who told him that a "train of light ambulances and wagons" had crossed the Oconee River that morning. When Harn-den questioned some white residents of Dublin about the wagons, they insisted that no such wagon train had passed through their town. Later that night Harnden talked to another Negro who confirmed that the wagon train had both Davis and his wife Varina aboard, and it was headed in the direction of Irwinville, Georgia.

Not long after this encounter, elements of the Fourth Michigan stumbled into the First Wisconsin. The two commanders learned for the first time that they were operating in the same area. Pritchard would later say that neither he nor Harnden agreed on a strategy to search independently for Davis. They had no orders assigning them to work together, but Harnden did tell Pritchard that he was going to ride to Irwinville to check out the Negroes' stories.

Pritchard and the Fourth Michigan rode toward Abbeville, Geor-gia, where he learned from a resident that a wagon train believed to be Davis's had already crossed the Ocmulgee River and was heading toward Irwinville, the same village that Harnden was going to visit. There were two roads heading to the town. Convinced from his last known location that Harnden would be heading down the westernmost road from Abbeville to Irwinville, Pritchard took the eastern road.

Pritchard arrived in Irwinville at 1:00 a.m. on May 10 and was surprised that he did not see Harnden's men already there. Posing as a Confederate officer assigned as rear guard to the wagon train, Pritchard knocked on some doors to ask where the camp was. Sleepy villagers, who apparently could not tell blue uniforms from gray late at night, told Pritchard that the camp was about 1.5 miles north of town, along the road that Harnden was supposed to be riding down.

Pritchard quietly rode his men back north along the westernmost road and found the camp that he now strongly suspected belonged to Davis and his party. The colonel sent a dismounted twenty-five-man detachment to the north to cut off any escape attempt in that direc-tion. He then sat down to wait for dawn because he thought it was so dark that any raid on the camp might allow some in the camp to slip into the woods unnoticed. He would wait a few hours until dawn's light would help illuminate the attack.

Just before dawn, Pritchard's mounted command rushed the camp. Pritchard wrote in his report:

The surprise was so complete, and the movement so sudden in its execution, that few of the enemy were enabled to make the slightest defense, or even arouse from their slumbers in time to grasp their weapons.

Then, before Pritchard could even find out whose camp he had captured, gunfire broke out on the north side of the camp. Pritchard rushed forward, sending out skirmishers to face what he thought were hidden Confederates. Muzzle flashes pierced the darkness in both directions. After several minutes of heavy firing, the colonel took note of the sound of the rifle reports. All of them sounded like Spencer repeating carbines, which he assumed only Federal cavalry had. Guessing that the two Union regiments were now engaging each other instead of hidden Confederate pickets, Pritchard ordered his men to stop firing. The colonel then boldly rode his horse into an open spot in the woods where he "hallooed" to them, asking them who they were, and received the reply, "First Wisconsin."

The First Wisconsin had been sneaking up on the camp from the north side at the same time the Fourth Michigan was attacking from the south. Two men were killed in the Fourth Michigan and one was wounded. Three men from the First Wisconsin were severely wounded. Pritchard would later officially blame the mistaken firing on a sergeant in the First Wisconsin for not giving a proper response to a challenge from a lieutenant of the Fourth Michigan when he spotted the Wisconsin men in the trees.

Davis's camp had not posted pickets and was not involved in the shooting. It was Jim Jones, a longtime loyal black servant to Davis, who was first awakened by the sound of Yankees firing on Yankees. Jones rushed into the center of camp, shouting alarm. At first, Davis thought the firing was the rumored renegade Southerners who he believed had been stalking the wagon train for at least a day. When Davis stepped outside his tent, he thought he could convince the renegades to respect him as their president. Instead, Davis saw the dark colors of Federal uniforms in the growing light.

The next minute or less of elapsed time would forever color Davis's reputation.

The president's first thought was to defend the camp and his family. He was torn between his lifelong nature to stand and fight his enemies and the entreaties of his loving wife to save himself. As he tried to sort out what to do in his own mind, Varina acted more impulsively and inadvertently set in motion a molehill of truth that would be turned into a mountain of lies.

According to a June 5, 1865, letter from Varina to her Yankee friend Montgomery Blair in Washington City, Varina traced the actions of her husband:

When he saw them [some Fourth Michigan cavalrymen] deploying a few yards off, he started down to the little stream hoping to meet his servant with his horse and pistols, but knowing he would be recognized, I pleaded with him to let me throw over him a large waterproof raglan which had often served him in sickness during the summer season as a dressing gown and which I hoped might so cover his person that in the gray of the morning he would not be recognized. As he strode off, I threw over his head a little black shawl which was around my own shoulders, seeing that he could not find his hat. After he started I sent my colored woman after him with a bucket for water, hoping that he would pass unobserved. He attempted no disguise, consented to no subterfuge.

Davis, writing in *Rise and Fall of the Confederate Government*, would remember the moment the Federals attacked differently than his wife. According to his memory, as he turned back into the tent to tell Varina that the Federals were upon them, she begged him to leave and make his way into the dark woods. Davis hesitated, saying that he lost "a few precious moments before yielding to her importunity."

Davis said he impulsively reached for what he thought was his raglan. He threw it over his shoulders, either anticipating that he would need it to keep warm if he escaped, or using it to hide his light-colored gray suit against the dark forest. By mistake, he had picked up his wife's raglan because it was "so very much like my own as to be mistaken for it. As I started, my wife thoughtfully threw over my head and shoulders a shawl."

Shawls were commonly worn by both men and women in the 1860s. President Lincoln had one draped around his shoulders on the night he was shot. It was not uncommon for a man to put a shawl over his head on a damp morning if he was not wearing a hat. Men in the 1860s usually wore some kind of head covering whenever they ventured outdoors.

Davis's story was that he put the raglan over his shoulders. Varina remembered that she threw the raglan over his shoulders. Both of them remembered that she threw the shawl over his head.

According to Burton Harrison, Davis's secretary who was now aroused and looking in the direction of Davis's tent, there was only one mounted soldier whose horse was standing near Davis's tent. By this time Pritchard ordered all his troopers, except for that one, to go toward the firing occurring on the north side of the camp, thinking his men were involved in a skirmish with Confederate guards.

That mounted man was stationed near Davis's tent, probably by chance because Davis's tent would have looked like any of the others in the camp, a large, white canvas tent. The trooper, either Corporal George Munger or Private Andrew Bee (both claimed to be the first to spot Davis) could not have been aware of who was inside the tent.

Harrison's version differs somewhat from both Varina's and Davis's stories. According to Harrison, Mrs. Davis emerged and talked to the soldier, trying to get him to move away from the tent. Harrison then walked up and talked to the man. Harrison said he was able to intimidate the Union trooper enough to get him to move his horse away from the tent several yards and to face Harrison, whose back was toward the center of the camp. According to Harrison, while he was talking to the trooper and keeping the man's attention away from the opening of the tent, the president slipped out of the tent and began walking alone toward the woods.

Neither Harrison's nor Davis's postwar stories mention a black woman following the president with a bucket as does Varina's story.

Harrison could not keep the trooper's attention long enough for Davis to get out of sight. Some sound caused the cavalryman to turn around in his saddle, which is when he glimpsed Davis walking toward the woods. The cavalryman spun his horse around and charged Davis, calling on the Confederate president (whom he never claimed to have recognized) to halt. When Davis kept walking, the Fourth Michigan man drew his carbine. Davis immediately stopped, threw off the shawl and raglan, and turned and moved aggressively toward the trooper. He intended to cup his hands under the trooper's foot in the stirrup and fling the man from his horse, something Davis called "an old Indian trick" that he had learned from his days in the Army.

As the Union cavalryman leveled his carbine at Davis, Varina rushed forward and threw her arms around her husband, obstructing the man's aim and putting her own life in danger. With his wife now in the line of fire, Davis decided to give up.

"Success depended on instantaneous action, and recognizing that the opportunity had been lost, I turned back, and the morning being damp and chilly, passed on to a fire beyond the tent," Davis wrote.

Pritchard of the Fourth Michigan Cavalry, now satisfied that the shooting was over, rode up to Davis and asked his identity. Davis did not give a false name. The hunt for the Confederate president was over. He had been fleeing for more than five weeks, but the official Union army search for him was not launched until just two weeks earlier, twelve days after Lincoln had died.

The capture of Jefferson Davis was accomplished. Though the officers of the First Wisconsin Cavalry and the Fourth Michigan Cavalry would squabble among themselves in official reports as to who was to blame for firing at each other, all would get equal credit for the success of the mission from Macon. Curiously, Yeoman, the Ohio spy within Davis's ranks who had kept Wilson informed about the direction Davis was fleeing, would not even be mentioned in the initial after-action reports. It was not until later that Wilson would push for Yeoman to collect part of the reward.

At some point after Davis's capture, according to Varina, perhaps not even the same morning, but possibly days later, Union soldiers from the Fourth Michigan were ransacking the family's luggage when a soldier somehow shot off his own hand by trying to pry open a trunk with a loaded carbine. (Assuming the shooting story is true, it is more likely that the soldier with the carbine shot off someone else's hand who was holding the trunk's lock for the first soldier. It would be difficult for a soldier to shoot off his own hand as described.)

Varina wrote in her postwar book about her husband:

Out of this trunk, the hooped skirt was procured, which had never been worn. No hooped skirt could have been worn on our journey, even by me, without great inconvenience, and I had none with me except the new one in the trunk.

Varina could not imagine at the time why the soldier would take her hoop skirt, but she would learn soon enough. United States secretary of war Edwin Stanton wanted it.

CHAPTER 10

"He Hastily Put on One of Mrs. Davis's Dresses"

DAVIS SHOULD HAVE STUCK CLOSE to Secretary of War John C. Breckinridge, or would-be sailors John Taylor Wood and Charles F. Thorburn. All three escaped the Federal attack on Davis's camp, and all three made it to freedom outside the United States.

After slipping away from the Federal patrols that captured the two remaining columns of Confederates who had been protecting Davis, Breckinridge headed deep into Georgia. His goal was Madison, Florida, a small town along the Florida and Georgia border. As it was far from Federally occupied cities along the coast such as Fernandina Beach, Jacksonville, and St. Augustine, the isolated town was a natural stop for Confederates trying to lose themselves in the interior of the state. From Madison, Confederates could move to either the east or the west coast below the Federals who were concentrated in bases along the northeast coast.

Wood escaped the raid on Davis's camp by appealing to the baser instincts of the cavalryman who captured him. Wood convinced the man to edge into the woods where he gave him several gold coins to look the other way. The cavalryman, at least honest in his susceptibility to bribery, did just that. He left Wood in the tall grass without reporting him. Wood simply waited for the Federals to leave with their real prize, Davis, before he, too, struck out for Madison.

Wood and Breckinridge surprised each other when both showed up in Madison. Finally free of Davis's slowness and unwillingness to move south as quickly as possible, the two men resolved to escape to Florida together and head to another country. Both had reason to fear the United States. Breckinridge had been a United States vice president. He feared being tried for treason. Wood had been one of the Confederacy's best commerce raiders. He feared being hung as a pirate.

While planning what to do next, Breckinridge heard Secretary of State Judah P. Benjamin had already passed through Madison and was heading for Florida's west coast. The man voted least likely to escape by the Confederate cavalry escort while still in South Carolina was already ahead of all the other escapees in Florida. Benjamin eventually made it to a plantation near Bradenton, Florida, on the west coast. He escaped by boat to Cuba and then to England, where he would become a very successful barrister, or lawyer. Unlike his fellow cabinet members, Benjamin never felt the urge to return to the United States. He would die and be buried in Paris, France, in 1884.

Wood and Breckinridge headed south through the north central part of the state until they met Colonel John J. Dickison, a Confederate cavalry leader so knowledgeable about the region that he was dubbed by both sides the Swamp Fox of Florida, in honor of Francis Marion, the original Swamp Fox of South Carolina during the American Revolution. Dickison took the pair to an eighteen-foot boat that he had sunk in a lake for just such an emergency. This boat was not the same boat Thorburn was bragging about because Dickison personally had hidden this craft after capturing it and removing it from a Union gunboat.

Wood and Breckinridge set off down the Indian River and entered the Atlantic where they endured stormy seas, Federal blockaders, and homegrown pirates during a run down Florida's east coast. After many adventures and near death experiences, the two aides to Davis who refused to abandon him made it to Cuba on June 11, 1865. Breckinridge would live abroad until returning to Kentucky in 1869. Wood would never quite trust that the United States government would not arrest him for his commerce raiding days. He moved to Nova Scotia and never returned.

Thorburn, the man with the plan and the boat, was not in camp when the Federals struck. He planned to leave early to move ahead to Florida so that he could prepare for Davis's arrival and he could finally show the president his hidden watercraft. Just hours before Lieutenant Colonel Benjamin Pritchard's men struck the camp, Thorburn ran into a Union patrol—or so he later said. Suspecting he was a Confederate, the patrol chased Thorburn and fired on him. Thorburn claimed he shot one cavalryman from his saddle, and the rest of the patrol faded back rather than deal with such a deadly shot.

If the Fourth Michigan or the First Wisconsin or any other roving Union patrol suffered such a loss on that night, they did not report it, which seems unlikely. Thorburn may have been a big talker and maybe a liar when it came to his escape, but he did reach Florida. He never got around to using the boat he claimed was waiting for Davis.

ONE PERSON WHO WAS CAPTURED with the Davis party that early May 10 morning does not show up in official reports. Neither Pritchard's nor General James H. Wilson's reports on the Davis capture mention the black child, Jim Limber, only the "four children" of the blood-related Davis family. The 4-year-old may have been counted among the unnamed "servants" who were captured, an inadvertent racist description on the part of the capturing Federals. Jim Limber was not a slave. He did not work for the Davis family. He was part of the Davis family.

It was on the ride to Macon that Varina's blood began to run cold when she noticed a certain Union officer take a particular interest in her black foster son.

According to Varina, an officer named Hudson "informed me that he intended to take our little Negro protégé for his own, and solicitude for the child troubled us more than Hudson's insults."

The officer's true name was Major Joseph S. Huston, the adjutant or chief staff officer of the Fourth Michigan Cavalry, from Paw-Paw, Michigan. After taking that initial, intense dislike to Huston, Varina became determined that if the Davis family could not keep Jim Limber with them, then she would find someone better than Huston—and higher ranking—who would raise a child she considered part of her family.

On the second day of the three-day ride back to Macon, slowed now because Pritchard insisted on using the same wagons that had so slowed Davis, the Fourth Michigan Cavalry passed the time of day insulting and threatening the Davis family. A scout rode in with a broadside (a public notice) announcing a reward of $100,000 for Davis's capture as a suspect in Lincoln's assassination. This broadside, based on the May 2 proclamation issued by President Johnson, was separate from the poster Wilson had printed mentioning that Davis was carrying millions of dollars in specie that could be divided among the people capturing Davis. Passing the poster around, the cavalrymen jeered even more, some breaking into song: "We'll hang Jeff Davis from a sour apple tree."

After having the poster waved in his face, Davis was not successful in calming his wife's fears that he would be charged with the assassination. He knew who was to blame for the accusation—President Johnson.

"The miserable scoundrel who issued that proclamation knew better than these men that it was false. Of course, such an accusation must fail at once; it may, however, render these people willing to assassinate me here," Davis told Varina.

The cavalrymen turned more menacing as the column drew closer to Macon. The children could sense it. Nine-year-old Maggie crept into her father's arms and held him closely as Davis recited Psalms from memory "which he repeated as calmly and cheerfully as if he were surrounded by friends."

Hearing Davis recite Bible verses did not calm the soldiers who "expressed in words unfit for women's ears all that malice could suggest."

It was 9:30 a.m. on May 13 before Davis had arrived in Macon, when Wilson sent the first telegram announcing Davis's capture back to Washington and Secretary of War Edwin Stanton.

Buried in the report were the lines:

The firing of this skirmish was the first warning that Davis received. The captors report that he hastily put on one of Mrs. Davis's dresses and started for the woods, closely pursued by our men, who at first thought him a woman, but seeing his boots while running suspected his sex at once. The race was a short one, and the rebel President was soon brought to bay. He brandished a bowie-knife of elegant pattern, and showed signs of battle, but yielded promptly to the persuasion of the Colt revolvers without compelling our men to fire.

Wilson was inaccurate in his own telegram. The two troopers who pointed their weapons at Davis had pointed Spencer carbines, not Colt revolvers.

The column finally arrived in Macon on the afternoon of May 13. When Davis alighted from the ambulance to walk into Wilson's headquarters, the Union guards standing at the door brought their rifles vertically in front of them to present arms, a military command of respect given to officers and dignitaries. Davis noticed the movement, but thought nothing more of the unusual demonstration of honor that had been afforded the man now accused of assassinating President Lincoln.

General Henry Halleck back in Washington was the first government official to comment on the rumors of Davis being in a dress. After getting a copy of the 9:30 a.m. telegram, Halleck sent a note to Stanton saying, "If Jeff. Davis was captured in his wife's clothes I respectfully suggest that he be sent north in the same habiliments."

That afternoon dinner was brought to the Davis family in their hotel room by a black servant who gave them flowers on their tray because, as he told Varina: "I could not bear for you to eat without something pretty from the Confederates." Varina kept one of the flowers as a keepsake of the man's "righteousness" for at least thirty-five years.

After dinner Davis had a private meeting with Wilson who never formally met Davis, but while a cadet saw him visit West Point as both the secretary of war and as a Mississippi senator.

Wilson said:

He looked bronzed and somewhat careworn, but hardy and vigorous, and during the conversation behaved with perfect self-possession and dignity. However petulant he may have been at the time of his capture and during his march to Macon, he had entirely recovered his equanimity.

The conversation drifted around to Davis's opinions of his generals. According to Wilson, Davis praised Lee as the ablest of his generals, but then, Davis being Davis, the Confederate president also commended Bragg for "high qualities and leadership, but as might have been expected, he spoke slightingly of Johnston, charging him with timidity and insubordination. He condemned Beauregard's military pedantry and deprecated Hood's heroic rashness."

Even in front of a real enemy like Union general Wilson, Davis could not resist the temptation to slam Confederate generals Joseph E. Johnston and Pierre Beauregard, his perceived enemies, who had been fighting for Davis and the Confederacy against his real enemies. And even in front of a skilled Union general who knew better, Davis praised the skills of Bragg, a military failure in nearly every campaign he attempted and whose only friend in the entire Confederacy was his president.

Davis even had opinions on Union generals. He liked the abilities of Ulysses S. Grant, William T. Sherman, and George Thomas, but said that "he expected more from McClellan, Buell, and Fitz-John Porter than they had performed."

"His comments and criticisms were clothed in excellent language and delivered with felicity and grace while his manners were stately and dignified without being frigid or repellent," said Wilson.

When the conversation drifted to Lincoln's death, Davis, without any prompting from Wilson, said that Lincoln was a "conscientious president. He did not hesitate to express his sorrow that a man of so much sensibility and kindliness had been succeeded in the presidency by Andrew Johnson, for whom he made but little if any effort to conceal his dislike, and whom he seemed to fear would be governed by a vindictive and unforgiving temper toward the Southern people."

Davis, insistent on speaking his unfiltered mind, was telling a general who reported to the United States secretary of war and subsequently to the president of the United States, that he had no use for the chief executive of the nation, the same man who now held the Confederate president's fate in his hands.

Davis sloughed off the charge, as issued by President Johnson, that he had anything to do with the assassination of Lincoln, with an accurate assessment of his future:

I have no doubt, General, the Government of the United States will bring a much more serious charge against me than that, and one which will give me much greater trouble to disprove.

He was predicting that he would be charged with treason.

At the end of the conversation, Davis told Wilson that he thought Pritchard had "treated me with marked courtesy and respect." If Davis was serious, he had changed his mind about the man who had formally taken him captive. At some point on the ride back to Macon, Davis complained that Pritchard did not have control of his men. He charged that the Fourth Michigan Cavalry ransacked his wife's baggage and spoke rudely in front of her and the children. It may have been at this time that Varina's hoop skirt was confiscated, but her own account is not clear on when the theft occurred.

Davis would soon have reason to change his mind again about Pritchard.

From Macon on May 14, the Davis family, including Jim Limber, was sent by train to Augusta, where they boarded an old, open-sided tugboat that would take them to Savannah. Also aboard the ship were Confederate vice president Stephens, suspected Lincoln assassination conspirator Clement Clay, and Confederate major general Joseph Wheeler, one of the last of the cavalry leaders to be captured. Clay had escaped Richmond with Davis, but left the cabinet in Danville, the first of Davis's friends to become frustrated with the slow pace of the escape.

Davis and Stephens met once on the deck on the morning after they boarded the tug as it headed down the Savannah River. It was not a reuniting of old friends. The two had not seen each other since Davis's rousing patriotic speech in February. The president and vice president exchanged pleasantries without smiling, embracing, or wishing each other luck for what was sure to be a lengthy imprisonment. Still, Stephens, who had never liked Davis, felt sorry for him.

"Much as I disagreed with him and much as I deplored the ruin which, I think, his acts helped to bring upon the whole country, as well as on himself, I could not but deeply sympathize with him in his present condition," wrote Stephens.

The tug continued down the Savannah and into the Atlantic toward Beaufort, South Carolina. Along the way Wheeler noticed that Pritchard so trusted his Confederate captives—or was so lax in his knowledge of securing prisoners—that he assigned only two guards over the sixty muskets the men had stacked before heading down below decks for dinner. Wheeler and nine other able-bodied Confederates discussed overpowering the guards, taking the muskets, and, then, hijacking the ship to head for the Bahamas. They asked Davis for permission to instigate the plan. Davis quietly refused the suggestion. Finally, Davis was ready to recognize that the war was over, and he was ready to face whatever punishment the North had in store for him.

When the tug stopped in Beaufort, everyone was transferred to a more seaworthy ship, the USS *William P. Clyde*. Just before leaving port, Varina learned that the entire region was under the command of Union brigadier general Rufus Saxton. Saxton was a Davis family friend since the 1850s when Secretary of War Davis assigned the young army officer to survey a route for a transcontinental railway that Davis envisioned. Varina conferred with her husband and made one of the hardest decisions of her life—to give up one of her children.

Varina wrote of Jim Limber:

My husband thought we might ask of him [Saxton] to look after our little protégé Jim's education, in order that he might not fall under the degrading influence of Captain Hudson [Huston]. A note was written to General Saxton, and the poor little boy was given to the officers of the tug-boat for the General, who kindly took charge of him. Believing that he was going on board to see something and return, he quietly went, but as soon as he found he was to leave us, he fought like a little tiger, and was thus engaged the last we saw of him. I hope he has been successful in the world, for he was a fine boy, notwithstanding all that had been done to mar his childhood.

Saxton and Davis might have been privately amused at the irony of Saxton being chosen by Davis to be Jim Limber's new foster father. Saxton was a dedicated abolitionist who organized the formation of the first two black regiments in the United States Army. The relationship between the two men could have been tense because Davis had once signed an order threatening execution of any white Union officer found in command of armed black soldiers. Now, the war over, the two men used their prewar friendship to put Jim Limber in a good home rather than let him leave in the arms of a man who Varina's motherly intuition sensed would be bad for him.

At least the Davis family thought they were putting Jim Limber in good hands. Saxton may not have been as interested in raising a black child as his own son as the Davis family thought an abolitionist might.

History seems to have swallowed up Jim Limber. Saxton was stationed in Portland, Oregon, in 1870, but Jim Limber does not show up as Saxton's ward in the 1870 census when he would have been ten years old. Neither does Jim Limber show up in the 1880 census when Saxton was stationed in San Francisco, and Jim would have been 20.

Saxton may have sent the boy to Massachusetts to live with another family, but if that happened, the family did not identify him by name as Jim Limber, Jim Davis, or Jim Saxton. No 10-year-old child bearing those names shows up in Massachusetts' 1870 census.

Varina was upset to hear, years later, that a Massachusetts newspaper had quoted a person identifying himself as a grown-up Jim Limber saying he would "bear to the grave the marks of the stripes inflicted upon him by us. I felt sure he had not said this, for the affection was mutual between us, and we had never punished him."

She did not identify the newspaper in her memoirs. If the man quoted was the real Jim Limber, he apparently did not write any articles for more prestigious national magazines such as *Harper's Weekly* or *Century Magazine* describing any mistreatment by the Davis family. Jim Limber's name does not show up in searches of magazines of the late nineteenth century that printed numerous and lengthy articles about the war from writers on both sides.

The trip north on the USS *Clyde* was surprisingly relaxing for the Davis family, despite the fact that they did not know where the journey would end, or how, or when the president would be taken from them. A least they had cabins, which the tug did not. None of the captured Confederates on board mention anything in their memoirs about being harassed or insulted from May 16 through May 19, when they arrived at Hampton Roads, Virginia. On the nineteenth the *Clyde* anchored off Fortress Monroe, a Union fort on the eastern end of the Virginia peninsula between the York and James rivers.

Fortress Monroe, the nation's largest stone fort and one of the most heavily armed, was distinctive in that it had never fallen into Confederate hands like most other U.S. forts in the South. It had been the base from which Union troops marched for the first major skirmish in the war, the Battle of Big Bethel, Virginia, on June 10, 1861. The next year the fort was the staging area for George McClellan's massive invasion of Virginia that turned into the Peninsula Campaign from March through August 1862. Afterward, Fortress Monroe had been the first place of refuge for escaping slaves, when Union general Ben Butler took them inside the fort, dubbing the refugees "contraband" of war.

The journey took three days, perhaps shorter than the War Department expected as the ship stayed at anchor for several more days, waiting for orders. On May 20, several prisoners, including Vice President Alexander Stephens, Postmaster General John Reagan, General Joseph Wheeler, and Davis's secretary, Burton Harrison, were taken off and put on board another ship that was bound for other Northern prisons. Soon, the only prisoners on board the *Clyde* were Jefferson Davis and Clement Clay and their families.

Davis must have thought the stay at Hampton Roads to be merely a stopping point on the way to Washington where he expected to be put into prison alongside the men and woman who had been arrested in the conspiracy to assassinate Lincoln. Three weeks earlier Judge

Advocate Holt said that he had found conclusive proof that Davis was involved in the plot. If Davis was the head of the plot, he surely would be tried as one of the murderers of Lincoln.

In a curious historical twist, the assassination trial had begun on May 10, the very day Davis was captured in Georgia. Testimony began two days later on May 12 when Davis and his family were still in wagons being taken to Macon.

On the afternoon of May 22, 1865, the day after Stephens and Wheeler had been removed, another tug filled with German soldiers approached the *Clyde*. Davis grasped his wife in a hug and whispered in her ear: "Try not to weep. They will gloat over your grief."

Varina was struck by how tall and stately her husband looked standing amidst the "undersized German and other foreign soldiers on either side of him" [more than half the Union soldiers who fought in the war were foreign born rather than native born Americans], and as we looked . . . our last upon his stately form and knightly bearing, he seemed a man of another and higher race, upon whom 'shame would not dare to sit.' "

Part of the reason for the delay in taking Davis ashore was to allow two officials from the War Department to supervise personally how he would be treated upon arrival.

One was 50-year-old General Henry Halleck, the ranking general in the Union army who had a reputation of being almost as incompetent for the United States Army as General Braxton Bragg was for the Confederate army. Why Lincoln kept Halleck as chief of staff is one of history's mysteries. One of Grant's subordinates once said of Halleck that since he was "unable to command one army so he was brought to Washington to command all armies."

After the near defeat at Shiloh, Halleck replaced Grant with himself, only to learn that few generals had a poorer sense of the battlefield than the general in chief. Still, Lincoln did not replace Halleck for the entire war, though the president did create a position for Grant that bypassed Halleck for battlefield decisions.

The other man waiting on the dock for Davis was Assistant Secretary of War Charles H. Dana, a former newspaperman. Dana had gained the trust of both Lincoln and Stanton to become their eyes and ears at the front. Dana would report back to them about his impressions of the generals they had chosen to lead their armies. Part of his job was to make sure that Grant did not relapse into such heavy drinking that he could not perform in the field. Grant, who normally shared Sherman's distrust of newspapermen, eventually came to like Dana.

The treatment of Davis under orders from Stanton as relayed by Dana would drastically change once the Confederate president was out of sight of his wife and family and the crew and other passengers on the *Clyde*. Surprisingly, the Davis family was not the only group of people on board the ship who were apprehensive about Davis heading toward the fort. The officers and sailors, even Pritchard and his cavalrymen, had grown accustomed to the quiet manners of Davis.

Had Davis known the cruelty the United States government planned for him, he might have taken Wheeler up on the idea of hijacking the ship and making for the Bahamas. Had Davis known the humiliation the United States government would heap on his character and reputation, he might have rushed for his pistols back on May 10 and gone down fighting as a Confederate martyr.

Presumably, the Davis family had not been shown any newspaper accounts of their arrest, even though they were in custody more than two weeks. Had Davis and Varina seen the cover of the Sunday, May 14, 1865, *New York Times*, they would have been shocked—not at the accurate main headline of "DAVIS TAKEN!" nor at the first incorrect subhead of "His Wife, Sister and Brother Secured" (Davis's sister and brother were not with him), but at the sixth and seventh subheads: "Cowardly Behavior of the Head of Southern Chivalry," followed by "He Puts on His Wife's Petticoats and Tries to Sneak into the Woods," and finally the last incorrect subhead, "Not Having Changed His Boots, the Brogans Betray Him."

The *New York Times* then saw fit to print what it considered news exactly as the United States government had given its editors. The entire article was a copied portion of Wilson's May 13 telegram to Stanton: "The captors report that he hastily put on one of his wife's dresses and started for the woods, closely followed by our men, who at first thought him a woman, but seeing his boots while he was running, they suspected his sex at once. The race was a short one, and the rebel President was soon brought to bay. He brandished a bowie-knife and showed signs of battle, but yielded promptly to the persuasions of Colt's revolvers, without compelling the men to fire."

There was no original reporting by the New York Times other than the inaccurate and misleading headlines. Varina's sister was with her, not President Davis's sister. Wilson's telegram made no mention of "petticoats," but it did say a "dress." Boots and brogans are two entirely different cuts of military footwear, but the civilian editors of the New York Times, none of whom had served in the army, did not know the difference.

Now that Stanton had given the dress story to the press, he had to produce evidence to support it. The first indication Varina had that something strange was afoot other than the earlier confiscation of one of her hoop skirts from her trunk came on May 24, the day after Davis walked down the causeway and disappeared from her sight into Fortress Monroe. Pritchard, under orders from Stanton, came to her and asked for the raglan Davis had been wearing. Varina readily gave it to him. Pritchard then came back the next day and asked for the shawl Varina had thrown over her husband's head. Varina and Virginia Clay, wife of Clement, presented both their shawls, thinking that such a request was so ridiculous that they would make light of it by forcing Pritchard into a guessing game. He correctly chose the shawl that the president was wearing in the dampness of the cool morning.

Varina could not have imagined what the confiscation of these three articles of clothing, the hoop skirt, the raglan, and the shawl, would mean to newspaper editors across the nation.

She would never have guessed that they would be part of a plot to damage her husband's reputation. Davis had been a volunteer soldier who had fought Indians in the Midwest. He had been the toast of Northern newspapers for having saved the day for the United States with his bravery at the Battle of Buena Vista during the Mexican War. He had been one of the most respected members of the United States Senate, invited to speak in many Northern venues.

On May 27, 1865, two days after Pritchard collected the shawl and seventeen days after Davis's capture, Harper's Weekly, one of the few newspapers with a national audience and distribution, followed the *New York Times*' example and printed the May 13 Wilson-to-Stanton telegram word for word. As it was a weekly news magazine dependent on stories from many places around the nation, *Harper's* needed a two-week lead time to carry the same story that the *New York Times* broke with just one day's notice from Stanton. Such long lead times were not unusual. It also took two weeks for *Harper's Weekly* to carry news about Lincoln's assassination.

The story that Davis was wearing his wife's dress when captured spread through the Northern newspapers within weeks, all based on Wilson's first telegram to Stanton. But Wilson may have started feeling regrets about that inflammatory telegram. In Wilson's official battle reports to Stanton written after the initial telegram, Wilson makes no mention of Davis being in women's clothes, or even being in a disguise.

That Davis was wearing—or had thrown over his shoulders—a raglan and that his wife threw a shawl over his head was not disputed by Jefferson or Varina Davis. That much of the story was also confirmed by witnesses Burton Harrison and John Reagan.

But all the Confederate witnesses angrily disputed the suggestion that Davis would don a dress in order to escape.

The story that Davis was in female disguise apparently started with Lieutenant Julian Dickinson, the adjutant of the Fourth Michigan Cavalry. If Dickinson made a written report on his involvement in Davis's capture to Pritchard or Robert H. Minty, his two immediate commanders, or to General Wilson, it did not make it into the *Official Records of the War of the Rebellion*. In fact, only one mention of Dickinson appears in the entire 138,579 pages of the *Official Records* published after the war, and that brief mention attests to the wounding of another lieutenant by the First Wisconsin Cavalry. Dickinson's report on the Davis capture could have been lost, but the only other mention of Dickinson comes in an 1867 report filed by Wilson telling the story of how Dickinson saw three female figures moving away from the Davis camp on May 10, 1865.

Yet, while any report from Dickinson on the capture of Davis is missing from the *Official Reports*, some basic elements of his postwar accounts of the capture appeared in the newspapers within days. These accounts seem to be based on the 9:30 a.m., May 13, 1865, telegram of Wilson to Stanton. One possibility is that Dickinson made a verbal report or a written report to Pritchard (since lost and not recorded in the *Official Records*) who passed it on to Wilson, who included the details told to him in the telegram Wilson sent to Stanton.

In his postwar account of the capture, Dickinson made sure he occupied center stage.

One account told by Dickinson in 1899 was given at a meeting of the Military Order of the Loyal Legion of the United States. In Dickinson's speech account of the capture, he says he was left in charge of Davis's camp with a few soldiers while the bulk of the detachment rushed north to investigate the shooting. Dickinson said he was questioning a man (later identified by him as Davis's secretary Burton Harrison) when Private Andrew Bee, the headquarters cook, pointed "to three persons in female attire, who, arm in arm, were moving rapidly across the clearing towards a thicket. Andrew called to me, 'Adjutant, there goes a man dressed in woman's clothes.'"

Dickinson then said that Corporal George Munger rode up to the three people and leveled his Spencer carbine at the man. Apparently Munger was the one who Davis said in his own account he considered flipping from his saddle by cupping the cavalryman's boot in his hand.

Dickinson said:

Davis had on for disguise a black shawl drawn closely around his head and shoulders, through the folds of which I could see his gray hairs. He wore on his person a woman's long black dress, which completely concealed his figure, excepting his spurred boot heels. The dress was undoubtedly Mrs. Davis's traveling dress, which she afterwards wore on her return march to Macon. At the time of the capture, she was attired in her morning gown and a black shawl covering her head and stately form, while her waiting maid was completely attired in black.

As an officer and a gentleman, Dickinson should have been familiar with the article of clothing called the raglan, a waterproof overcoat worn by the upper classes and named after British Lord Raglan, a hero of the 1855 Crimean War in Europe. Lord Raglan developed the overcoat without the seam that pulled the sleeves in toward the wearer's neck. Instead, the sleeves were left large and roomy. When worn by putting one's arms through the sleeves, Lord Raglan's garment would have billowed around the neck.

By 1865 men and women of the upper classes in both North and South were wearing the popular garment, which had been designed more than ten years earlier. There was little differentiation between men's and women's versions of the garment. All overcoats were meant to be big, bulky, and waterproof. The only true differences between men's and women's raglans were color, size, and presence or absence of sleeves.

Dickinson would have known the difference between a large overcoat and a dress. It seems unlikely that one could have been mistaken for the other, even in the early morning light. But Dickinson, a future lawyer, might also have seen the value in starting a good story that would both humiliate Davis and throw some favorable light on the storyteller who also was one of the first ones to claim that he was an integral part in the capture.

Still, even if Dickinson's account does not ring true, it is valuable because he was the only person known to mention seeing Jim Limber.

"There was also with the party a little colored lad about the same age as young Davis, and the two created considerable amusement for us by their wrestling exercises," Dickinson wrote.

Dickinson's account, upon which all other official versions seem to stem, simply does not sound plausible when taking into account the well-known character of Jefferson Davis.

Davis was convinced on the night of May 9 that the threat of the wagon train being attacked by renegade Confederates was now past. After more than a month on the run from Federal forces, Davis was ready to take the advice of others to separate himself from the slow-moving wagons and escape faster by horseback. He left his horse saddled and tied in the woods so that he could give his wife and children a fond, if quick farewell, before beginning a hard day's ride that could take him within another day's ride to Madison, Florida, about 110 miles to the south of Irwinville.

When Davis heard the shooting on the morning of May 10, he jumped up and dashed out of the tent fully clothed in the same suit he had been wearing for days. He would have stayed fully dressed from the night before so that he could make the most of the day riding rather than dressing.

If Davis's and Varina's accounts are to be believed, no more than a few seconds to no longer than a minute could have elapsed from the time Davis saw the cavalrymen in camp to him leaving the tent in answer to his wife's pleading with him to try to escape by walking into the woods. If Burton Harrison's account is more accurate of how he tried to distract the mounted soldier in front of Davis's tent, then there might have been two or three minutes before Davis tried to make for the woods.

Just as Jefferson slept in his gray suit, Varina almost certainly slept in her dress in anticipation of her husband leaving early that morning. No candles would have been lit inside the dark tent because everyone in camp was still asleep when the attack occurred. Davis would not have needed a candle to see into the pre-dawn darkness that soldiers were in his camp, but he would have needed a candle to see anything inside the dark tent. The darkness would have accounted for the wrong raglan being grabbed.

The suddenness of the early morning raid also supports Davis's account. If Varina had slept in her dress in order to see her husband off first thing in the morning, then there would have been no need for her to lay out an extra dress for herself, which would have had to have been the one Davis would have donned if Dickinson's story were true. But even if tall, skinny Davis had found a dress in the darkness belonging to his plump, short wife, it would have taken several minutes just to put the dress on to make a proper disguise. Women's dresses in those days had many buttons running up the front. Just touching the buttons and finding the buttonholes in the dark would have been a time-consuming task. Putting on a hoop skirt in the dark would have been impossible.

Not only would it have been physically impossible for Davis to put on one of Varina's dresses in the short amount of time he had before trying to escape, he would not have done it. He would rather have died.

Men in the 1860s, particularly Davis, strongly identified with the commonly accepted masculine traits of that time period of duty, honor, country, and bravery in battle. Davis exhibited a streak of bravery in his character dating back to when he was six years old when he protected his little sister from what he thought was a drunken lout walking down the same road the two children were taking. Davis had fought Indians while with the United States Army. He was wounded while fighting Mexicans, ignoring the wound so long that he almost passed out from loss of blood because he wanted to stay on the battlefield and lead his men.

Davis had stood tall against arrows, rifle balls, and artillery shrapnel. Dressing as a woman in a desperate and potentially humiliating attempt to avoid capture by a force of Union cavalry that were already in his camp and surrounding his camp's perimeter would not have entered Davis's mind. It would have been beneath his dignity. He would have rather died than be caught dressing as a woman.

The president did try to escape that morning by walking into the dark woods toward his tied horse. That seems to have been the extent of his escape plans that morning. It was Varina's actions of throwing the raglan on his back, throwing the shawl over his head, and sending her servant after him that created the impression among the Yankees that Davis was posing as a woman. Davis was not attempting a disguise at all, but his well-meaning wife's actions made his appearance seem to be a disguise.

After learning of the stories in the newspapers, Davis realized they were caused by his wife's actions, but being a dutiful husband unwilling to criticize a woman whom he loved, Davis blamed Wilson.

Davis wrote years later:

Wilson and others have uttered many falsehoods in regard to my capture, which have been exposed in publications by persons there present. . . . I will postpone, to some other time and more appropriate place, any further notice of the story and its variations, all the spawn of a malignity that shames the civilization of the age.

Davis never made good on that statement. He never directly addressed the stories.

The improbability and the impossibility of Davis actually dressing as a woman and trying to escape did not seem to deter the trained military officers who were assigned to capture him or the bureaucrats back in Washington who were still figuring out what to do with a defeated South. In fact, these men were the ones who made a conscious effort to spread the rumors.

According to Wilson, writing forty-seven years after the fact in his autobiography, the first he heard of Davis in women's clothing was when Minty, commander of the Fourth Michigan Cavalry, burst into his office in Macon: "On entering my office, this natty and dashing officer, hastily saluting, called out in an exultant tone: 'General, we have captured Jeff Davis, and by jingo, we got him in his wife's clothes!' "

"It flashed through my mind that Davis's capture would be hailed throughout the North as the end of the Rebellion and if he really were caught in his wife's clothes, it would overwhelm him and the Confederate cause alike with ridicule," wrote Wilson.

Wilson was right on that count.

Within days editorial cartoonists for the nation's newspapers and news magazines were producing cartoons that were all similar in nature. All showed Davis in a dress, sometimes wearing hoopskirts, wearing a bonnet, clutching a Bowie knife, and running through the brush with laughing Union soldiers close behind.

The detail of Davis waving a Bowie knife came from Wilson's first telegram to Stanton. Dickinson makes no mention of a Bowie knife in his 1889 speech, but he may have said something to Pritchard or Minty in 1865 and forgot about it by 1889.

No Confederate source mentions Davis even owning a Bowie knife. His common dress was a gray business suit. His pistols were kept in a saddle holster. Such a large, almost sword-like knife, named after the 1836 Battle of the Alamo martyr Jim Bowie, needed its own belt and sheath, which Davis did not wear. Bowie knives were found among private soldiers early in the war who posed with them for photographs, but few of those soldiers at the end of the war would have carried such a heavy weapon.

Postmaster General John Reagan, a former surveyor from Texas, did carry a large knife that Secretary of the Navy Stephen Mallory described in his writings as a Bowie knife. Perhaps the knife's confiscation from Reagan during the capture gave a sliver of confused truth to the story of Davis carrying one at his capture. Dickinson or someone saw a large knife being taken from a Confederate, so the detail was attached to Davis, but it is unlikely that a gentleman planter from Mississippi like Davis would have ever had any use for such a knife.

Based on Wilson's report to Stanton, songs were quickly written about the Davis capture with artwork depicting the same scenes on the sheet music. One song rushed into print in the summer of 1865 was "Jeff Davis in Petticoats" with one verse managing to work in the rumor that Davis had escaped with the Confederate treasury:

Jeff took with him, the people say,
A mine of golden coin,
Which he, from banks and other places,
Managed to purloin;
But while he ran, like every thief,
He had to drop the spoons.
And maybe that's the reason why
He dropped his pantaloons.

While Stanton contacted every newspaper he could to encourage the story, several Union soldiers knew the truth though they would not discuss it until years afterward at a time when men like Wilson and Pritchard were still telling the tall tale.

One officer of the Fourth Michigan Cavalry wrote an account of the attack in a postwar newspaper, but chose not to sign his name to it. In it the officer said:

Besides the suit of men's clothing worn by Mr. Davis he had on when captured Mrs. Davis' large waterproof dress or robe, thrown over his own fine gray suit, and a blanket shawl thrown over his head and shoulders. This shawl and robe were finally deposited in the archives of the war department at Washington by order of Secretary Stanton.

The story of the "hoopskirt, sunbonnet and calico wrapper" had no real existence and was started in the fertile brains of the reporters and in the illustrated papers of that day. That was a perilous moment for Mr. Davis. He had the right to try to escape in any disguise he could use.

Private James H. Parker, a member of the First Wisconsin Cavalry, the unit that killed two members of the Fourth Michigan in the early morning darkness, was so angry at the defamation of character Davis underwent after his capture, he wrote an article for the Southern Historical Society in 1877. Parker wrote his article for the Southern-leaning Society after reading an article by General James H. Wilson in the *Philadelphia Times*: "I am no admirer of Jeff. Davis. . . . I am full of Yankee prejudices; but I think it wicked to lie even about him, or, for the matter, about the devil."

Parker, who must have mingled with the Fourth Michigan Cavalry in order to observe what he saw, ticked off all the lies he had read in articles about Davis. According to Parker, the Confederate president did not have on "any such garment as is worn by women." Parker said Davis wore over his shoulders a "water proof article of clothing." He did not have a pail of water with him. In fact, Parker did not remember seeing anything in Davis's hands.

Parker wrote:

I defy any person to find a single officer or soldier who was present at the capture of Jefferson Davis who will say, upon honor, that he was disguised in woman's clothes, or that his wife acted in any way unladylike or undignified on that occasion. I go for trying him for his crimes, and, if he is found guilty, punishing him. But I would not lie about him, when the truth will certainly make it bad enough.

Even Dickinson found he had to defend himself when others were telling their version of the Davis capture with Dickinson as part of the story.

The book *Minty and the Cavalry* by Joseph Vale was published in 1886. Vale was a former member of the Seventh Pennsylvania Cavalry, part of the brigade that was left to picket the river in the event Davis had not passed over it yet. Since his unit stayed behind at the river, Vale was not on the scene when the Davis capture took place. Still, Vale claimed that Dickinson saw "an old lady" accompanied by a young lady come out of a tent in the captured Davis camp and ask permission to go to a nearby stream to get water. In this account Dickinson saw the old lady and granted his permission for them to get water. According to Vale, it was Private Andrew Bee who "was not pleased with Lieutenant Dickinson for having permitted them to pass, yet, as the privilege was granted, he let them go, but kept a sharp watch on their movements. After they passed him a few yards, the cloak of the old lady caught on a bush, which lifted it just enough to disclose a pair of cavalry boots and spurs."

When Dickinson saw that account in a copy of the book, he scribbled "Not so" in the margins, meaning he had not given permission for Davis/the old lady to get water. Dickinson later crossed out the name of Andrew Bee as the man responsible for stopping Davis.

Dickinson scribbled in the margins of the book:

Andrew Bee was cook at headquarters, a servant on detail as cook, no standing as a soldier. This letter was prepared from false statements. It is wholly false as regard the action of Bee and Lieut. Dickinson.

What angered Dickinson was that Vale's book accused him of being fooled by Davis into letting him escape in the first place. In Vale's opinion, Dickinson was a fool, not the hero that Dickinson claimed to be.

Three years later Dickinson gave his enhanced account of the capture of Davis to the Military Order of the Loyal Legion. Curiously,

Dickinson in his 1889 speech says it was Andrew Bee who saw Davis, but three years earlier, Dickinson had scribbled in the margins of the book *Minty and the Cavalry* that it was not Bee. Dickinson could not keep his own story about who was with him straight from one account to the next.

Some soldiers were less than impressed with the national media attention given to men who had done nothing more than go on a ride through the woods looking for a wagon train.

Captain Albert Potter, a member of the Fourth Michigan Cavalry who had stayed behind in Macon on other duties, wrote to his sister Amelia that Davis's capture was not much to be proud of:

> There was no bravery about it. Davis' whole party numbered only about 25 and we surprised them while in bed. And there would not have been a shot fired at all if the 1st Wisconsin Cavalry which was hunting for Jeff and came up after our regiment had taken him had not mistaken us for the enemy.

On May 19, Captain Potter wrote a letter to his father including the lines:

> I hear there are to be medals given to those who took a part in his capture—so far as the bravery is concerned, and all that which you will see in the papers, that is all nonsense. There was men along at his capture that never fired a gun since they came into the service. But the fact that they gobbled up old Jeff will be enough to put their name in history—us fellows that staid back claim the honor of belonging to the old Fourth Mich. Cavalry and are satisfied with that.

A good story dies hard.

In a 1902 edition of a Kalamazoo, Michigan, newspaper, Pritchard retold Dickinson's story of how Varina had come to the front of her tent to ask if her "old mother" could go get water. In Pritchard's version, the gullible soldier who does not recognize the Confederate president is not Lieutenant Dickinson, but Private Andrew Bee. According to Pritchard, Bee was a "gallant man" who would not refuse such a request to help an old woman.

Pritchard said in an interview with the newspaper:

> So she [the old woman] presently emerged from the tent, wrapped in a waterproof cloak, with a shawl around her head which had been drawn down under her chin and concealed all of her face except her eyes. It was learned later that Davis, who was the old mother, was so tall that he had to tie his wife's cloak around his waist. He had started for the spring when in some way the skirt caught on a twig. Corporal Munger and Pvt. James Bullard caught glimpse of a boot and commanded Davis to halt. His disguise was quickly discovered.

The higher up the command chain the story went, the more it seemed to cause remorse in its repeated telling and increasing number of lies told about Davis.

By 1912 and in the shadow of his life, Wilson seemed regretful for the role he played in Davis's national humiliation.

> Although both officers and men declared that when arrested Davis was endeavoring to escape in disguise, I gave no details and specified no particular articles of clothing. . . . So far as I know, no officer ever asserted that the Confederate chief was caught in crinoline or petticoats as worn in those days, and yet his friends everywhere hastened to deny the allegation as published in the newspapers, and many went so far as to declare that Davis was not disguised at all and that the whole story was a tissue of false-hoods.

Wilson ends his discussion of the tale of Davis's capture with the perfect excuse people use when they want to dissociate themselves from something of which they are not quite proud. It wasn't his fault the stories got started:

It can hardly be necessary to call further attention to the fact that I was not personally present at the capture of Davis, and therefore, did not see him until he arrived at my headquarters in Macon on the afternoon of May 13. I never saw the disguise and all I have related is consequently based upon verbal and official reports and the statements of the various participants in the event so of the time, and yet I have no doubt that I have given the truth with accuracy just as it occurred.

CHAPTER 11

"Place Manacles and Fetters upon the Hands and Feet of Jefferson Davis"

MAJOR GENERAL NELSON MILES must have wondered whom he had irritated at the War Department to draw his latest assignment: jailer of Jefferson Davis.

Born a farm boy in Massachusetts with little hope of going to college or winning a coveted appointment to West Point, an honor usually reserved for the sons of the privileged classes, Miles showed determination at an early age to become a soldier. At 17 years of age he moved to Boston where he worked in a crockery store in the daytime while reserving the evening to being tutored in military sciences by a Frenchman who had served in that country's army.

When the war started Miles, just 22, raised his own company, but his superiors thought he was too young to command respect of other men his own age. They put him in a staff command—a do-little job in his mind. He soon talked his way into a field command.

Miles was brave in battle, but unlucky enough to be wounded in four different battles in four different places on his body. Still he was tough enough that he survived all the wounds, any one of which could have killed him.

In May 1862 a Confederate musket ball grazed Miles' heel. In December 1862, another one passed through his throat and out his ear. He reported to his general while holding his throat closed with both hands. In May 1863 Miles took his third ball to his abdomen, a wound that killed most men, but left him paralyzed for several weeks. Still, Miles came back in order to receive his commission as a brigadier general. In June 1864 Miles suffered his fourth wound, yet another shot to a different part of his neck.

The reason such a brave, skilled field general was assigned to the desk job command of Fortress Monroe was that the war was over. The United States did not need all the generals it had commissioned over the previous four years, particularly those who had not gone to West Point and particularly those who had learned their military skills in night school. The United States Army was prejudiced against officers who had not learned their skills in colleges controlled by the federal government.

Miles wanted to stay in the army, so when the command of Fortress Monroe was offered, Miles reluctantly decided he would take what he considered a temporary assignment, which he had convinced himself was sure to be followed by a field command once his superiors realized what a commanding presence he was. Miles correctly guessed that the United States Army would soon need young, aggressive, experienced officers such as himself who could transfer what they had learned fighting Confederates to fighting Indians on the Western Plains.

As Davis walked down the causeway on May 22 into the fort, Miles grasped him tightly by the arm. It was a ridiculous gesture by Miles taking such formal, firm control of a single, exhausted, sickly prisoner who was flanked by scores of men armed with loaded muskets, not to mention that he was walking into a stone fort ringed with cannons that could sink ships at distances of more than a mile.

As the former cup and saucer sales clerk from Massachusetts pulled on the arm of the former United States senator from Mississippi, neither man could have guessed that both their lives were changing at that very moment.

Miles' public rough handling of Davis on the first day he met him was the start of an unhappy portion of the ambitious general's career. For the next year, Miles' treatment of Davis would be the focus of newspaper reports questioning how the nation was treating a man who was not formally charged with a crime. Miles would later wonder if the well-reported harsh treatment of Davis—which some observers regarded as torture—during the first week of the president's imprisonment played a role in cutting short Miles' grand plan for himself. At one time Miles believed a grateful nation would demand he be appointed secretary of war in the 1880s and an even more admiring nation would elect him president in the 1890s.

Davis could never have guessed that Miles' treatment of him once inside the fort's walls and away from prying eyes would actually make him a sympathetic figure with many Northerners. Davis believed he would soon face a court in Washington, fighting charges either that he planned the assassination of President Lincoln or that he led millions of treasonous Southerners who dared to defy the United States government. Davis assumed his stay at Fortress Monroe would be short and that he would soon board another ship bound for Washington City.

It would be two years before Davis would board another ship.

Davis was led into a hastily prepared cell that formerly was a casement for a cannon pointing toward the sea. The red brick walls were freshly whitewashed. Heavy iron bars were placed where the cannon's muzzle normally would have pointed. Two huge wooden doors locked by an iron bar through the handles walled off the casement from the long brick hallway. A desk, chair, and cot were all the furnishings in the cell. A candle burned on the table. A bucket sat in the corner for his waste. Another bucket held some drinking and washing water.

As Davis walked into the cell, two armed guards followed him. Two more stood outside the now barred wooden doors. Four more were stationed in the casements next to his. Six others guarded the entryway into the hallway from outside. Davis had more than a dozen armed guards personally watching him inside one of the most heavily armed forts in the nation garrisoned by more than a thousand men.

That night Davis discovered that the guards inside his cell were there to do more than watch him. They were there to make him as uncomfortable as they could. They were there to keep him from falling asleep.

According to written orders issued by Secretary of War Edwin Stanton and hand delivered to Miles by observers Assistant Secretary of War Charles A. Dana and Major General Henry Halleck, the guards were to pace up and down inside the room beside Davis's cot. The candle was never to be extinguished, even at night. An officer was detailed to walk into the cell and look at Davis every fifteen minutes to make sure that he had not escaped the guarded room during the previous fifteen minutes and, presumably, that no facsimile of Davis had taken the place of the real Davis in the previous fifteen minutes. No guard was to speak to Davis under any circumstances. When given his meals, Davis was to be allowed no implements other than a wooden spoon—even when the meal was a slab of meat.

The next morning, Miles followed through on another order from Stanton, hand delivered by Dana: "Brevet Major-General Miles is hereby authorized and directed to place manacles and fetters upon the hands and feet of Jefferson Davis and Clement C. Clay whenever he may think it advisable in order to render their imprisonment more secure."

Miles did not follow through on the order to manacle the hands of Davis, but he did have a blacksmith chain Davis's ankles together, an action that the emaciated Davis "violently resisted" according to Miles.

The leg irons placement was leaked to *The Philadelphia Evening Telegraph*. When other newspapers picked up the news, Davis drew some sympathy from Northerners who might otherwise be angry with him for the 360,000 Northerners who had lost their lives during the war. More important to the Republicans in power, their political sponsors were disturbed by the apparent torture of a man who had yet to be charged with a crime. Thurlow Weed, a New York City political boss, was one of several prominent Republicans who sent Secretary of War Stanton a note that the "irons were an error and an enormity . . . wholly unnecessary severity."

Fortress Monroe's post doctor, Dr. John Craven, examined the prisoner the day after the chains were put on Davis's ankles. What Craven saw shocked him.

Craven wrote:

He presented a very miserable and afflicting aspect. Stretched upon his pallet and very much emaciated, Mr. Davis appeared a mere fascine of raw and tremulous nerves—his eyes restless and fevered, his head continually shifting from side to side for a cool spot on the pillow, and his case clearly one in which cerebral excitement was the first thing needing attention. He was extremely despondent, his pulse full and at ninety, tongue thickly coated, extremities cold and his head troubled with a long-established neuralgic disorder.

When Craven suggested to Davis that he should stand up and exercise, Davis removed a blanket to display the chains and the skin that was being scrapped from around his ankles.

Craven instantly liked Davis. One of the doctor's first acts was to bring Davis some tobacco for his pipe. The act of lighting up seemed to bring new life into the Confederate president, making Craven realize that some of Davis's physical state he witnessed could be attributed to acute tobacco withdrawal.

The post doctor was not cowed by his superior officer. Craven warned Miles that if he did not remove Davis's shackles, the president's health would plummet from want of exercise. He might even be driven insane. After passing that note of warning along to Stanton, Miles received orders to remove the shackles. Five days had passed with Davis in chains. That was long enough for the details of what was happening inside the prison to make national news.

Stanton did not so much have a change of heart about the way he was treating Davis as much as he realized that news of the leg irons was not being favorably carried in all the Northern newspapers. Stanton's belief that the nation wanted Davis punished for the war had backfired. Even if some newspapers were calling for Davis's trial and execution, the issue of torturing someone held inside the nation's most secure fort made the Republicans seem vindictive toward a chained man who was a danger to no one.

From the moment Davis entered the prison, he and Varina were forbidden to contact each other by letter. Alarmed at the reports she was reading in newspapers that her husband was near death, on June 1, Varina sent Craven a letter begging him to ignore military protocol and to tell her about her husband's health.

Varina begged:

Would it trouble you to tell me how he sleeps—how his eyes look—are they inflamed? Does he eat anything? May I ask what is the quality of the food? Do not refuse my request. It seems to me that no possible harm could accrue to your government from my knowing the extent of my sorrow. And if, perchance, actuated by pity, you do not tell me the worst, the newspapers do, and then the uncertainty is agony!

Craven was touched by Varina's personal appeal. After looking at the unappetizing food Miles was feeding Davis and noticing that Davis, always the picky eater, was even refusing to look at it, Craven asked his own wife to prepare the meals for Davis from his own table. Miles, who constantly sent Stanton telegrams asking permission before he did anything for Davis, such as give him reading material other than the Bible, seems to have allowed Craven to carry in the homemade meals without asking the permission of the secretary of war.

While Craven would grow increasingly sympathetic to Davis, the mutual goodwill would not last more than a year. Craven was transferred from Fortress Monroe at the end of 1865. In the summer of 1866, Craven, using a ghostwriter named Charles Halpine, turned his personal diary into a book called *The Prison Life of Jefferson Davis*. Craven was a doctor who had no sense of politics, but Halpine, a Democratic Party activist, recognized the political value Craven's diary of Davis's treatment had.

Halpine used Craven's diary to create a virtual work of fiction disguised as fact in order to score Democratic points against the Republicans by making them appear to be heartless torturers of political prisoners. When Davis was given a copy of Craven's book, he was appalled reading quotes he supposedly made and actions he supposedly took.

While Davis hated Miles and believed he was being treated poorly by the Union general, he also had no desire for the nation to see him as a pathetic figure in prison. Trying to elicit sympathy was something a Southern gentleman simply did not attempt. Davis made notes in the margins of Craven's book as he read it line by line, often remarking "not true," and "never happened." Some of Halpine's "fiction distorting fact" as Davis called it, seemed inconsequential and even cast Davis in a favorable light, such as a made-up story that Davis kept a pet mouse in his cell, feeding him breadcrumbs. Other stories, such as a flowery description of Stonewall Jackson, Davis denied ever having said with a margin comment of "He [Craven] has attributed to me the opinion of someone else, not knowing what I thought, and only careful to fill his book according to programme."

Davis's reaction to Craven's book was one more example of the man's true character. Even though the book played a major role in creating sympathy for him with the Northern public, attracting the attention of men who would eventually bail him out of prison, Davis believed the truth needed no enhancement. Not knowing at the time that Halpine had made up the quotes in the book with Craven's name listed as author, Davis cut off all contact with Craven after the book came out in the summer of 1866. Davis even refused to accept Craven's letters that might have explained that Halpine was the man behind the book's publishing and its tall tales.

Within a week of removing the irons from Davis's ankles due to negative public opinion, Stanton received more bad news. One of the most famous and influential lawyers in the United States had volunteered to represent the imprisoned Confederate president.

Charles O'Conor was more than just a good courtroom lawyer; he was one of the best in the nation. He was also a Yankee, a resident of New York City, a city that he served as United States District Attorney in the mid-1850s. He was even willing to represent Davis at no charge.

O'Conor, a balding, 61-year-old with chin whiskers, was striking to look at and even more impressive in court. He was passionate about his religion and his political beliefs. He was a Catholic who was sensitive to the discrimination against his faith and a Democrat who angered the Radical Republicans by remaining a strong states' rights advocate as had many other New York politicians.

He was also politically savvy. O'Conor knew that any letter to Davis offering to represent him would be opened and read by Stanton.

O'Conor wrote in his first letter of June 2, 1865:

Gentlemen who have no personal acquaintance with yourself, and who never had any connection by birth, residence, or otherwise with any of the Southern States, have requested me to volunteer as counsel for the defense in case you should be arraigned upon an indictment which has been announced in the newspapers. No less in conformity with my own sense of propriety than in compliance with their wishes, I beg leave to tender my services accordingly.

Davis, also knowing that his return mail would be opened and read, replied:

After my capture as a prisoner of war the proclamation publicly accusing me and offering a reward for my arrest reached the section where I then was. Since my arrival here all knowledge of passing events has been so rigorously excluded that I am quite ignorant as to any proceedings instituted against me, as well as the character of the evidence on which they could have been founded, and consequently cannot judge what kind of testimony will be required for my vindication.

Davis even managed to work in one of his rare attempts at humor in the reply letter: "Though reluctant to tax you with the labor of coming here, I must, for the considerations indicated, request you to obtain the requisite authority to visit me for the purpose of a full conference."

What would turn out to be a two-year struggle to free Jefferson Davis from prison had begun.

☆   ☆   ☆

WHILE DAVIS WAS LANGUISHING in Fortress Monroe, the show trial of the Lincoln conspirators in Washington was rushing to a foregone conclusion. Some, maybe all the seven men and one woman on trial for Lincoln's death, would be executed. While he was not in the courtroom, the United States government was doing what it could to make sure that the absent Davis was considered just as guilty as the conspirators on trial for plotting the death of Lincoln.

The trial was not in civilian court, even though Lincoln was a civilian and the crime had taken place in a public place. Instead, Attorney General James Speed, at the constant insistence of Stanton, issued a lengthy ruling that declared the assassination of the commander in chief during war created the need for a military tribunal. A military tribunal of twelve men, all combat veterans but minor officers who had served in the field, were selected to be judge and jury.

Curiously, two of the most famous officers selected to serve on the tribunal, generals David Hunter and Lew Wallace, had both incurred the wrath of the Lincoln administration early in their military careers. Neither one was in favor with General Ulysses S. Grant, the general over all armies.

Hunter had angered Lincoln by issuing his own emancipation proclamation to the slaves in the captured Port Royal section of South Carolina in March 1862. Lincoln rescinded the order out of fear that other slave-holding Union states like Missouri, Kentucky, and Delaware would join the Confederacy. Later Hunter was replaced in the field when he lost some battles in the Shenandoah Valley.

Wallace was blamed by Grant for being late to engage the Confederates at Shiloh, Tennessee, in April 1862. Wallace had been on the far side of the battlefield and was unaware that Grant's surprised army was in full retreat. Even though he followed Grant's vague orders and the arrival of Wallace's troops saved Grant from disaster, Grant considered Wallace's response too slow. He transferred Wallace out of his sight. In August 1864 Wallace got a second chance to impress Grant. Wallace used his own discretion to save Washington City from capture by rallying a thrown-together command at the Battle of Monocracy, Maryland. Even though it was Grant's fault that the Confederates had been able to penetrate Union lines almost to the grounds of the Executive Mansion in Washington itself, Grant still refused to forgive Wallace.

The conspirators' defense attorneys argued that there was no precedent for military officers to try civilians. They argued that even convening the trial violated at least two articles of the Bill of Rights since no grand jury had been called to indict the accused. The defense declared that since only Congress can declare war, it followed that only Congress could create a military tribunal. The tribunal had been created solely by the administration, principally by Stanton, with no input from Congress.

The defense attempts to stop the trial fell on deaf ears in the wake of Lincoln's death. If the defense counsels thought the public would rise up in protest of an illegal trial conducted by the United States government, they were sorely disappointed. The public, which had eagerly anticipated the end of the manhunt for John Wilkes Booth, was ready to see the conspirators tried and executed.

Legal or not, constitutional or not, the Johnson administration, under the influence of Stanton, declared the trial be conducted by military tribunal. The defense counsels could defend their clients or not under those conditions. The only trial the civilian defendants would get would be in a courtroom filled with United States Army officers.

The head judge for the trial was 58-year-old Judge Advocate General Joseph Holt, a clean-shaven man with a mop of straight, white hair. Like Davis and Lincoln, Holt was a native of central Kentucky. He had never lived anywhere but the South when he arrived in Washington City to take on a succession of cabinet posts in the administration of President James Buchanan.

Lincoln had appointed Holt as the nation's first judge advocate general, head of the army's lawyers, even though Holt had no military training. All the previous lawyers heading the army's legal department were career military men with the rank of colonel.

After Lincoln's death, Stanton turned to Holt not as a prosecutor or a judge, but as an investigator. He did not disappoint. Without revealing his sources or presenting his evidence, presumably gathered from whatever records had not been destroyed by the Confederates upon the abandonment of Richmond, Holt assured Stanton and President Johnson that Davis was the mastermind behind the Lincoln assassination.

Holt and Stanton were determined to cast as wide a net as necessary throughout the nation to bring in anyone who had anything remotely to do with the death of the president. No one was too insignificant to avoid suspicion. Stanton arrested Edman Spangler, the man who held Booth's horse outside Ford's Theater. He arrested wounded Confederate general William Payne at home because conspirator Lewis Powell had once taken a room with one of Payne's relatives and used the alias Paine. Confederate John Singleton Mosby, a famed partisan ranger who earned the nickname "The Gray Ghost" for his daring raids behind Union lines, was suspected since Powell had briefly served in his command. Stanton even accused Mosby of donning a disguise and having dinner with Booth, a claim that was so wild that no one but Stanton believed it.

Mosby was not arrested, but many more were. Investigations of links to Booth were conducted until the numbers arrested were weeded out to the ten who would be put on trial. Nearly four hundred witnesses would be called for the two-month trial before the same man who had conducted the investigation.

Even though Davis was not in Washington or in the prisoners' docket in this trial and the testimony about him and links to the Lincoln assassination had yet to be given in this trial, some newspapers were calling for the Confederate president to be separately tried both for the assassination and for treason.

The May 26, 1865, edition of the *Chicago Tribune* debated itself about which would be better, trying Davis for the assassination before a military tribunal or trying Davis for treason before a jury of citizens since "the greater the war, the greater the treason." The newspaper wanted to make it easy for average citizens to understand what the trial would be about. Blaming Davis for the deaths of Northerners was easy to explain in print.

Yet the *Chicago Tribune* worried that putting Davis on trial for treason would "elevate him to a certain kind of dignity, by putting him on a par with revolutionists of all countries."

During the Lincoln assassination trial in May and June, the prosecution built a case against Davis using the testimony from three men: Richard Montgomery, James Merritt, and Sandford Conover. Conover was presented by the prosecution as an amazing spy for the Union who was in just the right place at all the right times to see Lincoln conspirators like John Wilkes Booth, Lewis Powell, and John Surratt meeting in Canada with Confederate Secret Service agents like Jacob Thompson, George Sanders, and Clement Clay.

The United States government prosecutor confidently told the court and the newspapers that Conover was such a good spy that not only could he mingle with the top agents of the Confederate government in Canada, but he could also wrangle a job with the Confederate government in Richmond. According to the United States government, Conover was in just the right place at all the right times to overhear and read about the Richmond side of plots against the Union being planned in Montreal. According to the United States government, Conover was a super spy the likes of which the nation had never seen.

Most damning to Davis was Conover's testimony that he was in the room in Montreal when Jacob Thompson received a letter from Davis suggesting that Lincoln be killed. According to Conover, Thompson dramatically tapped the letter, smiled, and said, "This makes it right."

Many of the nation's newspapers reported Conover's testimony implicating Davis by copying the government transcripts. The newspapers accepted as gospel every word Conover said. The newspaper editors believed everything the United States government told them, even going along with the idea that the three men must testify in secret in order not to reveal their true identities to any former revengeful Confederates.

The reporter for *Harper's Weekly* wrote in its June 17, 1865, edition:

This testimony is very important, and is conclusive as to the complicity of the rebel authorities in the assassination, as also in other most heinous plots against the lives of our citizens. The object for the reservation of the testimony was to secure the safety of the witnesses.

Still, the magazine wanted to cover its bases just in case some evidence was presented in court that Davis was not guilty. The last paragraph in the same issue read:

In regard to the testimony implicating Davis and the rebel agents in Canada in the assassination, it is very plain that, being so circumstantial, it can easily be proved to be false. Until rebutting testimony, it must stand as true.

Midway through the trial, the *Chicago Tribune,* which had pushed for Davis to be tried for both the assassination and the treason, began to suspect the testimony of the three self-styled Union spies. Over time, the newspaper editors decided to remain vague about whether the three witnesses could be trusted.

It is vain to attempt to impeach these witnesses by the petty charges that informers, spies, renegades, etc. are never reliable. If they were fit to be the associates and confidential agents of Davis and Thompson, they are fit to be witnesses in their trial in a court of justice. Davis and Thompson selected them as their associates. By this act the accused placed the witnesses on a level with themselves. Many criminals can only be proved such by the evidence of presented or real accomplices. The latter are never, the former are seldom, of the highest character, but either are esteemed fit to convict criminals of a still deeper dye.

The newspaper said it was not sure if the witnesses were telling the truth about Davis and Thompson, but the *Chicago Tribune* did accept the fact that the three witnesses knew the Confederate president and head of the Secret Service in Canada.

The slow-to-build suspicions of the newspaper editors that the government was not being straight with the truth would come back to haunt them.

There was one witness at the trial who even Davis could not deny had been in the same room with him.

That was Lewis F. Bates, the man in Charlotte, North Carolina, in whose home Davis had been invited to stay on his escape south. According to Bates, who testified on May 30, not long after Davis was freed of his irons, Davis was excited to hear about Lincoln's assassination. Bates said that on April 19, after hearing of the assassination while inside his house in Charlotte, North Carolina, Davis turned to Secretary of War John C. Breckinridge and attempted to adapt his own version of an old quote from *Macbeth*, which philosopher Samuel Johnson had also said, "If it were to be done at all, it were better that it were well done; and if the same had been done to Andy Johnson, the beast, and to Secretary Stanton, the job would then be complete."

"No remark was made at all as to the criminality of the act," testified Bates.

What Bates omitted in his testimony was that he was not present on the porch of his house when Davis actually received the telegram from Breckinridge informing him about Lincoln's assassination. Bates' fanciful testimony was that Davis and Breckinridge were discussing the Lincoln assassination in the home of a stranger who both of them probably knew had been born in Massachusetts. There was no cross-examination of Bates to ask him why the supposed chief conspirator in the nation's now most famous crime, who was on the run from Federal cavalry, would openly claim in the presence of a Yankee that he was happy the crime had been done.

Bates' testimony was followed by the presentation of numerous documents and supposedly found Confederate orders that implied the Confederacy was advocating terrorism against the Union. One was a plan to use bombs aboard mass transit such as steamships to terrorize the populace and disrupt the nation's commerce. Another was a plan to burn New York City using incendiary devices planted in hotels. Another was a plan to introduce "pestilence" into the North by selling yellow fever-infected clothes to unsuspecting citizens.

What the prosecutors could not know was that yellow fever was spread by mosquitoes, not by infected clothes, but that was not discovered until the turn of the twentieth century by Dr. William Gorgas, son of Confederate general Josiah Gorgas.

The last charge against Davis presented at the Lincoln conspirators' trial was that he issued orders to starve Union prisoners of war intentionally.

One particularly incriminating piece of evidence in the prosecutor's mind that showed Davis was involved in the assassination was a summer 1864 letter to Davis from a Confederate lieutenant offering to "rid my country of some of her deadliest enemies, by striking at the very heart's blood of those who seek to enchain her in slavery." A letter supposedly from Davis's personal secretary, Burton Harrison, to the Confederate president was read in court detailing how the lieutenant would like an interview with Davis so he could explain his plan in more detail.

No proof was offered that Davis or Harrison ever met with the lieutenant. No lawyer for the president was there to ask how a letter suggesting assassination of "enemies" could have been missed during the Confederate cabinet's burning of important records and letters just before the fall of Richmond.

Not presented in court because there was no way the Union prosecutors could have known about it was the story of how Davis had totally rejected the idea of kidnapping Lincoln when it was presented to him in the summer of 1862. The idea was from Major Walker Taylor, a nephew of Davis's former father-in-law, General Zachary Taylor. William Preston Johnston, Davis's aide, writing after the war, said that Davis totally rejected Taylor's idea, even complimenting Lincoln in saying that he was "an Indian fighter and a Western man" who would fight any such abduction. Davis's estimation of Lincoln's record as a soldier was in error. In reality, Lincoln served only ninety days in the militia during the Black Hawk War and never even saw an Indian during his service. Lincoln joined the state militia to pad his military resume—a practice common to many politicians who wanted the newspapers to recognize that some candidate running for office had served in a war.

Davis dismissed the idea of killing Lincoln out of hand.

Johnston wrote that Davis said in the summer of 1862:

I could not stand the imputation of having consented to let Mr. Lincoln be assassinated. Our cause could not stand it. Besides, what value would he be to us as a prisoner? Lincoln is not the government of the Federal power. He is merely the political instrument there.

The United States government's chief prosecutor John Bingham, who delivered his closing argument on June 29, 1865, made it clear to the court that he believed Davis was part of the conspiracy, even though the Confederate president was not yet on trial. Bingham repeated Bates' testimony that Davis had spoken positively of Lincoln's death.

Bingham said in court:

It only remains to be seen whether Davis, the procurer of arson and of the indiscriminate murder of the innocent and unoffending, necessarily resultant there from, was capable also of endeavoring to procure, and in fact did procure the murder, by direct assassination, of the President of the United States and others charged with the duty of maintaining the Government of the United States, and of suppressing the rebellion in which this archtraitor and conspirator was engaged.

The official papers of Davis, captured under the guns of our victorious army in his rebel capital, identified beyond question or shadow of doubt, and placed upon your record, together with the declarations and acts of his co-conspirators and agents, proclaim to all the world that he was capable of attempting to accomplish his treasonable procreation of the murder of the late President, and other chief officers of the United States, by the hands of hired assassins.

Bingham mentioned Davis seventy-four times in his closing summation of the case against the men and the woman who were on trial for their lives. At one point Bingham said John Wilkes Booth was in a possession of a letter that could only be deciphered by use of a cipher machine that had been captured from Davis's office in April. He did not explain how Booth could have written the letter without a matching cipher machine in his own possession or why the cipher machine from Richmond was not produced in court.

Bingham said in front of the attentive military officers:

Whatever may be the conviction of others, my own conviction is that Jefferson Davis is as clearly proven guilty of this conspiracy, as is John Wilkes Booth, by whose hand Jefferson Davis inflicted the mortal wound upon Abraham Lincoln. His words of intense hate, and rage, and disappointment, are not to be overlooked—that the assassins had not done their work *well;* that they had not succeeded in robbing the people altogether of their Constitutional Executive and his advisers; and hence he exclaims, "If they had killed Andy Johnson, the beast!" Neither can he conceal his chagrin and disappointment that the War Minister of the Republic, whose energy, incorruptible integrity, sleepless vigilance, and executive ability had organized day by day, month by month, and year by year, victory for our arms, had escaped the knife of the hired assassins. The job, says this procurer of assassination, was not well done; it had been *better* if it had been well done.

Bingham used 32,773 words in his summation before getting to the last paragraph where he said he would "pray the Court, out of tender regard and jealous care for the rights of the accused, to see that no error of mine, if any there be, shall work them harm."

What Bingham was hinting at was that newspaper reporters were finally starting to question the evidence presented in the case. There seemed to be a problem with some of the witnesses. With a little digging, the problem turned into a disaster.

Montgomery, Merritt, and Conover, the men who swore there was a Confederate Secret Service connection with Booth in Canada, lied in their sworn testimony.

Their stories began to unravel when the court reporter leaked their supposed secret testimony to his hometown newspaper. Judge Advocate Holt was then forced to release their testimony to all the newspapers. Some of the more curious ones began their own investigations of the three witnesses, something the United States government had not done before presenting them as star witnesses in the nation's most important trial.

The reporters found numerous inconsistencies in their testimonies. In many instances the reporters found documentation, sometimes in

Confederate newspapers, that key "conspirators" like Clay and Thompson were often in the South on days the three government witnesses testified they were meeting with them in Canada. Conover had even testified that he had become fast friends with Thompson at least a full month before he could have met him.

None of the three witnesses were in the employ of the United States government, which had plenty of spies working in Canada keeping well-known Confederate agents like Clay and Thompson under surveillance. In fact, Conover, which was one of many aliases the man used, was not a spy at all. He was a freelance newspaper reporter who apparently made up most of his news stories off the top of his head. The master spies were anything but master spies. They were con men who had been elevated to the status of important men by the intense, fawning interest in them by the United States government.

In 1862 Holt read Conover's exciting, bylined account in the *New York Tribune* of a plot to kidnap President Lincoln. According to the article, Conover uncovered the plot while operating as a Union spy in the Confederate government.

Working on the assumption that newspaper reporters and editors are honest men who do not lie, Holt met with Conover more than three years after reading that article to learn if this exciting master spy knew of any other plots against Lincoln, including the just completed one. Only too happy to oblige, Conover told Holt the assassination as directed by Booth was plotted in Canada. To bolster his story, Conover told Holt he could deliver two other men who could back him up on the details of how Clay and Thompson planned Booth's attack. Those two men were his friends Montgomery and Merritt. Conover would coach his bewildered friends on who was who in the Confederate Secret Service in Montreal, what to say happened when, and who met whom.

Now after they had sworn oaths and testified on behalf of the United States government, the stories of the three men were falling apart. What was the government to do? Rather than immediately arrest the three perjurers and charge them with giving false testimony in a United States government courtroom, Holt did what he thought best. He told them not to say anything to anyone. The chief judge in the Lincoln assassination trial told his star witnesses to keep quiet and out of the public eye during the rest of the trial.

The problem for the federal government was that Jefferson Davis, Clement Clay, Jacob Thompson, George Sanders, and several other Confederates had been prominently and continually accused over the two-month trial of being directly responsible for Lincoln's death. They were publicly declared guilty, but now the weight of evidence against them collapsed into a pile of lies told by three men whose credibility had been easily shredded. The United States government knew the truth of the case, and the nation's newspapers were beginning to suspect the truth, even though the trial was not yet over.

Prosecutor Bingham decided he could not backtrack on the accusations against the Confederates who were not yet in front of him. He just needed more time to find more concrete evidence against the accused. Bingham decided to go ahead with his summation as if nothing had happened to impute the honesty of his witnesses. Time was on his side. Two of the key conspirators, Davis and Clay, were in prison, where they would stay until the government was ready for them. Their pleas of innocence could be easily silenced. Two others, Thompson and Sanders, had both escaped to Europe. Their fleeing seemed to make them guilty. Those two would not be returning to the United States at any time soon to defend themselves publicly.

Instead of ever going public with a reason why the accused Confederates were not also brought into the courtroom to stand trial, Holt and Bingham just stopped talking about them. Instead, Holt and Bingham concentrated on convicting and punishing the ten prisoners they already had on trial. That was no challenge. The military tribunal considered the evidence for just one day and then convicted all ten. Four, David Herold, who had fled with Booth; Mary Surratt, who owned the rooming house where the plot was discussed; George Atzerodt, who had lost his nerve about attacking Vice President Johnson; and Lewis Powell, who had attacked Seward, were all sentenced to die. The other six were sentenced to various prison terms to be served in Fort Jefferson, a sprawling brick fort in the Gulf of Mexico, more than one hundred miles northwest of Cuba.

The United States government would later quietly try to arrest the three men who lied to the military tribunal. Conover was arrested, but he escaped into the teeming tenements of New York City. He was never rearrested.

☆   ☆   ☆

THROUGH THE REST OF THE SUMMER of 1865, Davis's health was of constant interest to Miles, Stanton, and the Northern press. Miles filed weekly reports describing the president's appetite, his moods, and even the presence of carbuncles on his legs.

Not all Northern newspapers were sympathetic to the incommunicado incarceration of the former United States senator.

The *New York Times* took to task the *New York Herald* and the *Philadelphia Inquirer* for printing articles that questioned why Davis was being kept in a fort casement and being denied any time in the outdoors. The *New York Times* said it was "much amused at the manufactured folderol" when its competing newspapers made it seem that "Jeff is in the hands of brutish tyrants rather than Christian gentlemen; that he is being worn away by the upper and nether stones of official restriction and prison torture, instead of enjoying to his full capacity every comfort which the necessary caution and watchfulness of his guardians will permit."

The *New York Times* noted that a lamp was kept on in Davis's cell twenty-four hours a day, but that "was done as a matter of precaution rather than annoyance." The newspaper described that Davis's food was better than Union prisoners got, but added with more than a touch of sarcasm that Davis's meals were not "strawberries and cream and boned turkey and mince pie."

In a strange twisting of the truth, the *New York Times* said it was inaccurate that no letters of sympathy were passed along to Davis. His family frequently writes to him, the news article said. It was not until readers searched deep into the article that they learned from the *New York Times* that those letters were not given to Davis. The *New York Times* said that a military officer kindly read all the letters to the president and then passed along any details of family information that was necessary for Davis to know.

The *New York Times* ended its piece on the health of Davis by claiming that he was in "better condition today than he has been in five years."

Harper's Weekly was no more sympathetic. The June 10, 1865, edition reminded readers that "the circumstances of Davis's capture show a greater degree of pusillanimity and cowardice. He was taken disguised in a woman's hood and cloak, so desperate were his fears."

The weekly news magazine also chose to focus on Davis's food:

At noon, yesterday he threw his soup, bread and meat from him, exclaiming, in a loud and angry voice, "that he was not accustomed to such living, and would not put up with it."

So far as possible the Government will of course hesitate to compromise its own dignity by treating with any unnecessary dignity any of its state prisoners.

Harper's Weekly had just told its readers that the United States government would never torture prisoners in its care.

CHAPTER 12

"He Is Buried Alive"

THE OPINION OF MOST NORTHERNERS on the future of Jefferson Davis was found in the May 23, 1865, edition of the *New York Herald*:

At about three o'clock yesterday, all that is mortal of Jeff'n Davis, late so-called President of the alleged Confederate States, was duly, but quietly and effectively committed to that living tomb prepared within the impregnable wall of Fortress Monroe. The 22nd of May, 1865, may be said to be the day when all of the early aspirations of Jeff'n Davis ceased. . . . No more will Jeff'n Davis be known among the masses of men. . . . He is buried alive.

On May 29, 1865, New York's United States senator Edwin D. Morgan wrote President Andrew Johnson a letter questioning if Davis was a traitor under existing laws, but insisting that if Davis was not a traitor, he could still be executed for other crimes such as a supposed massacre of black troops at Fort Pillow, Tennessee, or the starvation of prisoners of war:

The country is impressed with the importance of punishing Jefferson Davis legally and promptly. Grave doubts exist whether this can be accomplished by a trial for treason. . . . His complicity with the assassination plots, etc. etc. these are crimes in violation of the laws of war to be tried by court martial.

On that same day, before receiving Morgan's letter, Johnson issued an amnesty proclamation for most Confederates if they would take an oath of allegiance to the United States. He excepted those above the rank of colonel and leaders of the "pretended Confederate government."

O'Conor was refused permission to see his client very soon after he volunteered to represent Davis. The government, just now struggling to find some legitimate reason to hold Davis, told his lawyer that the Confederate president was not a prisoner of the United States government, but a prisoner of war held by the United States Army—which was different.

Attorney General James Speed wrote a letter to O'Conor saying, "This prisoner has not yet been handed into civil custody, and that so long as he may remain in his present military custody as a prisoner of war, the government cannot consent to allow anyone to visit him."

Speed had just told Davis's attorney that even though he was the highest legal official in the Johnson administration, he did not have the power to tell the United States Army to release one prisoner in its custody.

All through the summer and fall of 1865, even with the knowledge that all the assassination conspiracy testimony about Davis's links to President Abraham Lincoln's assassination were perjured by the three self-proclaimed spies, Northern congressmen and newspaper editors demanded Davis be put on trial. Some suggested the gallows whether or not there was a trial.

Harper's Weekly attacked one of the nation's best-known abolitionists, Gerrit Smith, in its June 24, 1865, edition after Smith suggested that clemency be granted "the rebel leaders."

> Davis's offense is carefully and explicitly described in the fundamental law and the penalty unequivocally determined by statute. . . . The fate of Davis individually, as of any single criminal, is of very little importance; but it is very important that this country should decide how it will regard treason and punish traitors. Those who oppose the execution of Davis plead that Davis "simply committed treason." True; and Booth simply committed murder. The law awards the same penalty for both offenses.

Former Massachusetts congressman Amasa Walker spent most of his July 18, 1865, letter lecturing Johnson that it would be instructive for the nation's citizens to see how harshly the United States dealt with a single citizen who dared to resist the omnipotent power of the federal government.

Walker insisted that treason was the crime for which Davis should be tried, not conspiracy to assassinate Lincoln. Walker wanted to make an example of Davis:

So that the people may understand that the government recognizes such a crime, and if convicted, as he cannot fail to be, that he shall be punished, so that the people may understand that such is the fate of Traitors. I do not say what the punishment should be, but whatever it is, let it be executed promptly and fully. You may rely upon it that the people will be greatly mortified and disappointed if the great chief of the rebellion is never arraigned for the crimes against the nation's life.

Tiring of getting unsolicited advice from current and former members of the House and Senate, Johnson brought the issue up of what to do with Davis at his cabinet meeting on July 21, 1865.

Opinions varied.

Secretary of State William Seward, now back in office after the April knife attack, wanted Davis tried before a military commission for treason because he feared a civilian court might not convict him. Postmaster General William Dennison wanted Davis tried for the assassination before a military commission, just as the known assassination conspirators had been tried. Secretary of the Treasury Hugh McCulloch wanted to delay a trial, but he wanted it held before a military commission. Secretary of War Edwin Stanton, who had been so sure that Davis was involved in Lincoln's assassination back in May, now wanted him tried for treason before a civilian court. Secretary of the Navy Gideon Welles also voted for a treason trial before a civilian court. Secretary of the Interior James Harlan at first said it would be better to pardon Davis quickly rather than risk a civilian trial that might acquit him. Later, Harlan would vote with Seward to try Davis before a military commission.

Attorney General James Speed did not take a stand at this point because he was conferring with other lawyers in the private sector to see what they thought was possible. All the other cabinet members voted to try Davis for treason with the majority voting for a civilian court.

Some newspapermen did not want to wait for a trial.

A correspondent to the *Chicago Tribune* who identified himself only as P.H.N. compared Davis to hyenas or lions in the August 2, 1865, edition:

They simply act out the nature that is in them; but such men as well as such animals are too dangerous to roam at large and should be destroyed to secure the peace and safety of more civilized people.

In August, Johnson tried to get Chief Justice Salmon Chase involved, hoping he would shed some legal light on the chances of the United States government getting a conviction in a federal civilian court. Chase refused even to meet with Johnson. Welles wrote down in his diary that he considered his former cabinet colleague Chase to be "cowardly and aspiring." Welles speculated that Chase refused to offer an opinion about trying Davis because he feared presiding over such a trial.

Even though he was chief justice of the United States Supreme Court, the highest office a judge could hold, Chase still harbored a twenty-year dream of being elected president. Welles speculated that Chase believed if he presided over Davis's treason trial and Davis was acquitted, it would doom Chase's own chances of ever reaching the Executive Mansion.

On October 2, 1865, Johnson virtually demanded an answer out of Chase so that planning the legal strategy to try Davis could begin. Chase reluctantly described one problem he had already determined. Any treason trial would have to be conducted where the treason had occurred. That meant the trial would have to be conducted in the

South since Davis had not led any Northern states out of the Union. Chase then said since Virginia, the residence of Davis for most of the war, was still under U.S. military control and undergoing Reconstruction, it was his legal opinion that civilian courts could not operate in a state that was under martial law.

There were ironies now working against the United States trying Davis in a civilian court. Lincoln wanted all the Southern states to be readmitted into the Union after they met some conditions such as abolishing slavery. Lincoln envisioned the rapid restoration of state legislatures and courts staffed by men who were once again loyal to the Union even if they had been Confederates. Lincoln never suggested putting the South under extended military control.

If Lincoln had not been shot and killed in mid-April, his mild civilian Reconstruction policies for all the states then willing to return to the Union would have been put in place within weeks. If the civilian courts had reopened and if Lincoln wanted to go through with a trial of the Confederate leaders (which he did not), Davis could have been tried for treason almost immediately after the war in a Southern civilian court.

Now that Lincoln was dead and the Radicals had installed military governments in all the South, there were no operating civilian courts. The military would have to allow the civilian courts to be created in order to hold a trial. Chase worried that the public spectacle of the United States Supreme Court formally asking permission of the United States Army to create civilian courts would look like the real government in the land was now the military.

Other politicians had the same worry. Back in April, some Radicals spread rumors that General William T. Sherman was planning to march on Washington City to take over the government in a military coup. Chase believed that compromising the image of the courts, particularly his own United States Supreme Court, might give the Sherman coup story legitimacy.

What made the situation even more confusing for President Johnson, Stanton, and the rest of the cabinet was that some Radical Republican members of Congress were against the idea of punishing Davis. Both Senator Charles Sumner of Massachusetts and Representative

Thaddeus Stevens of Pennsylvania, the two most influential Radical members of Congress, personally did not want to put Davis on trial.

That did not mean they were Davis's friends. Sumner was expedient as well as a little vicious in what was best for the country. Sumner bluntly told friends that he felt "regret that Jeff Davis was not shot at the time of his capture."

When Judge Advocate Holt tried to show Stevens the evidence that Davis planned the assassination of Lincoln, Stevens said of Davis and Clay: "I know these men, sir. They are gentlemen and incapable of being assassins."

Stevens finally looked at the evidence against Davis and called it "not credible."

☆   ☆   ☆

ONE OF THE BEST-KEPT SECRETS of the Johnson administration was that few men in the highest levels of the government believed Davis had done anything illegal or unconstitutional in leading the South out of the Union.

McCulloch, writing his memoirs after the war, claimed in a few revealing paragraphs that Johnson and the cabinet knew they had put themselves in an untenable position long before they were willing to admit it to the public. If McCulloch's memory was accurate and his tale truthful, the United States government in the form of President Johnson and his cabinet knew in the summer of 1865 that it had no case against Davis.

McCulloch wrote:

The legal question, "Has Mr. Davis been guilty of such acts of treason that he can be successfully prosecuted?" was submitted to the attorney general [James Speed], who, after a thorough examination of it and consultation with some of the ablest lawyers in the country, came to the conclusion that Mr. Davis could not be convicted of treason by any competent and independent tribunal, and that therefore he ought not to be tried. The conclusion was undoubtedly correct. It was a revolution which had been attempted by the Southern States—a general uprising of the people of the South against the Government. It was a war in which they had been engaged—war of such proportions that belligerent rights had been accorded to them by foreign nations. The same rights had been acknowledged by the Government in exchanges of prisoners and other acts. They could not, therefore, be charged with treason, nor could one of their number be singled out and legally convicted of the crime.

McCulloch compared the South's secession to the American Revolution from Great Britain, which he said was a shared opinion of the cabinet.

Going further, McCulloch said the United States government had made a mistake by formally recognizing the Confederate States government by entering into agreements to exchange prisoners. In McCulloch's view—and the view of Johnson's cabinet—the United States could not charge anyone with treason if the United States government was willing to negotiate with anyone from another country at war with the United States.

Davis's lawyer O'Conor, who had no access to McCulloch's or the Johnson cabinet's thoughts, still knew the Johnson administration was in a quandary about what to do with Davis. He decided to take advantage of the confusion both to alleviate the prison conditions of his client and to set up a legal charge that he was confident he could defend against in a federal court.

In a November 1, 1865, letter to Johnson, O'Conor pleaded:

My aim in addressing you is to mitigate the personal sufferings of Mr. Davis. His physical health has long been precarious. This is well known and needs no proof. To one in his bodily condition a long imprisonment may become in effect, an infliction of the death penalty.

I propose that he be withdrawn from his present custody and charged with treason before a committing magistrate. Let bail be accepted. I will myself enter into a recognance for his appearance not exceeding my whole estate.

O'Conor already knew—at least in his own legal opinion—that secession could not be proved treason, but he was hoping that Johnson, a tailor by training, would spend little time researching the legal arguments and would free Davis on bail. O'Conor trusted Davis implicitly that he would not attempt any escape and would not jump bail. If O'Conor's offer had been accepted and if Davis had fled to Mexico or England, O'Conor's entire estate would have been confiscated by the federal government.

O'Conor's attempt to maneuver the United States into charging Davis with treason and then bailing him out did not work—at least immediately. Johnson did not react to the O'Conor letter. Davis remained at Fortress Monroe.

While the Johnson administration spent most of 1865 pondering the situation in which they had placed themselves by not following Lincoln's wishes of allowing Davis to escape, Congressional politicians hungry for press attention kept demanding action.

Congressman Sam Moulton of Illinois submitted a resolution to the House on December 17, 1865, asking why Davis had "not been tried for his treason against the government; and if any, what obstacles [were] in the way of the speedy trial of this great criminal."

Congressman William Lawrence of Kentucky decided that Moulton had not gone far enough. Two days later Lawrence issued his own resolution calling for Davis to be tried and for the issue of secession to be settled forever by that trial:

> Jefferson Davis, a representative man of the rebellion, should have a fair and impartial trial in the highest appropriate civil tribunal of the country, for the treason, most fragrant in character, by him committed, in order that the Constitution and the laws may be fully vindicated, the truth clearly established and affirmed that treason is a crime, and that the offense may be made infamous; and at the same time that the question may be judicially

settled, finally and forever, that no State of its own will have the right to renounce its place in the Union.

The following day, December 20, 1865, Senator Jacob Howard of Michigan, introduced a resolution in the United States Senate, asking Johnson "why he [Davis] had not been put upon his trial" for treason.

On January 16, 1866, Senator Howard submitted an even more inflammatory resolution that included that Davis be "charged with the crimes of having incited the assassination of Abraham Lincoln, President of the United States, and with the murder of soldiers of the United States held as prisoners of war during the rebellion, and other cruel and barbarous practices in violation of the rules and usages of civilized war."

By this time it was well known that Davis's three accusers in the May 1865 Lincoln assassination trial had lied about knowing of Davis's complicity in Lincoln's murder. Nine months later, Howard was repeating the charges on the floor of the Senate. Some senators must have thought that Howard's charges were overwrought. Senate rules dictated that Howard's resolution be read a second time on February 2, but no second reading of the resolution appears in *The Journal of the Senate*.

☆   ☆   ☆

THOUGH HE MAY HAVE BEEN FIGURATIVELY BURIED ALIVE, Davis was not out of sight and out of mind. Throughout the rest of 1865 and into 1866, the newspapers periodically ran reports on his health. Davis was never healthy in his entire adult life. He developed herpes simplex that had blinded him in the left eye while in the United States Army in the 1830s. He caught malaria on his honeymoon during his first marriage, and stress would often bring the disease back to provoke racking fevers more than twenty years after he had contracted the disease. He was shot in the foot in Mexico, a seeping wound that took months to heal. He suffered from headaches and painful neuralgia of his face for at least thirty years He was an insomniac, which was exacerbated by the constant shuffling back and forth of his armed guards walking past his cot. He had poor digestion—when he chose to eat. His wife had struggled with his refusal to eat "enough to feed a bird" during her twenty years of marriage to him.

Other than having an iron will and a determination to prove that he was right and everyone else was wrong, there was very little reason for Davis even to be alive if all the things that were wrong with him were added up.

Yet, he did live, even though Davis often frightened his concerned Dr. Craven and his ambitious jailer Major General Nelson Miles with occasional bouts with illness. The constant flow of information about what was wrong with Davis finally led Stanton on July 22, 1865, to order Miles to remove the guards from inside Davis's cell. Stanton also had Miles remove the candle lantern that burned twenty-four hours a day since the president's confinement in May.

Stanton was simply still not ready to leave Davis in a jail cell from which there was a possibility of escape. He removed the two guards from inside the cell, but kept the others who constantly walked by Davis's cell door to make sure he had not slid through the barred window.

Stanton's telegram to Miles would have infuriated Davis if he had read it because Stanton suggested the ending of the sleep deprivation practices if they were "inconvenient to him [Davis]."

In the same order, Stanton ordered Miles to give Davis any reading material he wanted, to let him exercise in the open air, and for Miles to visit with Davis daily so his health could be even more closely monitored. Davis was still not allowed to talk to anyone but Miles and Craven. It was not until August, three months after his capture, that Davis was allowed to write to his wife.

In Davis's first letter to his wife, he tried to calm her fears about his health, claiming that what she read in the newspapers was false. He praised Craven (Craven's book would not come out until 1866) saying, "I am deeply indebted to him and can assure you that while I am under his charge you need have no apprehension that any thing which is needed will be wanting."

Davis's health improved some from May through the late summer, but not enough to convince Craven that he would long survive. Craven came to believe the cold, damp casemate would eventually grow even colder with the coming winter, and Davis might be in danger of dying of some lung problems. Along with the now consolatory Miles, who constantly worried that his career would be derailed if Davis died on his watch before ever reaching a courtroom, Stanton finally agreed to allow Davis to move to Carroll Hall, a barracks on the post. He left the casemate on October 2, 1865, and moved into a second-floor room. The room was an officer's quarters modified with bars on the window and door.

☆　☆　☆

EVEN THOUGH THE WITNESSES AGAINST DAVIS in the Lincoln conspiracy trial had been proved liars, some powerful men were still not willing to absolve Davis of any involvement in the assassination.

Judge Advocate Holt sent a letter to Stanton on December 21, 1865, objecting to Stanton's endorsement of letting Burton Harrison, Davis's personal secretary, out of prison. Nearly six months after the known Lincoln conspirators had been hanged, and after his hand-picked witness Conover was proved a liar, Holt's letter to Stanton dredged up mention of the 1862 letter from the Kentucky lieutenant who offered to "rid the nation of its enemies." Holt still believed the letter was evidence that Davis and Harrison collaborated on the Lincoln assassination. In Holt's view, letting Harrison out of prison was a mistake.

Holt wrote to Stanton:

To ask that faith be reposed in a party resting under imputations not only of the deepest dishonor and the most intense disloyalty, but also of the gravest crime, is, it is submitted, as unconscionable as it would be unfortunate for the Government to favorably consider such a request.

Stanton, still smarting from his trust in Holt's presentation of Conover as a foolproof witness, ignored Holt. Harrison was freed.

No one in official capacity in the Union was yet willing to be so forgiving to Davis. Miles still believed Davis was a security risk. On December 28, 1865, Davis objected to an officer taking down some red tape holding up his mosquito netting over the second floor window of his barracks. When Davis called Miles "an ass" in the presence of the other officer for issuing the order to remove the tape, Miles rushed to the telegraph office to send a report to Stanton.

"I directed it [the red tape] to be removed from his cell, when he took occasion to make use of the profane and vulgar language. His becoming so much enraged at its being removed leads me to believe that he desired it for improper uses, as it is long enough to reach from the ramparts to the moat, and strong enough to draw up a longer cord," wrote Miles.

Major General Miles, a four-times wounded combat veteran who had been nominated for, and would eventually receive, a Congressional Medal of Honor for valor on the battlefield and a man who had dreams of being president, had tattletaled to Secretary of War Stanton that an emaciated, unhealthy man more than twice his age had called him a bad name.

All through the summer, fall, and winter of 1865, Varina wrote worried letters asking her husband about his health. Not knowing that his letters were heavily censored, Varina was puzzled that he did not give her details about his newer, better quarters. If he was living in better surroundings, why did the newspapers always report him to be in poor health, she would ask.

Davis finally got Varina to understand that she should not believe everything she read in the newspapers. Davis told his wife that newspaper reporters and editors often lied while insisting that they were reporting the news.

Davis said:

It is true that nothing happened which does not somehow pass to newspaper correspondents, but as is usually the case with monopolies they abuse their privilege by perverting their knowledge and building a superstructure with but little regard for the foundation. You say the papers tell you every thing, but I warn you that the things they tell are not realities.

Davis was allowed his first visitor on December 9, 1865. Reverend Dr. Minnigerode, who had last seen the president walking out of his Richmond church to begin his escape south on April 2, brought Davis a communion wafer. Among Davis's other visitors that December were Charles O'Conor and George Shea, another of his self-appointed lawyers, who were preparing for what they assumed would be Davis's eventual trial for treason. Varina was still barred from visiting her husband.

Early in April 1866, Attorney General Speed, under pressure to do something constructive to move the trial along, conferred with prosecutors William M. Evarts and John H. Clifford. Clifford hinted that one way Davis could be convicted would be to pack the jury with former slaves who almost certainly would feel some sort of animosity toward a man who had owned slaves and believed that slavery was good for black people. If they did not pack the jury box with men they knew would vote to convict Davis, Clifford suggested that the federal government could find itself losing the case. In that event, he warned, the just concluded war in which 360,000 Union soldiers had died would be on trial rather than Davis. If Davis won, the Northern public would be asking why the Union had invaded the South in the first place.

While planning trial strategy, Speed still felt hamstrung by Chief Justice Salmon Chase's reluctance to preside as senior judge in a state still under military rule. Speed's prime concern was what kind of judge would be presiding over the case. Chase was well respected by his peers. Judge John Underwood, the presiding federal judge for Virginia, was not. Underwood, a 59-year-old native of New York City was a Tammany Hall politician who had moved south after marrying his wife from Virginia. He was appointed a judge by Lincoln, but he was not respected in Virginia by citizens or by his peers. At various times, Underwood had made public comments about how backward he found Southerners to be. Underwood was the one who hinted to Clifford that he would be willing to pack the jury with freedmen.

☆　☆　☆

WHILE ALL THE LEGAL MACHINATIONS were going on behind the scenes, Davis waited in his second-story cell. His favorite thing to do other than walk around the fort was to read letters from his family, which were now flowing more freely. Davis was amused to get a letter from Varina from Montreal, Canada, on April 14, 1866, informing him that Jefferson, Jr., had learned to fight. Davis's oldest son had traded punches with another boy who accused his father of wearing petticoats. Varina also had to explain that the children were now picking up English expressions such as "dear fellow" now that they were living in Canada.

It was not until May 3, 1866, nearly a year after their separation that Davis and Varina saw each other again after Varina had personally appealed to Johnson. In retaliation for all the letters she had been sending to the newspapers blaming him for her husband's poor health, Miles forced Varina to wait more than six hours before she was finally taken to see her husband. Even then three officers were in the room. She could only see her husband through the barred window. They were not allowed to embrace each other.

Varina wrote:

Through the bars of the inner room I saw Mr. Davis's shrunken form and glassy eyes; his cheek bones stood out like those of a skeleton. Merely crossing the room made his breath come in short gasps, and his voice was scarcely audible.

Knowing that Varina would be there, Johnson also sent Secretary of the Treasury McCulloch to Fortress Monroe to check on Davis's health. It was the first time since Assistant Secretary of War Charles Dana had watched Davis enter the fort in May 1865 that anyone in the administration had personally seen Davis. Johnson tried to influence McCulloch's visit before he left Washington by calling Davis "the head devil among the traitors, and he ought to be hung, but he should have a fair trial, and not be brutally treated while a prisoner."

Instead of meeting a devil, McCulloch found that there were "few men more gifted than Mr. Davis." He was charmed by the Confederate president, who, in his opinion, did not look at all as bad as the newspapers were saying he did. McCulloch found himself sympathizing with Davis when the Confederate president explained how he was kept in chains for the first five days and then in a damp, always-lit casemate for more than two months.

McCulloch wrote:

He had the bearing of a brave and high-bred gentleman, who knowing that he would have been highly honored if the Confederate States had achieved their independence, would not and could not demean himself as a criminal because they had not.

Varina took the opportunity of meeting McCulloch to send a thank-you letter back to Johnson along with a report from Dr. George Cooper. Cooper replaced Craven as the fort's doctor back in January 1866.

Cooper's report did not make Miles happy. It said Davis was not in as good health as McCulloch thought he was. Enclosing Cooper's medical report in her thank-you note, Varina asked Johnson to grant Davis permission to roam the fort both night and day so that he could get more fresh air than came in from the barred windows in the cell where he was forced to spend most of his time.

Then, on May 8, 1866, the case against Davis entered a new phase. A year after Speed had told the cabinet that Davis should not be charged with treason, the United States government in the form of United States Attorney L. H. Chandler in Norfolk, Virginia, indicted Davis for treason. Instead claiming that seceding from the nation was treason, Chandler based his indictment on a July 1862 law making it illegal for anyone to make war against the United States.

The indictment is filled not with legal jargon, but with religious imagery.

The indictment charged that Davis:

Owing allegiance and fidelity to the United States of America, not having the fear of God before his Eyes, not weighing the duty of his said allegiance, but being moved and seduced by the instigation of the devil and wickedly devising and intending the peace and tranquility of the United States . . . incited insurrection, rebellion and war against said United States of America . . . and most wickedly, maliciously, and traitorously, did ordain, prepare, levy and carry on war against the United States.

The words "wickedly" and "traitorously" are used at least three times each in the four-page indictment.

Without any explanation why, the indictment named June 15, 1864, as the single date when Davis carried out his rebellion against the United States, more than three years after the war actually started.

June 15, 1864, was a historic day during the war. But it was actually a day demonstrating incompetence in the Union general officer ranks rather than a day when peaceful Southern citizens were enticed by a devilish Davis to rebel against the United States.

It was on June 15 that Union major general William F. Smith ordered Major General Winfield Scott Hancock's Second Corps of 16,000 men to capture a long line of trenches protecting Petersburg, Virginia. The trenches were manned by only 3,000 Confederates, so Hancock's corps easily took the trenches. Smith was so surprised at how quickly his men had done their job that he held back from advancing on Petersburg out of fear that the ease of capture was actually a trap set for him. Despite Hancock's pleas to let his men advance, Smith failed to follow through on his advantage, thinking that the entire Army of Northern Virginia lay hidden in the woods and was waiting to pounce on his advancing men. Instead of rushing forward to capture Petersburg, Hancock's troops sat around the easily captured trenches waiting for orders from Smith that never came.

By the end of the day, Confederate reinforcements were rushed down from Richmond to hold back Smith's Federals. Thanks to Smith's reluctance to advance, Petersburg was saved from capture. The war would last another nine months—not because of anything Davis had ordered Virginia's citizens to do that could constitute treason, but because Smith had failed to act. And, technically, Davis was not the person who should have been charged. It was General Robert E. Lee, not Davis, who rushed the reinforcements from Richmond to Petersburg.

The nation's newspapers were not necessarily overjoyed to hear that an indictment had finally been filed. *Harper's Weekly* wondered what would happen if Davis was found innocent of any charge resembling treason.

The newspaper said on May 26, 1866:

Is it worth while for the Government of the United States to have placed itself in such a ludicrously humiliating position? If the jury be packed, the trial is a farce. If it be free, there is the chance and the probability of this humiliation.

A few paragraphs later, the newspaper voiced its biggest fear, creating a martyr out of Davis.

If the accused be convicted he is not disgraced. His offense is political, and no reasoning can persuade men to regard political offenses as crimes. . . . To hang him would be an error as huge as to try him. . . . Hang him and he becomes a living power to sedition, and an eternal remorse to the country.

The editor ended that article with a plaintive plea to the Judiciary Committee of the House to find some evidence that Davis intentionally harmed prisoners of war or that he was guilty of assassinating Lincoln. Then, the newspaper reasoned, they could execute Davis without trying to prove that secession was treason.

On June 5, 1866, Davis's attorneys reacted to the May indictment by brashly asking if the United States government intended to try the case, implying that the indictment was filed as an attempt to buy time for the government to come up with a more provable charge.

William B. Reed of Philadelphia, another attorney friend of O'Conor who was working at no charge to Davis, asked in open court, "What is to be done with this indictment? Is it to be tried? This is a question, perhaps, which I have no right to ask. Is it to be withdrawn or is it to be suspended? If it is to be tried, may it please your honor, speaking for my colleagues and for myself, and for the absent client, I say with emphasis, and I say it with earnestness, we come here prepared instantly to try that case, and we shall ask for no delay."

Major J. S. Hennessey, an assistant prosecutor filling in for Chandler, who was absent to tend to a "domestic calamity," admitted he had no idea what the government intended to do with Davis. He would get back to the court on that question. The next day Hennessey returned and said that the federal court had to apply formally to the military in order to get Davis into its custody and that would take time. Besides, Hennessey said, it was too hot to hold a trial in Richmond in May. It would be better for Davis's "delicate state of health" to wait until October.

"[Until then, Davis] will be enjoying the cool breezes of the sea at Fortress Monroe, instead of inhaling the heated and fetid atmosphere of a crowded court-room," said Hennessey.

James T. Brady, another of Davis's New York attorneys, could not resist figuratively poking a stick in Hennessey's eye for the federal government's ludicrous excuse for not being ready to put Davis on trial:

Although it may be very hot in Richmond, it is infinitely worse where he is. . . . From my own experience in the city of Richmond, whose hospitality I have enjoyed certainly, I would be happy to remain here through the heats of summer or the frosts of winter. We can only say that we are entirely ready.

Judge Underwood covered for Chandler, who was still absent, saying the prosecuting attorney was so busy right now that it made more sense to try the case in October, and besides, "it would be much more comfortable for the counsel and Mr. Davis himself" to wait until fall.

Then, Underwood said something strange for a sitting judge in the employ of the United States:

I may say to the counsel that Mr. Davis will in all probability at that time be brought before the court, unless his case shall in the meantime be disposed of by the government, which is altogether possible. It is within the power of the President of the United States to do what he pleases in these matters, and I presume the counsel for Mr. Davis would probably find it for the interest of their client to make application directly to the government at Washington.

Oddly, Underwood, who reported to Chase and knew his boss's reluctance to try the case personally out of fear that it would damage his future presidential aspirations, had told Davis's attorneys to ask Johnson to pardon Davis so the case could be dismissed.

Just when the attempt to try Davis could not get more complicated, it did. In July 1866 Speed resigned in protest as part of the Radical Republican effort to pressure Johnson to give up his control of Reconstruction to Congress. Speed was replaced by Henry Stanbery, a 63-year-old lawyer from New York City who was a contemporary of O'Conor.

Stanbery had no more influence over convincing Chase to sit for a trial of Davis than Speed had. But Stanbery was willing to push harder for some resolution of the case. Ignoring the fact that Virginia was still under military occupation, Stanbery openly suggested that since the war had ended more than a year earlier, there was no reason why Davis should be in military hands. Apparently without conferring with Chase, who he knew would continue his stalling tactics, Stanbery suggested to Johnson that Davis be transferred to civilian custody.

Stanton objected, insisting that if Davis were released into civilian hands he would be housed in a civilian jail. Stanton insisted that moving the Confederate president from Fortress Monroe either would make it easier for Davis to break out of jail himself or would allow an armed band of former Confederates to break into the jail to free him.

Stanton once again was being disingenuous. Virginia was still under military occupation. Former Confederates could not even wear brass buttons on their coats, much less organize themselves into an army to mount an attack to free Davis from custody.

Moreover, Davis did not want to be sprung from prison. He wanted to go on trial. He did not care whether he was in custody in a federal fort or in a state jail. He wanted to be in a courtroom. Jefferson Davis wanted his day in court to prove to the United States that it was wrong and he was right.

Several historical sources, including men who had personal contact with Johnson in the fall of 1866, say that Johnson wanted to release Davis on bail, but he never could bring himself to sign the papers. By this time Johnson was under heavy assault by the Radical Republicans in Congress who wanted to take over Reconstruction policies. Johnson feared that his release of Davis on bail could result in impeachment proceedings being filed against him.

No one in the federal government was yet ready to give Davis his day in court.

☆　☆　☆

ONCE THE INDICTMENT WAS FILED in Underwood's court, Davis's lawyer O'Conor went to Chase to find out if the government would free Davis on bail. Chase pointed out that military rule was still in effect in Virginia, indictment or no indictment. As long as the state was under martial law, he did not intend to try Davis in a civilian court. Chandler's indictment had been filed without any regard to Chase agreeing to hold a trial. Chase suggested the attorneys go back to Underwood to seek bail.

When Davis's lawyers asked Underwood for bail, the judge, whom Chase did not believe was competent, surprised them. He dredged up the May 2, 1865, presidential proclamation accusing Davis of being behind Lincoln's assassination. While he acknowledged that the witnesses against Davis were "impeached," Underwood said that did not mean that Davis was not guilty of the crime.

Underwood said to the stunned lawyers:

If Davis and his associates are innocent of the great crime of which they were charged in the President's proclamation, it is due to them that a thorough investigation should be made, that they may be relieved from the suspicion that now rests upon them. If, on the other hand, they are guilty, it is due to justice, to the country, and to the memory of him who was the victim of a foul conspiracy, that the originators should suffer the just penalty of the law. The committee [of the U.S. House] are of the opinion that the work of investigation should be further prosecuted.

More than a year after Conover and his cronies had been proved liars, Underwood was still not convinced that Davis had been falsely charged. A federal judge was taking his cues, not from case law or his boss, the chief justice, but from a committee of the House of Representatives led by Radical Republicans who desperately wanted to believe that Davis was an assassin against all evidence to the contrary.

Underwood denied bail.

Varina took the indictment in stride, preferring to concentrate on getting her husband better living conditions. She followed up her first letter to Johnson with another one on May 19 where she complained that Miles would not even let her walk with her husband.

Impatient to get action, and perhaps sensing that McCulloch, a cabinet member, was on her side, Varina asked to meet with Johnson personally to plead her case for better living conditions for her husband. On May 24, 1866, she got a personal audience with Johnson. Johnson told her that he had already sent out orders granting her wishes.

Perhaps in a bit of a gamble that Johnson would not get angry at press accounts covering Davis, Varina started sending the reports of Dr. Cooper to friendly newspapers. She made it clear that the evil person in this morality play was not Johnson, the president, but Miles, the general in command of Fortress Monroe.

After reading one of Cooper's reports, the *New York World* wrote:

It cannot be read by any honorable and right-minded American, no matter what his sectional feelings or his political opinions may be, without a sickening sensation of shame for his country and a burning flush of indignation against the persons who have prostituted their official position to inflict upon the American name an ineffaceable brand of disgrace by the wanton and wicked torture of an invalid lying a helpless prisoner in the strongest fortress of the Union.

Miles, more used to dealing with Confederate soldiers who were shooting lead balls into his body than furious wives of former Confederate presidents, begged Stanton to let friendly newspapers into the prison so they could see Davis for themselves. Stanton turned him down. The secretary of war did not want Davis speaking to anyone outside of the government's control.

All Miles could do to defend himself was to ask his subordinate officers to write letters supporting his actions. He gathered those letters together and published his own pamphlet declaring that Davis was healthy and well treated while under his care.

☆   ☆   ☆

BY THE SUMMER OF 1866 many newspaper editors were editorializing for the government to do something, anything, about Davis.

On June 12, 1866, Horace Greeley in his *New York Tribune* ran through the list of charges against Davis that had never been acted upon including Lincoln's assassination, killing prisoners of war, and treason.

Greeley wrote:

> The *Tribune* admonished the Government of the absurdity of its position, not daring, seemingly, to prosecute a great criminal against whom it had officially declared it was possessed of evidence to prove the crime.

Greeley, an ardent abolitionist who had famously admonished Lincoln in 1862 for not making ending slavery the object of the war, was now ready to do what he could to set the Confederate president free.

While some newspapermen like Greeley were trying to set Davis free, congressmen were still trying to figure out a way to put him on trial. Representative George Boutwell of Massachusetts introduced a resolution on April 8, 1866, restating the charges that Davis, Clay, Thompson, Tucker, and Sanders were implicated in Lincoln's murder. Boutwell's resolution instructed the House Committee on Military Justice to "inquire whether there is probable cause to believe any of the persons named in said proclamation [Johnson's of May 2, 1865] are guilty" and "if so, whether any legislation is necessary in order to bring such persons to a speedy and impartial trial."

What Boutwell was trying to do was force Chase to hold a trial. Up until this point, Chase had insisted that civilian courts had no rights to existence in a state ruled by the military. Boutwell was saying that the Congress could change any old law or create new laws in order to make Chase put the case on a federal court docket.

The wording of Boutwell's resolution was significant in that he asked the Judiciary Committee to determine if Davis and the supposed Confederate Secret Service agents demonstrated any probable cause to believe that they were guilty of treason and if any legislation was necessary to try the men on that charge.

The distinction was subtle and glaring at the same time. Boutwell had asked a Congressional committee to determine if the men were guilty—not if there was enough evidence to bring the men to trial to determine if they were guilty. Boutwell's resolution wording implied that Congress already knew the men were guilty, and the Congress should be willing to create any laws to confirm they were guilty in a court of law.

The resolution was tabled at the time, but on June 10, 1866, Boutwell introduced another resolution focusing solely on Davis. Boutwell persisted in charging Davis not only with treason but with Lincoln's assassination:

> Whereas it is notorious that Jefferson Davis was the leader of the late rebellion, and is guilty of treason under the laws of the United States; and whereas by the proclamation of the President of May, 1865, the said Davis was charged with complicity in the assassination of President Lincoln, and said proclamation has not been revoked nor annulled: Therefore, Be it resolved, as the opinion of the House of Representatives, that said Davis should be held in custody as a prisoner, and subjected to a trial according to the laws of the land.

The vote was 105 yeas, 20 nays, and 58 not voting.

Among those voting no was Thaddeus Stevens. Stevens, who wanted to confiscate Southern land, was so irritated at the House's action that he went on record saying he would volunteer to defend Clement Clay if any trial were to take place.

Newspapers were growing increasingly worried that any trial of Davis would also put the United States on trial for not letting the seceded South go in peace.

The *Harper's Weekly* July 14, 1866, issue contained an article headlined: "Is Ours A Valid Government?" The newspaper's editors warned readers that using Davis's trial to prove secession was illegal and dangerous.

"Suppose the court should solemnly decree that secession is constitutional. What then? Are we deliberately to submit to perish?" the newspaper asked. "There could be no more suicidal folly than to commit the decision of the validity of our national existence to any court."

Harper's Weekly decided that "organic law," which it deftly and subtly described as the power of the federal government to destroy anyone who opposed it, had settled forever the question of secession. The newspaper was willing to concede that the federal government had supreme power over its citizens, and it would not be wise to put that question before any court.

"Let the organic law declare that no State under any plea whatever shall secede, and it will matter little whether the late rebel States revoke, or rescind or repeal or annul or declare void their acts of secession, or whether the Supreme Court decided that the Government has or has not a right to exist," the newspaper concluded.

☆　　☆　　☆

IN SEPTEMBER 1866, Johnson did both the federal government and Miles a favor when he replaced Miles as commander of Fortress Monroe with Brigadier General Henry S. Burton. As much as Davis and Varina hated Miles and he hated them, Burton got along famously with his prisoner. Davis and Burton had much in common. Burton was only ten years younger than Davis and a West Point graduate as well, while

Miles was more than thirty years younger than Davis and learned his military training from books. Both Burton and Davis had fought in the Mexican War, although Davis's duty was in Mexico, while Burton fought in California. On a more somber note, Burton had also been in charge of two Union prison camps and knew that keeping prisoners alive in camps that were plagued with overcrowding was no easy task. Burton likely sympathized with the false charges being made against Davis that he intentionally starved Union prisoners, and he should be executed in retaliation for their deaths.

While Miles seemed to go out of his way to irritate Varina, Burton did everything he could to accommodate her. Burton allowed Varina and the youngest Davis child, "Pie Cake," to live in the same building as the president. Davis was still a prisoner, but at least he now had family to keep him cheerful.

Miles had mixed feelings about leaving Fortress Monroe. It was a duty he had hated from the beginning. He had been a soldier, not a jailer. Yet the reassignment looked to the public like Johnson had given in to public complaints of Miles' treatment of Davis. It looked like Varina's letter-writing campaign had worked. Miles felt humiliated; his Army career had been ruined by a pious prisoner and his pushy, plump wife.

After leaving Fortress Monroe, Miles got his wish of going west to fight Indians. Miles spent the next thirty years in that capacity, participating in the capture of both Chief Joseph and Geronimo. His tactics were controversial. His record was tarnished by the 1890 bloody attack on women and children at Wounded Knee, South Dakota. Miles would reach the army's highest rank, lieutenant general, during the Theodore Roosevelt administration. Roosevelt would push him out of office after growing tired of his peacock nature.

☆ ☆ ☆

BY FALL 1866, Johnson had grown weary waiting for Chase, who still objected to military control of Virginia, to agree to hear the case. Over the summer Congress had specifically authorized the federal courts to hold session in Virginia, effectively taking away any legislative excuse Chase might offer to get involved in the case. Armed with that new law, Johnson sent a letter on October 6 to the new attorney general, Henry Stanbery, asking him if he saw any reason why Davis could not be tried in the civil courts.

Stanbery replied that there was no reason why Davis could not be tried, but he pointed out that Congress had also reduced the number of Supreme Court justices from nine to seven and Chase might not have the time to sit as a judge. Stanbery sent a note off to prosecuting attorney Chandler asking him why Davis had not been turned over to civilian authorities.

Chandler replied that Fortress Monroe was the safest place for Davis, citing the possibility that he might escape. Besides, Chandler said, the fort was comfortable, and if Davis was moved to a state jail, his health might fail.

Even though wealthy Northerners were willing to put up more than one million dollars in bail, Judge Underwood still was unmoved. Bail was not granted.

When Davis celebrated his second Christmas away from three of his children in 1866, he was touched that many people wished him, Varina, and baby Pie Cake well. The child received many handmade dolls sent to her in care of the commander of Fortress Monroe.

The most unusual gifts Davis received that Christmas of 1866 came from the only country that had officially recognized the Confederacy during the war. That country was The Vatican, the tiny Catholic principality surrounded by Rome.

Pope Pius IX had corresponded several times with Davis, a devout Episcopalian, during the war. Davis had initiated the correspondence in 1863 when he wrote the Pope asking him to discourage European Catholics from joining the Union army in exchange for immediate American citizenship.

The Pope sent Davis an autographed photograph of himself with an inscription in Latin: "Come unto me all ye that labor and are cast down; and I will refresh you." Attached to the frame was a crown of thorns woven by the Pope's own hands.

Davis was deeply touched by the Pope's obvious intention of comparing the suffering of Davis to the suffering of Jesus by the gift of the crown of thorns. Davis appreciated that so righteous a man as the leader of the Roman Catholic Church would recognize him "when the invention of malignant was taxed to the utmost to fabricate defamations to degrade me in the estimation of mankind."

Christmas 1866 with Varina and Pie Cake was brighter than Christmas 1865 when Davis was denied all visitors.

But as the turn of the year to 1867 grew closer, the federal government still had done little or nothing to try the Confederate president for crimes it insisted he had committed. Davis, in prison now for a year and a half, was anxious to get his day in court, to exercise his rights under the Sixth Amendment to the U.S. Constitution:

> In all criminal prosecutions, the accused shall enjoy the right to a speedy and public trial, by an impartial jury of the State and district wherein the crime shall have been committed, which district shall have been previously ascertained by law, and to be informed of the nature and cause of the accusation; to be confronted with the witnesses against him; to have compulsory process for obtaining witnesses in his favor, and to have the Assistance of Counsel for his defense.

The United States government was violating prisoner Davis's rights under the Constitution. That fact was growing increasingly and embarrassingly clear even to the average reader of a daily newspaper. But until the United States president, the attorney general, the rest of the cabinet, and the chief justice of the Supreme Court figured a way out of the mess they had created for themselves, Davis would stay right where he was. He would stay imprisoned in Fortress Monroe.

CHAPTER 13

"The Government Is Unable to Deal with the Subject"

IT IS DIFFICULT FOR A LAWYER to plan a defense for a client when the prosecution has no idea if the accused has actually committed a crime, and the only thing the prosecution is sure of is that it wants to keep the accused in prison until it comes up with a crime with which it can win a conviction.

That was the situation facing Davis's attorney Charles O'Conor early in 1867.

The May 2, 1865, proclamation from President Andrew Johnson accusing Davis of conspiracy in the assassination of President Lincoln had never been withdrawn, even though the witnesses against Davis in the conspiracy trial were proved liars. There was an earlier indictment filed in the District of Columbia that was withdrawn once the federal government realized the District had never seceded from the United States, thus had not been influenced by Davis to commit treason. There was another indictment in Norfolk, but that was apparently so misdrawn that court employees expunged all traces of it from court records so effectively that even historians of the nineteenth century counted it as "lost to history." The only current indictment in 1867 was the one from May 1866 that charged Davis with personally inciting war against the United States on a specific day in 1864 more than three years after the war had actually broken out.

O'Conor and the team of volunteer lawyers who had rushed to his side—all from Northern states—could not believe that any prosecutor would move forward with such a seemingly ludicrous proposition that the government could pick out one day in which a single person caused an entire region of the nation to incite war.

The indictment Davis expected and wanted to be issued against him—treason against the United States for the act of secession—was discussed in the president's cabinet in the summer of 1865, but no formal, specific charges laying out how Davis had practiced treason by secession were filed in the year and a half that elapsed since Davis's capture.

Most members of the Johnson administration and the Congress wanted something to happen. Davis, his family, his defense counsel, his friends, and most Southerners wanted something to happen. Newspaper editors wanted something to happen. The general public in both North and South wanted something to happen.

Nothing was happening. The government appeared paralyzed when it came to figuring out what to do with Jefferson Davis.

O'Conor said:

If the government has any fixed design in respect to [Davis], it is totally unknown to me. All is conjecture; but there is a prevailing impression that the government is unable to deal with the subject and is patiently awaiting some providential extrication from its doubts.

With the charge of complicity in the assassination of Lincoln all but dead except in the hearts of congressmen who wanted to make speeches about the martyred Lincoln, all the government's uncertainty revolved around a central question: Was secession treason?

Treason is mentioned in the Constitution as "levying War against them [United States], or in adhering to their Enemies, giving them Aid and Comfort."

Treason was and is generally defined as attempting to overthrow the government of one's own country or assisting its foreign enemies to achieve that same goal.

The problem the United States had was proving that states leaving the government was the same as states trying to overthrow the government. When South Carolina started the wave of secession in December

1860, its secession documents made no mention of changing the government in Washington. Indeed, South Carolina declared it had "resumed its separate and equal place among nations." In December 1860 South Carolina's politicians were not even sure that any other states would follow them to become a confederation of any kind. Rather than instantly align itself with any other states, South Carolina was declaring itself free of all the United States, north and south.

When each of the following ten Southern states left the Union from January through April of 1861, four after Lincoln demanded that they provide regiments to invade the other Southern states, each state declared that it was dissolving its compact with the Union. None of the secession documents mentioned trying to change the established government in Washington. None threatened to invade and capture the nation's capital. No Southern state used its secession documents to describe any action on its part that fit the classic definition of treason.

Once the war started, even the act of firing on Fort Sumter might not have fit the constitutional definition of "levying war" against the United States. In December 1860, before there was a Confederacy, South Carolinians considered Fort Sumter a foreign presence in the harbor of the new independent nation of South Carolina. In the minds of South Carolina's politicians, it was then a sovereign state, no longer part of the United States, and was perfectly within its right to demand the surrender of a foreign nation's fort that rested within Charleston's harbor.

Now in 1867 there was one glaring reason that federal government officials did not have clear-cut evidence that secession in 1860 and 1861 was unconstitutional. In 1863 the United States admitted a state into the Union in a manner that was clearly in violation of the Constitution.

When Union-leaning western counties in Virginia met in their own secession convention in Wheeling in western Virginia after the start of the war, they applied to the United States to be admitted into the Union. West Virginia was admitted into the United States as a state on January 1, 1863. Most Northerners considered admitting the new state a public relations coup—a portion of a slave state so loyal to the Union that it was willing to secede from its own state.

The problem is that West Virginia was—and still is—an illegal state according to the U.S. Constitution. Article IV, Section 3 of the Constitution is a clause covering the formation of new states reading:

New States may be admitted by the Congress into this Union; but no new States shall be formed or erected within the Jurisdiction of any other State; nor any State be formed by the Junction of two or more States, or parts of States, without the Consent of the Legislatures of the States concerned as well as of the Congress.

Virginia's legislature from 1861 to 1865 was not about to grant its rebellious western counties permission to join the United States. When the clear violation of the Constitution was pointed out to Lincoln he breezily replied:

It is said the admission of West Virginia is secession, and tolerated only because it is our secession. Well, if we can call it by that name, there is still difference enough between secession against the Constitution, and secession in favor of the Constitution.

Secession itself is not mentioned in the Constitution, but it had been part of national political debate for more than seventy-five years.

The New England states first threatened to leave the Union when the Northwestern territories (today's American Midwest stretching from Ohio to Minnesota) were admitted into the nation as western frontier territories after Great Britain surrendered claim to them after signing the Treaty of Paris in 1783. New England's objections were purely political. The urban centers of Philadelphia, Boston, and New York did not want to share voting power with the great unwashed trappers and settlers who would be pouring into the new lands.

The Northeast grumbled again in 1803 when President Thomas Jefferson bought the Louisiana Purchase. Still smarting from the creation of the District of Columbia in the South as part of the deal with the southern states to let the national government pay for war debts from the Revolution, New England secessionists proposed that the seven

Northeastern states secede and form a new nation with New York City as its capital. Nothing came of the threat.

The idea of secession came up again in 1814 when the Northeastern states held a convention in Hartford, Connecticut, to draw up proposed amendments to the Constitution that would strongly endorse states' rights. While the Hartford Convention document did not specifically threaten secession, it was discussed as an option if the United States refused to consider amending the Constitution to give New England more power.

What drove this dissatisfaction with the federal government were laws preventing New England from trading with England during the War of 1812. New England saw nothing wrong in trading with the enemy of the United States during a time of war. By the time the delegates of the Hartford Convention reached Washington to present their demands, the War of 1812 was over. The United States won and England lost, leaving New England looking foolish for trying to side with an enemy of the nation.

The idea of secession came up again for the fourth time, the first in the South, in the 1830s when South Carolina threatened to secede over the issue of having to pay high tariffs on imported and exported goods in order to protect the industries of New England. President Andrew Jackson, a native Southerner but a staunch believer in national government, threatened to invade South Carolina if it left the Union and did not pay its taxes to the federal government. South Carolina backed down and accepted a tariff compromise, but the issue still simmered below the surface for the next thirty years.

South Carolina carried through on its thirty-year threat in December 1860.

Once the war began, The Thirty-seventh Congress sought to develop a punishment for its definition of treason when in July 1862 it passed a joint resolution H.R. 110 calling on the president to "seize and confiscate the property of rebels" as a means to "suppress insurrection [and to] punish treason and rebellion." It was this resolution that formed the basis of how the Federal District Court picked June 15, 1864, as the date when Davis formally supported rebellion.

☆　☆　☆

WHILE PROVING SECESSION from the Union was treason was a theoretical and legal problem facing the nation after the war, the United States soon realized that during the war it had unintentionally recognized the legitimate existence of the Confederacy. Some legal minds now worried that the nation had committed a political and constitutional mistake that had given men like Davis a legal opening to prove that what they had done was not treasonous.

The mistake the United States of America made was to agree to exchange prisoners with the Confederate States of America.

The reluctance of one warring nation to recognize another warring nation when it came to the formal exchange of prisoners was not new. Great Britain had not wanted to exchange prisoners formally during the American Revolution because it feared a formality would embolden the rebels who called themselves Patriots. The generals in the field on both sides, including George Washington for the Patriots, made several informal exchanges without any official sanction of the practice by either government.

Less than one hundred years later the roles were reversed. Now it was the United States government that did not want to recognize the rebels from the South as a real government. The sticking point was that after any battle, both sides had prisoners. The Northern politicians knew that the public would not stand for their government refusing to exchange their loved ones when the only question was one of semantics: did the Confederacy exist or did it not exist?

Reluctantly, but carefully, the United States began to exchange captured soldiers. The first prisoner exchange was rather gentlemanly. The surrendered Union garrison at Fort Sumter was allowed by the Confederates to fire a one-hundred-gun salute to the American flag before they boarded a ship for New York City.

Once larger battles like Manassas were over in July 1861, the details became messier. Confederate officers were the first to offer exchanges, but Union officers were wary that accepting their own men back into the ranks meant official recognition of the enemy. In October 1861, Grant, then a virtually unknown brigadier general in Missouri refused the offer of one of his Confederate opponents to exchange prisoners, saying, "I recognize no Southern Confederacy."

As the number of prisoners began to mount on each side as more battles were fought, battlefield exchanges became more common. The opposing generals often did not ask permission from the civilian administration. As many of them knew each other from prewar service in the army, they simply worked out their own arrangements.

Then on December 13, 1861, General Henry Halleck, writing from Washington so that he probably cleared the idea with Secretary of War Edwin Stanton, had a brainstorm—simply exchange the Confederate prisoners immediately and then try all the thousands of men later for treason for fighting against the United States.

Halleck wrote:

After full consideration of the subject I am of the opinion that prisoners ought to be exchanged. This exchange is a mere military convention. A prisoner exchanged under the laws of war is not thereby exempted from trial and punishment as a traitor. Treason is a state or civil offense punishable by the civil courts; the exchange of prisoners of war is only a part of the ordinary *commercial belli* [open and mixed warfare].

The formal prisoner-of-war exchange process began in January 1862, but still the United States government was wary about recognizing the Confederacy. Finally, on July 22, 1862, after General Robert E. Lee captured thousands of Federals during the Seven Days Battles east of Richmond, the Union army's major general John A. Dix signed an agreement with Confederate major general Daniel Harvey Hill to create a formal means of exchanging prisoners. The first provision was that a general was worth sixty privates and each lower-ranking grade officer would reduce the number of privates exchanged. The lowest-ranking officer, a second lieutenant, was worth three privates. Prisoners were to be exchanged within ten days of their capture.

The *New York Times* was ecstatic that the federal government was exchanging Confederates for Union men. The newspaper did not care that such exchanges resulted in a de facto recognition of the Confederacy: "The principle of exchange has now been accepted by our Government," read one article.

The exchange process worked well enough for just over a year but was finally stopped on May 25, 1863. The Union insisted at the time the reason for halting the exchanges was that the Confederate government was threatening to execute captured black soldiers. But that was a disingenuous excuse. Large numbers of United States Colored Troops would not go into combat for another several months. Few black soldiers, if any, had been captured, so the Confederacy's threat to harm them had yet to be realized.

The more realistic reason for halting the exchanges was that some influential Union generals such as Ulysses S. Grant realized that paroled Confederate soldiers were often rejoining the ranks of the Confederate army. The Union army was sometimes fighting the same men it had just captured and released. Grant suggested that keeping the Confederates in prison camps would greatly benefit the Union army since the pool of potential recruits into the Southern armies was less than a quarter of what it was for the North based on the male population of both regions.

The Union strategy worked. Starting in the summer of 1863, Confederate armies began to shrink in enlistments, while more blacks and immigrants were recruited into the Union army's ranks. At the same time, the numbers of Confederate and Union prisoners began to mushroom as the battles became larger, the clashes came more often, and the geography under attack by the Union grew exponentially.

The explosion in prison populations on both sides was devastating. By the summer of 1864, prison camps for both sides were overflowing, resulting in high death rates from disease. The death rate for prisons on both sides hovered around thirteen percent with some individual prisons experiencing death rates as high as twenty-seven percent.

One Confederate, Major Henry Wirz, the commander of Camp Sumter located near the small town of Andersonville, Georgia, would be charged with war crimes and intentionally starving prisoners. Wirz, a native of Switzerland who had been crippled in combat, was given a show trial in Washington, not long after the Lincoln conspirators, and found guilty.

At one point, O'Conor thought about trying to defend Wirz as well as Davis, but he quickly realized that associating Davis with a prison commander he had never even met could be disastrous for his own case.

"If we should send counsel to defend Wirz, it would leak out that we had done so, and from that moment, Mr. Davis would in effect be on trial," O'Conor wrote to Varina on September 13, 1865.

Even with no evidence tying Davis to Wirz, the United States tried to link the two.

After Wirz had been convicted of war crimes, unidentified representatives from the United States government asked him to implicate Davis so that a formal charge of war crimes could be created on which to try the Confederate president. Two nights before Wirz was sentenced to hang on November 10, 1865, a number of civilians went into his cell. According to R. B. Winder, who was in the cell across from Wirz, the civilians offered to free Wirz if he would say that he was acting on personal orders from Davis to starve the Federal prisoners.

Wirz refused, insisting that he had never met Davis or received any orders from him. Winder said he heard Wirz tell the men that he considered it treason to the South to implicate anyone in a crime falsely that had not happened—the intentional mistreatment of Union prisoners.

Wirz hanged two days later.

Even if Wirz had agreed to accuse Davis falsely to spare his own life, there was hard evidence that could have been produced in Davis's defense. At one point in 1864, Davis tried to send Vice President Stephens to Washington to reopen prisoner exchanges, but the United States government officially refused him safe passage. O'Conor suspected he would find documents in both Union and Confederate archives to prove that the United States had refused an attempt by the Confederacy to ease the number of Union prisoners being held in Southern prisons.

The United States finally gave up on any strategy to charge Davis with war crimes involving intentionally harming Union prisoners of war. The evidence was clear. Davis did all in his power to help the prisoners. With the documents that could be produced and without Wirz's verbal testimony, if the United States government had tried to charge Davis with intentional murder by starvation of captured men, O'Conor would have made the government look foolish.

☆   ☆   ☆

THE UNITED STATES was running out of options. The government had nothing with which to charge Davis.

The Confederate president was not guilty of assassinating Lincoln. He was not guilty of murdering or mistreating prisoners of war. He was not guilty of treason in the classic definition of the word in that he had not tried to overthrow the government. He had simply resigned from the United States Senate, and accepted a draft to be president of an entirely new country that was not the United States. That was difficult for prosecutors to prove was a crime.

Even if the government had manufactured some crime with which to charge Davis, the chief justice of the Supreme Court did not want to bring him to trial. From the very beginning of the legal dispute right through its end, Chief Justice Salmon Chase did not want the United States Supreme Court to ask permission of the United States Army to set up civilian courts.

Early in January 1867, Davis's attorneys decided to try again to make something happen. Davis's attorney George Shea sent Chase a letter asking for an interview to discuss applying for a writ of habeas corpus to transfer Davis from military control to the Federal District Court in Richmond.

Chase suggested that the writ be presented to Judge John Underwood and to the surprise of Davis's attorneys, Underwood agreed. An order was written out to General Burton to deliver Davis to the Richmond courthouse on May 13, 1867. After more than two years of the United States government refusing to let Davis out on bail or to transfer him even from military authorities to civilian, suddenly, that was happening.

The seemingly matter-of-fact approval by Judge Underwood for Davis to appear in court within two weeks made Davis's attorneys suspicious. When Johnson sent his own note to the commander of Fortress Monroe on May 8 ordering him to turn Davis over to the court, they were somewhat relieved and hopeful that something constructive in the case was about to happen.

O'Conor, who had told Underwood and Chase in the fall of 1866 that he could raise one million dollars in bail, rushed to get those pledges in place. Davis's attorney, recognizing the power of public perception in such a high-profile trial, tried to recruit men who were known for being antislavery in sentiment and who were well recognized by the general public. Gerrit Smith, an abolitionist who had bankrolled John Brown's raid on Harpers Ferry, Virginia, in November 1859, agreed to appear personally in Richmond to sign his pledge of bail money. Cornelius Vanderbilt, whose shipping fleet had delivered supplies to Union armies, also agreed to post bail for Davis.

On May 12, 1867, two days past the anniversary of his capture, Davis boarded a ship at Fortress Monroe to head up the James River to Richmond. It was the first time he had been outside the walls of his prison since Major General Nelson Miles had seized him by the arm and led him into the whitewashed casemate nearly two years earlier.

The newspapers covered Davis's trip from the moment he stepped through the sally port. Some were less than kind in their observations, even to Varina.

The *Philadelphia Inquirer*, which had printed a large, faked composite image of Davis in a dress in one of its May 1865 editions, now commented that Varina was "a lady never called a beauty with a complexion so dark that she might pass for a quadroon [one-quarter black]. She has too much flesh for gracefulness."

A major American newspaper, covering the release of the former Confederate president from prison, had just called his wife fat and implied, without any evidence, that she was part Negro.

On May 13, 1867, at 11:00 a.m., at about the same time of day when a year earlier Underwood told Davis's attorneys that it was too hot to hold court, the Federal District Court of Virginia opened its session in Richmond. Underwood presided. Justice Chase was not in attendance. He still refused to hold court in a state that was controlled by military occupation. A jury of twelve men, half of them black, had already been selected by the judge. Courtroom observers wondered if Underwood had followed through on his earlier suggestion that he could pack the jury with black men who would vote to convict a former slave owner of anything the judge wanted. The black and white men sat side by side in the jury box. There was no segregation.

When Underwood asked the Federal prosecution to state its case, William Evarts, one of the private lawyers hired to try the case, said something unexpected:

It is not its [federal government] intention to prosecute the trial of the prisoner at the present term of the court.

District Attorney Chandler then suggested that bail be set at $100,000. O'Conor stood and said he had ten men in the courtroom who would sign for $10,000 each. Horace Greeley, the man who had editorialized about freeing Davis for nearly two years, was the first to sign the bond. Davis and Greeley had never spoken. Indeed, Davis had never met any of the Northerners who were signing his bond.

When the bond was signed, Underwood dismissed the court and released Davis after instructing his attorneys that a court date would be set sometime in the future. The two-year struggle to bring Davis to trial had turned into a perfunctory legal exercise that still was not resolved, but which had freed Davis on bail. The entire proceeding was over in less than a half hour. After two years in prison, Jefferson Davis was still awaiting his speedy trial as promised by the U.S. Constitution, but he was now free on bail.

As Davis stepped into the streets of Richmond, a rebel yell erupted from the crowd of men who also removed their hats. Davis immediately returned to his hotel where he faced his wife as a free man for the first time in two years.

"You have been with me in my sufferings, and comforted and

strengthened me with your prayers. Is it not right that we now once more should kneel down together and return thanks?" Davis asked his wife. They went into the adjoining room and knelt.

Not all newspapermen were as happy with the release of the Confederate president as Greeley had been to sign Davis's bond.

The *San Francisco Chronicle*, which boasted that it was the first daily newspaper to report that Lincoln had been shot, charged in large subheadlines: "Arch Traitor Released On Bail, A Sickening Travesty of Justice, The Farce Prearranged in Washington, Another Example of the Way A. J. [Andrew Johnson] Makes Treason Odious." The newspaper called Davis the nation's "greatest criminal" and claimed that Davis was "treated like Napoleon returning from Elba. The whole affair has assumed a melodramatic effect with Davis as star attraction." Later in the article the newspaper wrote: "We cannot properly characterize this high-handed outrage."

Though Davis had just been released on bail and the federal government intended to try him at some point in the future, there were no travel restrictions placed on Davis. The same day Davis was released from court, he and Varina boarded a steamship bound for Montreal, Canada, to see his children.

When time for the trial neared again, the newspapers began to question if what they had been pushing for over the past two years was really a good idea.

The *New York Times* said:

The forthcoming trial is likely to do us damage and discredit. . . . If Davis is convicted, he will not be punished . . . if he is acquitted, as he may be, the consequences, especially in the Southern states would be still more injurious. . . . We believe the whole country would be relieved if the whole proceeding could be dismissed.

Davis returned to the courtroom in Richmond on November 26, 1867, only to hear the federal government request a continuance in the case. That was granted with court again scheduled for March 26, 1868. This time Davis headed to Mississippi to visit his relatives. When

March 26 arrived, Davis was back in court again, but once again the federal government requested a continuance until May 2, 1868 because it wanted to prepare a new indictment for treason that would replace the oddly worded one from the previous year.

Another delay cropped up in March 1868 when the impeachment trial of President Johnson began in Washington. This was one trial that Chase could not avoid. He presided over a trial that found Johnson not guilty of the crime of asking Stanton to resign from his office.

O'Conor grew frustrated and went to Washington again to get a definitive trial date. This time he was given November 23, 1868, as the date that the treason trial for Davis would begin. Davis left for a European trip.

At some time after taking the case, O'Conor developed a friendship with some unnamed member of the Johnson administration who kept him apprised of the thinking toward Davis within the cabinet. In an April 18, 1868, letter to Davis, O'Conor told his client that his source within the administration was telling him that some high official in the administration was responsible for dragging the case out so long.

O'Conor said:

Most certainly, someone has carefully nursed the prosecution with an earnest vice to prevent it from falling through. I think it highly probable that the same scheming individual has been the actual guide and direction of Mr. Johnson as to his own case, both in the offense and defense.

In the same letter, he warned Davis that the newest attorney general, William Evarts, the same man who had once been part of the prosecution team, was "ambitious" and would be looking for some way to bring Davis to trial because "he wishes to succeed."

On July 4, 1868, President Johnson issued a blanket amnesty for all Confederates—except those under indictment for treason. Only Davis was affected. He did not care. He still wanted that day in court.

The November 1868 election of Ulysses S. Grant as president concerned O'Conor. On November 19, O'Conor warned his fellow lawyers on the defense team that the same unnamed person within the Johnson administration would probably carry over into the Grant administration, which could result in continuing problems in dismissing the case against their client.

O'Conor wrote to Robert Ould, William Reed, and Thomas Bayard, all three volunteer lawyers on the Davis defense team:

> I have long believed that but for the influence of a particular individual, Mr. Davis would never have suffered so long or so severe an imprisonment.
>
> There is reason to fear that individual may possess influence with the incoming administration, and I have already seen reason to believe that he has put his veto upon any discontinuance or relinquishment of the prosecution.
>
> The chief justice has no effect on this person. He [Chief Justice Chase] is not disposed to advance his views and I know of no wish on his part to have Mr. Davis tried or molested.
>
> The chief justice may intervene with strong hand and dismiss the prosecution for the default in not bringing it to trial.

The "individual" who O'Conor never named in any of his letters who kept the case against Davis alive for more than two years almost certainly was William Seward, the secretary of state for Lincoln, Johnson, and Grant. After recovering from his knife wounds inflicted by Lewis Powell on the same night that Lincoln was shot, Seward returned to cabinet meetings as the strongest advocate for trying Davis under a military tribunal. That was the same method that had quickly convicted and hanged Powell and the other conspirators. During the early part of the conspirators' trial, Davis's name was frequently mentioned as being the mastermind of both Lincoln's death and the near death experience of Seward.

That someone else in the cabinet would be feeding information about Seward to the lawyer of Davis was not surprising. Seward was not a popular member of Lincoln's cabinet. Secretary of the Navy Gideon Welles wrote in his diary in 1861 while the cabinet members were still learning about each other that Seward assumed he would shove Lincoln aside and "take over the reins and manage things as he pleased." Welles went on to say that Seward thought the coming war "was a mere party contest with which he and Thurlow Weed [a local New York City political boss] could dispose of as easily as some of their political strifes in New York City."

Chase and Seward had a particular dislike of each other. Like Seward, Chase had dreams of being nominated president in 1860 before upstart Lincoln captured the prize from both of them. According to Welles, there was "perpetual rivalry and mutual but courtly distrust" between the two men. It would have been natural for the severely injured Seward, who believed Davis to be part of the plot that scarred him for life, to be at odds with Chase, who wanted to find a way to try to release Davis from custody.

No matter how much Seward wanted to bury Davis, he had no real power over the courts. On November 30, 1868, Chase and Underwood finally sat on the bench together to decide the case. After Congress had passed a law detailing the reinstatement of state courts, Chase had given up his objections to trying a case in a state that was still under military rule.

Ironically, after so many delays brought about by the government, Davis was going to get his day in court, and he was not even in the same hemisphere. On advice of his attorney, Davis remained in London where he was trying to start a cotton trading business.

The reason Chase was finally taking on the trial after nearly three years of refusal was that he finally saw a way out of the legal mess that would not come back as blame on him should Davis win an acquittal.

By modern-day standards, Chase's actions in November 1868 would be highly unethical and perhaps illegal—if what he had done had become public. He would likely have avoided impeachment by the Congress because the definition of "high crimes and misdemeanors" that make up impeachable offenses are whatever the party in power decides they are. As Chase was a Republican himself, the Republican-controlled Congress likely would not have brought charges against him.

According to letters by O'Conor Chase rigged the case against Davis in advance of the court date by meeting exclusively and privately with some of Davis's attorneys and telling them what defense of Davis he would accept. The prosecution was not invited to the meeting. Such *ex parte* [Latin for by one party] meetings between judges and only one of the opposing counsels are considered unethical by modern judicial standards.

The chief justice had found a way out to extricate both Davis and himself from the trial. The strategy he used was citing a recently passed amendment to the Constitution.

The Fourteenth Amendment had gone into effect on July 28, 1868. One of its provisions was that no one could hold an elective office if they had sworn an oath in the past to uphold the Constitution but had then participated in a rebellion. That portion of the amendment was intended to keep former Confederates from holding office.

Before the trial opened, Chase called Davis's attorneys O'Conor and Shea to a private meeting, without the United States district attorney present. Chase told the defense attorneys that they should look at defending Davis by citing the Fourteenth Amendment. If they pursued that angle, he would rule that Davis had already been punished by the enforcement of the clause in the Fourteenth amendment that he could no longer hold office in the United States government.

O'Conor and Shea went back to develop their strategy based on what Chase had told them. Davis was not consulted because he was still in Europe and unreachable before the court was to open.

Armed with Chase's verbal commitment that he would rule in favor of Davis if they pursued the Fourteenth Amendment as a defense, Davis's attorneys produced evidence that Davis had sworn to uphold the Constitution when he was first elected to the United States House in 1846. Since he had served as Confederate president, he could no longer hold office without violating the Fourteenth Amendment. O'Conor argued that since Davis could no longer hold federal office, that ruling was punishment enough for whatever Davis had done to incur the wrath of the federal government. O'Conor was essentially reading from a script provided by the chief justice of the United States Supreme Court.

United States district attorney Chandler, who had not been privy to the private conversation Chase had held with Shea, tried to argue that the Fourteenth Amendment merely set forth qualifications for holding some future elected federal office. Not being able to run for office was no punishment, and punishment was not intended to be part of the Fourteenth Amendment. The two sides argued the true intentions of the Fourteenth Amendment before Chase and Underwood adjourned the court to consider their rulings.

On December 5, 1868, Chase and Underwood delivered their opinions. Underwood, who also had not been invited to the chat between Chase and Shea, agreed with the prosecution: the amendment was not meant as a punishment, but merely as a means of establishing who could run for public office.

Chase disagreed, saying that Davis was already being punished under the Fourteenth Amendment so that putting him through any other punishment would be akin to forcing Davis into double jeopardy, trying him twice for the same crime. As the court was divided, the case was then ordered to be settled by the United States Supreme Court in its next session. The final resolution had not been found, but at least Davis had won a draw in court.

Two days after the ruling, O'Conor wrote a revealing letter to his client Davis, still in England, explaining the strategy. In the letter O'Conor repeated his earlier theory that Davis was being victimized by a "particular individual" within Johnson's cabinet who was responsible for Davis's two-year ordeal of being in prison without being charged or tried. According to O'Conor's source that man was insisting to the administration that Davis be tried for treason.

O'Conor still did not name that individual in the letter, but he did hint at who his contact was within the Johnson cabinet. O'Conor continually referred to getting information from the cabinet from a "Mr. E." That was probably William Evarts, the current attorney general who would see Seward in every cabinet meeting.

Davis is warned in the letter from O'Conor that the matter is not over yet since Chase and Underwood split their decisions. The split decision meant that Davis's case would automatically be appealed to the full Supreme Court. O'Conor says that Mr. E has "admonished me that there was no just ground to hope for a voluntary abandonment of the prosecution." With that statement, O'Conor almost certainly identifies Mr. E as Attorney General Evarts since Evarts could drop all charges against Davis if he wanted to do so, but doing so would have offended old political pro Seward.

The most amazing part of the letter came in the last third when O'Conor assured Davis that Chase was in the pocket of the defense.

O'Conor bluntly told Davis in the letter that Chase was "thoroughly enlisted" in dismissing the case against the Confederate president.

"His judgment is with you; his fancy is excited; he says a judicial determination of this point in your favor would furnish a magnificent chapter in our history," O'Conor wrote in the December 7, 1868, letter.

While O'Conor's letter traveled the Atlantic Ocean, Evarts, probably "Mr. E," who had just warned O'Conor that the case was not over, began to have second thoughts about his ability to prosecute the case. After hearing Chase say that Davis had already suffered enough by not being able to run for office again, Evarts envisioned the case going before the United States Supreme Court with Chase actively and openly campaigning the other justices to free Davis from double jeopardy. If that happened, Davis would not only get his day in court but would win in the biggest court in the land—the United States Supreme Court. What would be even more embarrassing for the United States was that Davis would win his case by using the Fourteenth Amendment, which was supposed to punish Confederates, not free them from prison.

Sometime in the weeks after December 7, Evarts approached O'Conor with the offer that he would enter a *nolle prosequi* [agreement not to prosecute] if O'Conor and his defense team would drop the matter entirely and not appeal the case to the Supreme Court. Without consulting with Davis, who was still in Europe, O'Conor agreed to give up Davis's day in court in exchange for a promise that no matter who was elected president, representative, or senator in the future that Jefferson Davis would never be put on trial for being president of the Confederacy.

On Christmas Day, 1868, Johnson issued a blanket amnesty that finally included Davis. For the first time in three and a half years, Davis was not being accused by the United States government of being an assassin, a murderer, or a traitor.

Varina was happy, but Davis was disappointed. He had wanted to clear his name and prove that forming the Confederacy was a constitutional means of protesting the actions of the Untied States government. He would never get his trial to prove that he was right and all those millions of Northerners were wrong.

Even if Chase had not been around to rig the outcome, O'Conor was confident that he could have won a trial that tried to define secession as treason. In a February 2, 1878, letter to Davis, O'Conor outlined what his legal strategy would have been in the courtroom.

O'Conor wrote to Davis that he had

stored my mind with a knowledge of the decisions and dicta of courts and eminent persons—tending to support our cause. This was very necessary, for the precise points of law involved were essentially novel, and thus ceptible of little aid from judicial precedents.

What constituted treason at the common law was quite immaterial and the just construct of English statute law on that subject prior to the revolution was not doubtful or obscure. The Constitution adopted that construction and settled in English adjudications. In that view of the case, you could not be convicted unless it was for having levied war.

The case then resolved itself into the inquiry whether in any interpretation of the phrase you have levied war. [O'Conor underlined for emphasis].

O'Conor said:

My position was that if you had, that was merged in the war which was waged [O'Conor underlined for emphasis] by both parties. It might be safely admitted that this merger could not have taken place without an acknowledgement by the United States government that a public war existed. I intended to insist that such an acknowledgement was made.

O'Conor's argument was that if Davis and the Confederates had waged an insurgent war—a war of terror—against the United States, he might have been committing treason against the nation. But since the United States had retaliated almost immediately after the bloodless battle of Fort Sumter, April 12, 1861, by invading and threatening all the Southern states, the United States settled the question that the Confederacy was not engaged in terrorism against the United States.

A further argument that O'Conor would have made had the case gone to trial was that by calling for volunteers to invade the South and later in the war by exchanging prisoners with the South, the United States had recognized the Confederacy as an entity separate from the United States. The United States had treated the South as a foreign country almost from the beginning of the war, not withstanding Lincoln's refusal to meet with any of the Confederacy's leaders to discuss peace terms.

The two sides were waging war against each other. It was a legitimate war fought between legitimate nations.

O'Conor's court arguments would have been that it was the reactions of the United States, not the Confederacy, that had made the American Civil War, or the War for Southern Independence, a true war between two regions. Before the war had even started, Davis had said to the North in his inauguration speech: "All we ask is to be left alone." The United States had responded by trying to resupply Fort Sumter, followed by the call for volunteers to invade the South, followed by numerous incursions onto Virginia soil, including early battles in June before the first major battle at Manassas on July 21, 1861.

In the end, after three and a half years of legal jousting, O'Conor believed Davis had not committed treason and was confident he would prove the man's innocence in court. More importantly, all the legal minds in the Johnson administration also believed Davis had not committed treason, and they were afraid that they would not be able to prove his guilt in court.

The United States government had captured Davis, imprisoned him, humiliated him, and tortured him for a short period of time, but they had not been able to prove that he had done anything illegal or unconstitutional. The war that had claimed more than 620,000 American lives had ended with a clear winner, the United States, but the nation had not been able to find a reason to blame the war on Jefferson Davis.

☆   ☆   ☆

THE SICKLY, anorexic, neuralgic, headache-plagued, malarial Davis with his one blind eye would live another twenty-one years, dying on December 6, 1889, at the age of 81. That was one day beyond the anniversary of the day Chief Justice Salmon Chase issued his ruling from the bench that finally set Davis free without any concern that he would ever be tried in a court.

Davis, who always seemed near death in his two-year imprisonment, outlived most of his Union tormentors: Edwin Stanton (1868), Andrew Johnson (1875), William Seward (1872), and Jacob Howard (1871). His jailer, Major General Nelson Miles, lived until 1925, but he had been a much younger man than Davis when they first tangled.

As well, Davis also outlived most of his Confederate enemies like Alexander Stephens (1883) and Howell Cobb (1868). Davis's most personal enemy, Joseph E. Johnston (1891) did get the last laugh on Davis. Johnston would die two years after Davis—and only after marching in the rain during the funeral for his old enemy and friend Union general William T. Sherman. Pierre Beauregard, another old Davis enemy, would not die until 1893.

Davis even outlived his newfound friends Horace Greeley (1872) and Gerrit Smith (1874) and his most loyal general, Robert E. Lee (1870).

He never got that trial he wanted, but Davis got his revenge by creating a forum to bash his old antagonists when he wrote a massive two-volume explanation and defense of the Confederacy called *The Rise and Fall of the Confederate Government*. Published in 1881, Davis spent only a few paragraphs on his capture and even fewer words on the two years he spent in prison. Instead, he used hundreds of thousands of words to accuse men like Joseph E. Johnston and P.G.T. Beauregard of contributing to the defeat of the Confederacy.

Davis reveals himself and his stubborn nature in the two volumes. One of the most telling passages that demonstrates how the man could be self-delusional comes in volume 2. While writing about his escape through Georgia and South Carolina, Davis claims that had he made it to Alabama and his brother-in-law General Richard Taylor, he could have inspired Taylor's men to follow him to Texas where the Confederacy could have lived on in the Trans-Mississippi.

No book editor had the nerve to point out to Davis that his timeline was inaccurate. Taylor's army had already surrendered while Davis was still trying to escape through southern Georgia. Davis knew that while he was writing the book. He just refused to acknowledge what was a historical fact.

No one ever corrected Jefferson Davis. He was always right—always.

Acknowledgments

HISTORY WRITERS ALWAYS DEPEND ON others to help us produce books such as this.

My first thanks goes to Bob Williams of Jamestown, North Carolina, my friend of more than thirty years of reenacting. We both started with The Leon Rifles in Florida and are now with the Twenty-sixth Regiment of North Carolina in North Carolina. Bob read the manuscript to correct historical mistakes and to offer opinions on what needed to be strengthened. When he writes his own book, I will do the same for him.

Chris Hartley, another writer from Clemmons, North Carolina, will be coming out next year with the most comprehensive book on Stoneman's Raid ever published. Chris gave me some details on Stoneman's raid that still puzzle me. Had Stoneman and his subordinates checked out the rumors that Davis was in Greensboro, they might have captured him in that city. Had Davis been captured, President Lincoln would probably have pardoned him and the nation could have begun healing within weeks of Lee's surrender. Thanks too to Fergus Bordewich, a great writer of American history, for reading the manuscript and offering his insight. Thanks also go to writers Rod Grogg and Marc Leepson for reading it and offering comments.

The question of how ethical it was for Chief Justice Salmon Chase to meet in private with Jefferson Davis's attorneys I submitted to three lawyers in the Twenty-sixth North Carolina Regiment reenactment unit to which I belong. Thanks to Al Leonard of Tryon, North Carolina, Ed Fiorella of Norfolk, Virginia, and Brad Bush of Charlotte, North Carolina, for all sharing their opinion that what Chase did in 1868 would put him before an ethical review committee in 2008. Judge Richard Boner, a superior court judge in Charlotte, North Carolina, also agreed that Chase was out of bounds.

Nancy Ingalsbee, director of the Allegan County, Michigan, Historical Society, sent me some interesting archived articles on Allegan native son, Lieutenant Colonel Benjamin Pritchard, who was in the command of the Fourth Michigan Cavalry that captured Davis.

I also want to thank an Internet friend I have never met face to face, Mark Ruddy of Union City, Tennessee. Mark is the grandson of Captain Henry Albert Potter of the Fourth Michigan Cavalry. Mark graciously allowed me to quote from some letters his grandfather wrote about the capture of Jefferson Davis. He also alerted me to *Minty and the Cavalary* a book on the capture. Most important of all, and most interesting, Mark sent me photocopies of several pages in that book in which one of the officers involved in the capture disputed the author with margin notes.

Another two people I talked with by e-mail were Joel Craig, who had an otherwise unpublished account of Davis's capture on his website, and David Bright, who gave me some information on the condition of Confederate railroads in 1865.

John Coski, library director of the Museum of the Confederacy in Richmond helped guide me through the Davis trial preparation files. Heather Milne helped gather some photos. I have been a longtime member and financial supporter of the museum for years. Everyone should be. It is a great museum with fascinating artifacts and a fair, balanced interpretation of The War.

Thanks to Jim McQueen, Laurie Baumgarner, and the rest of the staff at my own Ashe County, North Carolina, library. They were always ready to help me find books and other sources. Other librarians who helped me include John Mohney at the Paw-Paw, Michigan, Public Library and Lisa Prolman at the Greenfield, Massachusetts, Library. Thanks also to Lynda Crist and the Papers of Jefferson Davis project at Rice University for preserving these important documents.

I also have to thank the staff at Appalachian State University Press in Boone, North Carolina. By paying just $10 for a researcher's card, I was given access to databases that provided much of the research I needed. Some pretty amazing databases are out there just waiting for writers to mine them.

Help from historians came from Diane Ross, a local historian from Paw-Paw; Peter Miller, a historian in Greenfield, Massachusetts; and Leo Mehalic and Deborah Goode from the United States Naval Academy. Richard Flowers, executive director of Beauvoir, the home in Biloxi, Mississippi, where Davis spent many years in retirement, helped with some details on the raglan and shawl that Davis was wearing at his capture. Both were destroyed by Hurricane Katrina and Beauvoir was severely damaged. I hope to visit it one day.

I also want to thank Lisa Marine, the business manager for the Wisconsin State Archives for helping gather some photos, as well as the staffs at the Michigan Historical Society and the Library of Congress who did the same.

Thanks to Joe Valley, my agent, for representing me on *The Politically Incorrect Guide to the South (and Why It Will Rise Again)* in 2007, and now this book. I hope we will find more projects in the future. Joe pushes you to write proposals that publishers want to see and books they want to publish.

Thanks to Michaela Hamilton, my editor at the Citadel Press. She recognized that while several books had been done on the flight of Jefferson Davis from Richmond, none had looked deep into the reasons why the United States government had never tried him for any crime. In May 1865 the United States government virtually assured the nation that Davis had conspired to murder President Lincoln. When that did not work, the politicians assured the nation Davis was guilty of treason. That did not work either. Until *Pursuit*, no book has looked deeply into the issue until now. Thanks, Michaela, for helping tell this story.

Finally, thanks to my wife, Barbara Gedemer Johnson, who acted as copy editor and who has never—well, rarely—objected to walking around battlefields.

Source Notes

Chapter I: "Nothing Short of Dementation"

2 **"with Patrick Henry, 'Victory or death'":** Jefferson Davis, speech given at African Church in Richmond, February 6, 1865, at www.TeachingAmericanHistory.org.

3 **In an 1858 speech:** Jefferson Davis, speech given at Faneuil Hall in Boston, October 11, 1858, in Dunbar Rowland, *Jefferson Davis, Constitutionalist: His Letters, Papers, and Speeches*, vol. 3 (Mississippi Department of Archives and History, Jackson, 1923) pp. 314–32; also at www.jeffersondavis.rice.edu.

4 **"successfully make war upon them":** Ibid.

5 **"bring disaster on every part of the country":** Varina Davis, *Jefferson Davis, Ex-President of the Confederate States of America: A Memoir by His Wife*, vol. 1 (Belford, New York, 1890) p. 695.
Davis scoffed: Ibid., 8.
"They know not what they do!": Ibid., 10.

7 **"more depressed than before":** Ibid., 19.

8 **"dreary cloud":** *Richmond Examiner* (October 26, 1864): 1.
"incompetence": John B. Jones, *A Rebel War Clerk's Diary at the Confederate States Capital* (Lippincott, Philadelphia, 1866) p. 461.

9 **"scheme":** Ibid., 466.
"term of service": Ibid., 471–72.

10 **"securing peace to the people"**: Carl Sandburg, *Abraham Lincoln: The War Years*, vol. 4 (Harcourt, Brace, New York, 1939) p. 33.

change in wording: John J. Nicolay and John Hay, "The Hampton Roads Conference," *Century Magazine* (October 1889): 847.

11 **Grant wrote**: Ulysses S. Grant, *Memoirs*, quoted in Sandburg, p. 235.

12 **"march across Georgia to be his last"**: Jefferson Davis, African Church speech, February 6, 1865.

"moved to their profoundest depths": Alexander H. Stephens, *A Constitutional View of the Late War Between the States*, vol. 2 (National, Philadelphia, 1870) p. 623.

"did not believe could be realized": Ibid., 625.

13 **"nothing short of dementation"**: Alexander H. Stephens, *Recollections of Alexander H. Stephens: His Diary Kept While a Prisoner at Fort Warren, Boston Harbour, 1865* (Doubleday, New York, 1910) [June 21, 1865] p. 241.

predicted would arrive: Jefferson Davis, African Church speech, February 6, 1865

15 **"toward us," Longstreet later wrote**: James Longstreet, *From Manassas to Appomattox: Memoirs of the Civil War in America* (Lippincott, New York, 1908) p. 605.

"find necessary in and about Richmond": *Official Records of the War of the Rebellion* (U.S. Government Printing Office, Washington, D.C., 1880–1901) ser. 1, vol. 46, pt. 3, p. 1378.

18 **"want of time to pack and transportation"**: Ibid.

20 **"selfish hearts may do"**: Charles Minnigerode, sermon, January 1, 1865, Charles Wynne, printer, 1865; from the Documenting American South digital collection at docsouth.unc.edu/imls/minnigerode.

"later, according to circumstances": *Official Records*, loc. cit.

21 **"as impenetrable as an iron mask"**: Mrs. Burton Harrison, *Recollections Grave and Gay* (Scribner's, New York, 1911) p. 207.

"a scrap of paper": Katherine M. Jones, ed., *Ladies of Richmond, Confederate Capital* (Bobbs-Merrill, Indianapolis, 1962) p. 270.

"was noted to walk unsteadily": Ibid., 271.

CHAPTER 2: "The Direful Things"

22 **"mass of hurrying fugitives":** *Richmond Whig* (April 5, 1865).
"General Lee may not have troops": John B. Jones, *Rebel War Clerk*, p. 466.

23 **"General Hardee":** Ibid., 527–28.
"most incredulous": Sallie Anne Brock Putnam, *Richmond During the Civil War: Four Years of Personal Observation by a Richmond Lady* (G. W. Carleton, New York, 1867); reprinted in Katherine M. Jones, *Ladies of Richmond*, p. 272.

24 **"Hail, Columbia, happy land":** Lloyd Lewis, *Sherman: Fighting Prophet* (Harcourt, Brace, New York, 1932) p. 503.
barrels of flour were selling at $700: John B. Jones, *Rebel War Clerk*, p. 381.
"had no relish for them": A. R. Tomlinson's memoirs, quoted in Burke Davis, *To Appomattox: Nine April Days, 1865* (Rinehart, 1959) p. 13.
"consciously preach of it": Mrs. William A. Simmons, diary, reprinted in Katherine M. Jones, *Ladies of Richmond*, p. 264.

26 **"not be such a hell of a shower after all":** Stephen Mallory, diary, quoted in Joseph T. Durkin, *Stephen R. Mallory: Confederate Naval Chief* (University of North Carolina Press, Chapel Hill, 1954) p. 338.

27 **Benjamin was sitting on top of a box:** W. H. Swallow, "Retreat of the Confederate Government from Richmond to the Gulf," *Magazine of American History* (June 1886): 596–97.
"say everything at once": Warren Spencer, ed. "A French View of the Fall of Richmond: Alfred Paul's Report to Drouyn de Lhuys, April 11, 1865," *Virginia Magazine of History and Biography* (April 1965): 181–82.

28 **Once Davis dismissed the meeting:** John H. Reagan, *Flight and Capture of Jefferson Davis,* in Annals of the War (Times Publishing, Philadelphia, 1879) p. 151.

29 **Davis went back:** Hudson Strode, *Jefferson Davis, Tragic Hero: The Last 25 Years, 1862–1889* (Harcourt, Brace & World, New York, 1964) pp. 168–69.

"trend of Confederate travel": Virginia Clay-Clopton, quoting her husband's exchange with Davis, in her memoir, *A Belle of the Fifties: Mrs. Clay of Alabama* (Doubleday, New York, 1905) p. 244.

30 **"board a ship to a foreign country"**: Varina Davis, *Jefferson Davis*, vol. 2, p. 577.

36 **pending evacuation of the cabinet**: Robert E. Lee, telegram, in *Official Records*, loc. cit.

"All troops will be directed to Amelia Court House": Robert E. Lee, telegram to John C. Breckinridge, in ibid.

38 **asked to spend the night in town**: William H. Parker, *Recollections of a Confederate Naval Officer, 1841–1865* (Scribner's, New York, 1883) p. 268.

"years," Parker wrote: Ibid., 269.

39 **the cabinet's nervousness**: Ibid., 270.

40 **"the general ruin"**: Edward M. Boykin, *The Falling Flag: Evacuation of Richmond, Retreat and Surrender at Appomattox* (E. J. Hale, New York City, 1874) p. 11.

"A scene that beggars description": Ibid., 12.

41 **"to share with his necessities the last morsel"**: Ibid., 13.

As Gary himself passed over the Mayo Bridge: Clement Sullivane, "The Fall of Richmond: The Evacuation," in Robert Underwood Johnson and Clarence Clough Buel, eds., *Battles and Leaders of the Civil War: Retreat with Honor*, vol. 4 (Century, New York, 1887; reprint: Castle, Secaucus, N.J., 1990) p. 726.

CHAPTER 3: "My Husband Will Never Cry for Quarter"

42 **Davis wrote to his son**: Jefferson Davis, letter to Jefferson Jr., in Hudson Strode, *Jefferson Davis: Private Letters 1823–1889* (Harcourt, Brace & World, New York, 1966) pp. 142–43.

43 **"that everyone agrees with him"**: Varina Howell Davis, letter to her mother, Margaret Howell, *The Papers of Jefferson Davis*, vol. 11, Lynda Lasswell Crist, ed. (Louisiana State University Press, Baton Rouge, 2003) pp. 52–53.

exclaimed to her mother: Ibid.

46 **"nature had designed me to be"**: Jefferson Davis, letter to his sister Polly, in J. T. Lasswell, "Jefferson Davis Ponders His Future, 1829," *Journal of Southern History*, 41, no. 4 (November 1975): 520.

47 **"made a favorable impression"**: Henry W. Hilliard, *Politics and Pen Pictures at Home and Abroad* (Putnam, New York, 1892) p. 132.

48 **life in the House of Representatives**: Varina Davis, *Jefferson Davis*, vol. 1, p. 245.

"Sir I make no terms" Jefferson Davis, quoted in William C. Davis, *Jefferson Davis: The Man and His Hour* (HarperCollins, New York, 1991) p. 126.

49 **"your country's service"**: *The Papers of Jefferson Davis*, vol. 2, James T. McIntosh, ed. (Louisiana State University Press, Baton Rouge, 1974) pp. 415–16.

failed to dissuade him: Varina Howell Davis, letter to her mother, in ibid., p. 400.

"how patiently Jeffy always bears suffering": Ibid., 419–20.

52 **"guardian of the whole country"**: Varina Davis, *Jefferson Davis*, vol. 1, p. 685.

"maintain which he was ready to sacrifice": Ibid., 697.

53 **"beef and supplies of all kinds"**: Varina Davis, *Jefferson Davis*, vol. 2, p. 574.

"a place of safety": Ibid., 575–77.

54 **"force your assailants to kill you" her husband said**: Ibid., 577.

"make for the Florida coast": Ibid., 576.

"the destruction of constitutional liberty": Ibid., 575.

55 **"food from here"**: Ibid., 577.

"Only clothes": Ibid.

59 **"He looked as though"**: Ibid.

60 **"arguing from the signs"**: Varina Davis, letter to Gen. John S. Preston, Varina Howell Davis Papers, Museum of Confederacy; reprinted in Katherine M. Jones, *Ladies of Richmond*, p. 267.

61 **"public or private enemies"**: Jefferson Davis, letter to Gen. Braxton Bragg, Jefferson Davis Papers, Tulane University.

CHAPTER 4: "Not Abandon to the Enemy One Foot of Soil"

63 **"great calamity and wrong"**: H. W. Bruce, "Some Reminiscences on April 2, 1865," *Southern Historical Society Papers,* vol. 9 (May 1881): 5.

"many and sad were the commentaries": Stephen Mallory, "The Last Days of the Confederate Government," *McClure's Magazine* (December 1900–January 1901): 102; reprinted in Peter Cozzens, ed., *Battles and Leaders of the Civil War,* vol. 5 (University of Chicago Press, Chicago, 2002) p. 670.

64 **"general gobble"**: Mallory, "Last Days," in Cozzens, p. 671.

"without ever reaching a satisfactory point": Ibid.

"redeemed from far gloomier reverses": Ibid., 672.

"no . . . appearance of despair": Bruce, "Some Reminiscences" [story 5].

65 **"mental exhaustion"**: John S. Wise, *The End of an Era* (Houghton Mifflin, Boston, 1900) p. 415.

"pitch of intense excitement": Ibid.

"after violent convulsions": Ibid., 416.

66 **"haggard expression came to his face"**: John Esten Cooke, *A Life of General Robert E. Lee* (D. Appleton, New York, 1883) p. 452.

"surprise and regret": Robert E. Lee, letter, in *Confederate Veteran*, vol. 7 (1889): 223.

"supplies were in depot or not": Jefferson Davis, *The Rise and Fall of the Confederate Government*, vol. 2 (D. Appletton, New York, 1881) p. 676.

68 **"as much of sorrow as of joy"**: Mallory, "Last Days," in Cozzens, pp. 672–73.

"hospitality of the patriotic citizens": Jefferson Davis, *Rise and Fall*, vol. 2, p. 676.

71 **"from the city of Richmond"**: Jefferson Davis, "Proclamation from Danville, Va., April 4, 1865," in Rowland, *Jefferson Davis, Constitutionalist*, vol. 6, pp. 529–31.

76 **"enthused by the assurance"**: John H. Brubaker, *The Last Capital: Danville, Virginia, and the Final Days of the Confederacy*

(Danville Museum of Fine Arts & History, Danville, Va., 1979) p. 32.

76 **"utter no complaints"**: Raphael Semmes, *Memoirs of Service Afloat During the War Between the States* (reprint: Blue & Gray Press, Secaucus, N.J., 1987) p. 816.

77 **"his great admiration and love"**: *Davis Papers*, vol. 11, p. 500.

78 **"except as encouraging exhortation"**: Varina Davis, quoted in Rowland, *Jefferson Davis, Constitutionalist*, vol. 7, p. 538.

"disaster, he was wholly unprepared": Mallory, "Last Days," in Cozzens, p. 673.

79 **"clothing for your Army"**: *Davis Papers*, vol. 11, p. 526.

"We have lonely two alternatives": Edward Porter Alexander, *Fighting for the Confederacy* (University of North Carolina Press, Chapel Hill, 1989) p. 531.

80 **"fire bell in the night"**: Mallory, "Last Days," in Cozzens, p. 675.

81 **"falling sick by the wayside"**: Parker, *Recollections*, p. 272.

84 **"appear awaiting an opportunity"**: Joseph T. Durkin, S.J., ed., *John Dooley, Confederate Soldier: His War Journal* (Georgetown University Press, Washiington, D.C., 1945).

85 **"make sure of their going"**: Frederick Seward, *Reminiscences of a Wartime Statesman and Diplomat* (Putnam, New York, 1916) pp. 254–55.

86 **"out of the country unbeknown to me"**: Hugh McCullouch, *Men and Measures of Half a Century* (Scribner's, New York, 1888) p. 408.

Chapter 5: "Let Them Up Easy"

90 **"of travel and many bloody battles"**: William T. Sherman, *Memoirs of William T. Sherman*, vol. 2 (D. Appleton, New York, 1875) pp. 326–28.

Johnston wrote a letter to Lee: *Official Records*, ser. 1, vol. 47, pt. 1, p. 1055.

91 **"the war would be prolonged"**: Sherman, *Memoirs* (reprint: Penguin, New York, 2000) p. 681.

91 **"had so much of it!" Lincoln said:** Dixon David Porter, *Incidents and Anecdotes of the Civil War* (D. Appleton, New York, 1885) p. 289.

"leaders, such as Jeff. Davis, etc.": William T. Sherman, *Memoirs of the War of the Rebellion* (reprint: Library of America, New York, 1990) p. 812.

92 **"say so openly":** Ibid.

93 **"charity for all, malice toward none":** Abraham Lincoln, Second Inaugural Address, March 4, 1865.

"government de facto": Sherman, *Memoirs* (Penguin reprint) p. 682.

"pursuit of a treacherous and dangerous enemy": Edwin Stanton, letter to Abraham Lincoln, April 3, 1865, Lincoln manuscripts, Library of Congress.

"I can take care of myself": Sandburg, *Lincoln: The War Years*, vol. 4, p. 177.

95 **"yell of defiance," Crook remembered:** Ibid.

"We were all so aware of the danger": Ibid.

"Porter in the whole proceeding": Ibid., 178.

96 **"let them up easy":** Ibid., 183.

102 **"interfere with your work":** Ibid., 227.

103 **dream actually been a vision of something:** Ibid., 182.

"always thought 'Dixie' was one of the best tunes": Ibid., 208.

104 **"treating the rebel organizations":** Doris Kerns Goodwin, *Team of Rivals: The Political Genius of Abraham Lincoln* (Simon & Schuster, New York, 2005) pp. 729–30.

105 **"safe-return to their homes":** Sandburg, p. 227.

106 **the rebels had to be punished:** Ibid., 234.

"the great majority of the Northern people": Ulysses S. Grant, *Personal Memoirs of U.S. Grant*, vol. 2 (Charles L. Webster, New York, 1886) pp. 510–11.

Chapter 6: "A Miss Is as Good as a Mile"

110 **One resident remembered:** Memorabilia of the Congregation at Salem, 1865, Moravian Archives, Winston-Salem, N.C., quoted

in Ina Van Noppen, *Stoneman's Last Raid* (North Carolina State Press, Chapel Hill, 1961) pp. 40–41.

111 **"about to leave"**: Jefferson Davis, letter to John C. Breckinridge, *Davis Papers*, vol. 11, p. 483.

112 **"galloping to Salisbury"**: *Greensboro Patriot* (March 23, 1866), quoted in Ethel Stephens Arnett, *Greensboro, North Carolina: The County Seat of Guilford* (University of North Carolina Press, Chapel Hill, 1955) p. 394.

"A miss is as good as a mile": Burke Davis, *The Long Surrender* (Random House, New York, 1985) p. 62.

113 **"it would have encountered a universal disbelief"**: Mallory, "Last Days," in Cozzens, p. 676.

114 **passed over that same bridge**: Captain H. K. Weand, "Our Last Campaign and Pursuit of Jefferson Davis," in *History of the Fifteenth Pennsylvania Volunteer Cavalry*, Charles H. Kirk, ed. (Higginson, Salem, Mass., 1907) p. 502.

less than two miles from the burning bridge: Ibid., 503.

116 **"clear knowledge of the situation"**: Alfred Norman, *The Military Operations of General Beauregard in the War Between the States* (Harper & Brothers, New York, 1884) p. 391.

117 **"to revive the spirit and hope"**: Jefferson Davis, letter to Zeb Vance, *Davis Papers*, vol. 11, p. 532.

in his postwar memoirs: Joseph E. Johnston, *Narrative of Military Operations During the Late War Between the State*s (D. Appleton, New York, 1874) p. 397.

118 **"resistance with the means at our command"**: Mallory, "Last Days," in Cozzens, p. 678.

"We have not a day to lose": Ibid.

119 **"like snow before the sun"**: Ibid., 679.

"I concur": Ibid.

"suspension of active operations": Johnston, *Narrative*, p. 400.

120 **"The delay was fatal"**: *Official Records*, ser. 1, vol. 46, pt. 1, p. 1266.

121 **join up with Johnston's army**: Robert E. Lee, Jr., *Recollections*

and Letters of General Robert E. Lee (Doubleday, New York, 1905) pp. 156–57

no interest in helping the Confederacy: *Official Records of the War of the Rebellion—Navy*, ser. 1, vol. 9, p. 252.

122 "ventured within reach of our guns": Semmes, *Memoirs*, p. 819.

123 "Everything is dark": Jefferson Davis, letter to Varina Davis, April 14, 1865, in Rowland, *Jefferson Davis, Constitutionalist*, vol. 6, p. 545.

CHAPTER 7: "Disastrous for Our People"

130 "to strike for the cause": Mallory, "Last Days," in Cozzens, p. 680.

131 "try to conceal his distress": Sherman, *Memoirs* [2nd ed.] (Charles L. Webster, New York, 1891) p. 837.
"men of that stripe": Ibid.

132 Harrison wrote of the event: Burton Harrison, "The Capture of Jefferson Davis," *Century Magazine* (November 1883): 136.

133 "to carry them to Nassau": Sherman, *Memoirs* [2nd ed.], p. 840.
"as soon as possible," Sherman wrote: Ibid, 842.

134 "It was not at all a seemly place": Harrison, "The Capture," 136.

135 "stabbed and is probably mortally wounded": John C. Breckinridge, telegram to Jefferson Davis, *Davis Papers*, vol. 11, p. 544.
"were constantly occurring": Mallory, "Last Days," in Cozzens, p. 681.

136 "much rather have heard of": Ibid.

137 "embodiment of malignity": Jefferson Davis, *Rise and Fall*, vol. 2, p. 683.

138 "If the men who had straggled": Jefferson Davis, letter to Varina Davis, in Rowland, *Jefferson Davis, Constitutionalist*, vol. 6, p. 556.

139 "have the world from which to choose": Ibid., 559–61.

140 "can hope to secure": Judah P. Benjamin, letter to Jefferson Davis,

April 22, 1865, in *Official Records*, ser. 1, vol. 47, pt. 3, pp. 821–23.

"the agreement into effect": George Davis, letter to Jefferson Davis, April 22, 1865, in ibid., 827–28.

141 "add the consciousness of power to their love of domination": John H. Reagan, letter to Jefferson Davis, April 22, 1865, in ibid., 823–26.

"shield them from useless war". Stephen Mallory, letter to Jefferson Davis, April 24, 1865, *Davis Papers*, vol. 11, p. 565.

142 "far better for us to fight": in Rowland, *Jefferson Davis, Constitutionalist*, vol. 6, p. 552.

"If I had 20,000 mounted men": Walter Brian Cisco, *Wade Hampton* (Potomac Books, Washington, D.C., 2004) p. 161.

143 Mallory wrote: Mallory, "Last Days," in Cozzens, p. 682.

"I cannot feel like a beaten man!": Harrison, "The Capture," 137.

144 "By your advice": Wade Hampton, letter to Joseph Johnston, in *Official Records*, ser. 1, vol. 47, pt. 3, p. 846.

145 "not have failed to remember the obligation": *Davis Papers*, vol. 11, p. 562.

146 "perilous for you and children to go with me": Jefferson Davis, letter to Varina Davis, April 26, 1865, in ibid., p. 566.

148 "The specie is estimated at $6,000,000": Henry Halleck, telegram to George Thomas, in *Official Records*, ser.1, vol. 45, pt. 3, p. 954.

149 "follow him [Davis] to the ends of the earth": George Stoneman, telegram to his generals, in *Official Records*, ser.1, vol. 49, p. 546.

Chapter 8: "We Are Falling to Pieces"

150 "We are falling to pieces": John Taylor Wood, diary, Southern Historical Collection, University of North Carolina, Chapel Hill, N.C.

"ever ready to defer": Mallory, "Last Days," in Cozzens, p. 682.

151 **touch on Reagan's shoulder:** John H. Reagan, *Memoirs of John H. Reagan* (Neale, New York, 1906) p. 210.
Reagan reluctantly agreed: Ibid., 209.

152 **"his pride would prevent":** Basil Duke, *Reminiscences of Basil Duke* (Doubleday, New York, 1911) p. 385.
her husband in Texas: Varina Davis, letter to Jefferson Davis, April 28, 1865, *Davis Papers,* vol. 11, p. 569.

154 **"having sat by its cradle and followed its hearse":** Richard Taylor, *Destruction and Reconstruction: Personal Experiences of the Late War* (D. Appleton, New York, 1879), p. 229.
"Central American Revolutions!": Parker, *Recollections,* p. 279.
Parker said: Ibid., 280.

155 **"After seeing the escort":** Ibid., 281.
"seemed to arouse him": Ibid.

156 **"seize a vessel of some kind":** Ibid., 282.

157 **"his resolution prevented him":** Rowland, *Jefferson Davis, Constitutionalist,* vol. 8, p. 171.

158 **"no mercy or forbearance":** Joseph Holt, speech, Joseph Holt Papers, Huntington Library, San Mario, Calif., quoted in William Hanchett, *The Lincoln Murder Conspiracies* (University of Illinois Press, Chicago, 1983) p. 63.
"attempted to kill Mr. Seward": Edwin Stanton, telegram to Major John Dix, in *Official Records,* ser. 1, vol. 47, pt. 3, p. 301.

161 **"to China!":** Reagan, *Memoirs,* p. 211.

163 **band of black cloth:** William C. Davis, *Diary of a Confederate Soldier: John J. Jackman of the Orphan Brigade* (University of South Carolina Press, Columbia, 1977) p. 167.

164 **cabinet was still in Greensboro:** Reagan, *Memoirs,* p. 214.

165 **"were in eager haste":** Mrs. M. E. Robertson, "President Davis's Last Official Meeting," *Southern Historical Society Papers* (July 1901): 291.

Chapter 9: "Success Depended on Instantaneous Action"

173 "going west of the Mississippi": *Official Records*, ser. 1, vol. 49, p. 516.

174 "movements of the party he was with": J. H. Wilson, "Pursuit and Capture of Jefferson Davis," *Century Magazine* (November 1889): 586.

175 "$100,000 REWARD in Gold": Edward Longacre, *Grant's Cavalryman* (Stackpole, Mechanicsburg, Pa., 2000) p. 281.

177 "Ocmulgee to follow and capture or kill him": *Official Records*, ser. 1, vol. 49, p. 527.

178 "authorities of an organized State": *Official Records*, ser. 1, vol. 47, p. 329.

179 check out the Negroes' stories: *Official Records*, ser. 1, vol. 49, pp. 517–18.

180 "in time to grasp their weapons": Ibid., 536.
reply, "First Wisconsin": Ibid.

181 "He attempted no disguise": Varina Davis, letter to Montgomery Blair, June 6, 1865, Blair Family Papers, Library of Congress.
"a few precious moments": Jefferson Davis, *Rise and Fall*, vol. 2, p. 701.

182 "my wife thoughtfully threw over": Ibid.

183 "fire beyond the tent": Ibid., 702.

184 her postwar book: Varina Davis, *Jefferson Davis*, vol. 2, pp. 640–41.

Chapter 10: "He Hastily Put On One of Mrs. Davis's Dresses"

187 "more than Hudson's insults": Varina Davis, *Jefferson Davis*, vol. 2, p. 642.

188 some breaking into song: William C. Davis, *An Honorable Defeat: The Last Days of the Confederate Government* (Harcourt, New York, 2001) p. 310.
"willing to assassinate": Varina Davis, *Jefferson Davis*, vol. 2, p. 642.
"which he repeated as calmly": Ibid.

189 "words unfit for women's ears": Ibid.
"the Colt revolvers": *Official Records*, ser. 1, vol. 49, p. 742.
honor that been afforded the man: Jefferson Davis, *Rise and Fall*, vol. 1, p. 703.
"captured in his wife's clothes": Henry Halleck, telegram to Edwin Stanton, *Official Records*, ser. 1, vol. 47, p. 741.
kept one of the flowers as a keepsake: Varina Davis, *Jefferson Davis*, vol. 2, p. 643.

190 "recovered his equanimity": James H. Wilson, *Under the Old Flag*, vol. 2 (D. Appleton, New York, 1912) p. 336.
"Hood's heroic rashness": Ibid., 337
"frigid or repellent": Ibid.
"unforgiving temper": Ibid.

191 "trouble to disprove": Ibid., 338.

192 "sympathize with him": Stephens, *Recollections*, p. 114.
ready to face whatever punishment: Joseph Wheeler, "An Effort to Rescue Jefferson Davis," *Century Magazine* (May 1898): 86.
of Jim Limber: Varina Davis, *Jefferson Davis*, vol. 2, p. 645.

193 "the affection was mutual": Ibid., 646.

195 "gloat over your grief": Ibid., 648.
"of another and higher race": Ibid.
"brought to Washington to command": Ezra Warner, *Generals in Blue* (Louisiana State University, Baton Rouge, 1964) p. 196.

197 *Times*, none of whom: *New York Times* (May 14, 1865): 1.

199 "Andrew called to me": Julian Dickinson, "The Capture of Jefferson Davis," speech read to the Military Order of the Loyal Legion of the United States, January 8, 1889; text at www.suvcw.org/mollus/warpapers/MIv1p179.htm.
"Davis had on for disguise": Ibid.

200 "wrestling exercises," Dickinson wrote: Ibid.

202 wrote years later: Jefferson Davis, *Rise and Fall*, vol. 2, p. 702.

203 "On entering my office": Wilson, *Under the Old Flag*, vol. 2, p. 331.
"would overwhelm him": Ibid.

204 "He dropped his pantaloons": "Jeff Davis in Petticoats," song lyrics, at www.civilwarpoetry.org.

205 **"in any disguise he could use"**: "The Capture of Jefferson Davis," unsigned article in Poughkeepsie, N.Y., *Eagle* (c.1880), at www.valstar.net/~jcraig.

205 **"wicked to lie"**: James H. Parker, "The Capture of Jefferson Davis," *Southern Historical Society Papers*, vol. 4 (August 1877): 91.

"would not lie about him, when the truth": Ibid., 92.

206 **"cavalry boots and spurs"**: Joseph Vale, *Minty and the Cavalry* (Edward E. Myers, Harrisburg, Pa., 1886) p. 552.

"Andrew Bee was cook": Marginal note by Julian Dickinson in a copy of ibid., p. 470.

207 **"after our regiment had taken him"**: Albert Potter, letter to his sister Amelia, May 14, 1865, at freepages.geneology.rootsweb. com/~mruddy/letters6.htm.

"belonging to the old Fourth Mich. Cavalry": Albert Potter, letter to his father, loc. cit.

208 **"disguise was quickly discovered"**: *Kalamazoo Saturday Gazette* (December 13, 1902): 1, collection of Allergen County, Michigan, Historical Society.

"a tissue of falsehoods": Wilson, *Under the Old Flag*, vol. 2, p. 332.

209 **"given the truth with accuracy"**: Ibid., 334–35.

CHAPTER II: "Place Manacles and Fetters upon the Hands and Feet of Jefferson Davis"

213 **"imprisonment more secure"**: *Official Records*, ser. 2, vol. 8, p. 565.

"violently resisted": Ibid., 571.

"an enormity . . . wholly unnecessary": Thurlow Weed, letter to Edwin Stanton, quoted in Burke Davis, *The Long Surrender*, p. 181.

214 **"neuralgic disorder"**: John J. Craven, *The Prison Life of Jefferson Davis* (Carleton, New York, 1866) p. 41.

215 **"you do not tell me the worst"**: Varina Davis, letter to John J. Craven, in ibid., p. 88.

216 **Davis made notes in the margins:** Edward Eckert, ed., *Fiction Distorting Fact: The Prison Life, Annotated by Jefferson Davis* (Mercer University, Macon, Ga., 1987) p. 67.

"**according to programme**": Ibid., 66–67.

217 "**beg leave to tender my services**": *Official Records*, ser. 2, vol. 8, p. 656.

"**required for my vindication**": Ibid.

220 "**a certain kind of dignity**": *Chicago Tribune* (May 26, 1865): 2.

221 "**safety of the witnesses**": *Harper's Weekly* (June 17, 1865).

222 "**criminals of a still deeper dye**": "The Proof Against Davis," *Chicago Tribune* (June 9, 1865).

223 "**No remark was made at all**": Lewis F. Bates, testimony, Lincoln assassination trial, transcript, pp. 46–47; reprinted in Edward Steers, Jr., ed., *The Trial: The Assassination of President Lincoln and the Trial of the Conspirators* (University Press of Kentucky, Lexington, 2003).

224 **explain his plan in more detail:** Letter, said to be from Burton Harrison to Jefferson Davis, read in court and entered in evidence against Davis, Lincoln assassination trial, transcript, p. 52; reprinted in Steers, *The Trial*.

"**merely the political instrument**": Henry T. Louthan, "A Proposed Abduction of Abraham Lincoln," *Confederate Veteran Magazine*, vol. 11 (April 1903): 157–58.

225 "**by the hands of hired assassins**": Summation of John Bingham, Lincoln assassination trial, transcript, pp. 351–402; reprinted in Steers, *The Trial*.

226 "*better* **if it had been well done**": Bingham summation, loc. cit, p. 402; reprinted in Steers, *The Trial*.

229 "**watchfulness of his guardians**": *New York Times* (July 28, 1865): 4.

230 "**so desperate were his fears**": *Harper's Weekly* (June 10, 1865).

CHAPTER 12: "He Is Buried Alive"

231 **"He is buried alive"**: *New York Herald* (May 23, 1865), quoted in Strode, *Jefferson Davis, Tragic Hero*, pp. 231–32.

"violation of the laws of war": Edwin Morgan, letter to Andrew Johnson, May 29, 1865, in *Papers of Andrew Johnson*, vol. 8 (University of Tennessee Press, Knoxville, 1989) pp. 134–35.

232 **"Davis 'simply committed treason' "**: *Harper's Weekly* (June 24, 1865).

233 **"never arraigned for the crimes"**: Amasa Walker, letter to Andrew Johnson, July 18, 1865, in *Johnson Papers*, vol. 8, pp. 433–34.

234 **majority voting for a civilian court**: George Fort Milton, *The Age of Hate: Andrew Johnson and the Radicals* (Coward-McCann, New York, 1930) p. 245.

"more civilized people": *Chicago Tribune* (August 2, 1865): 2.

refused to offer an opinion: Gideon Welles, *Diary of Gideon Welles, Secretary of the Navy Under Lincoln and Johnson* (Houghton Mifflin, New York, 1911) [August 22, 1865] p. 366.

236 **he felt "regret"**: Frederick J. Blue, *Salmon Chase: A Life in Politics* (Kent State University Press, Kent, Ohio, 1987) p. 263.

"I know these men": Thaddeus Stevens to Davis's lawyer George Shea, conversation reported in *Southern Historical Society Papers*, vol. 1 (April 1876): 325.

237 **"singled out and legally convicted"**: McCulloch, *Men and Measures*, pp. 408–9.

238 **"this great criminal"**: *Journal of the House of Representatives*, 39th Congress (December 18, 1865): 78.

239 **"renounce its place in the Union"**: Ibid. (December 20, 1865): 97.

"not been put upon his trial": *Senate Journal*, 39th Congress (December 21, 1865): 58.

"and barbarous practices": Ibid. (February 1, 1866): 127.

240 **"to him [Davis]"**: *Official Records*, ser. 2, vol. 8, p. 710.

"any thing which is needed": Jefferson Davis, letter to Varina

Davis, September 26, 1865, quoted in Eckert, *Fiction Distorting Fact*, p. xxvii.

241 **"consider such a request":** *Official Records*, ser. 2, vol. 8, p. 840.

242 **"a longer cord," wrote Miles:** Ibid., 841.

243 **"things they tell are not realities":** Jefferson Davis, letter to Varina Davis, December 2, 1865, quoted in Eckert, *Fiction Distorting Fact*, p. xxix.

why the Union had invaded the South: Clifford letter to Everts, May 28, 1866, referenced in Roy Franklin Nichols, "United States *vs.* Jefferson Davis, 1865–1869," *American Historical Review* (January 1926): 267.

244 **living in Canada:** Strode, *Jefferson Davis, Tragic Hero*, p. 278.

"his breath come in short gasps": Varina Davis, *Jefferson Davis*, vol. 2, p. 759.

"not be brutally treated": McCulloch, *Men and Measures*, p. 410.

245 **"not demean himself as a criminal:"** Ibid., 411.

"Owing allegiance and fidelity": Ibid., 297.

247 **"probability of humiliation":** *Harper's Weekly* (May 26, 1866).

"eternal remorse to the country": Ibid.

248 **"shall ask for no delay":** William B. Reed, statement to Judge John Underwood, quoted in Rowland, *Jefferson Davis, Constitutionalist,* vol. 7, p. 152.

"we are entirely ready": James T. Brady, statement to Judge John Underwood, quoted in ibid., p. 155.

"much more comfortable for the counsel": Judge John Underwood, quoted ibid.

249 **"the government at Washington":** Ibid., 156.

250 **"If Davis and his associates are innocent":** Judge John Underwood, statement, June 11, 1866, in ibid., p. 160.

251 **"It cannot be read":** *New York World* (May 24, 1866).

252 **"was possessed of evidence":** Varina Davis, *Jefferson Davis*, p. 787.

253 **"whether any legislation is necessary":** *Journal of the House of Representatives*, 39th Congress (April 9, 1866): 520.

254 **and 58 not voting:** Ibid. (June 11, 1866): 821–22.

"submit to perish?": *Harper's Weekly* (July 14, 1866).

257 "degrade me in the estimation of mankind": Strode, *Jefferson Davis, Tragic Hero*, p. 302.

CHAPTER 13: "The Government Is Unable to Deal with the Subject"

259 "extrication from its doubts": Charles O'Conor, letters in the James Mason collection, Library of Congress, quoted in William J. Cooper, Jr., *Jefferson Davis, American* (Alfred A. Knopf, New York, 2000).

"adhering to their Enemies": U.S. Constitution, art. 3, sec. 3.

260 "resumed its separate and equal place": "Declaration of the Immediate Causes Which Induce and Justify the Secession of South Carolina from the Federal Union," legal proclamation issued by South Carolina, December 24, 1860.

261 "as well as of the Congress": U.S. Constitution, art. 4, sec. 3.

"secession against the Constitution": Abraham Lincoln, December 31, 1862, Abraham Lincoln Papers, Library of Congress.

262 "suppress insurrection [and to] punish treason": *Journal of the House of Representatives*, HR 110 (July 20, 1862): 345.

264 "I recognize no Southern Confederacy": *Official Records*, ser. 2, vol. 1, p. 511.

"only a part of the ordinary *commercial belli*": Ibid., 526–27.

265 "accepted by our Government": *New York Times* (July 24, 1862): 4 (col. 3).

266 "Mr. Davis would in effect be on trial": Charles O'Conor, letter to Varina Davis, September 13, 1865, in Jefferson Davis Trial Preparation collection, Ellen Brockenbrough Library, Museum of the Confederacy, Richmond, Va.

268 "quadroon": *Philadelphia Inquirer* (May 16, 1867): 1.

270 "return thanks?" Robert McElroy, *Jefferson Davis: The Real and the Unreal* (Harper, New York, 1937) p. 586.

"We cannot properly": *San Francisco Chronicle* (May 14, 1867): 1.

"The forthcoming trial": *New York Times* (October 28, 1867).

271 "he wishes to succeed": Charles O'Conor, letter to Jefferson Davis,

April 18, 1868, in Davis Trial Preparation collection, Museum of the Confederacy.

273 **"dispose of as easily"**: Welles, *Diary*, p. 58.

According to Welles, there was "perpetual rivalry": Ibid., 139.

275 **Two days after the ruling:** Charles O'Conor, letter to Jefferson Davis, December 7, 1868, in Davis Trial Preparation collection, Museum of the Confederacy.

276 **"magnificent chapter in our history"**: Ibid.

278 **"acknowledgement was made"**: Charles O'Conor, letter to Jefferson Davis, February 2, 1878, in Davis Trial Preparation collection, Museum of the Confederacy.

Selected Bibliography

Books

Arnett, Ethel Stephens, *Greensboro North Carolina: The County Seat of Guilford County,* University of North Carolina Press, Chapel Hill, 1955.

Ballard, Michael B., *A Long Shadow: Jefferson Davis and the Final Days of the Confederacy,* University of Georgia Press, Athens, 1997.

Beauregard, P.G.T., *Military Operations of General Beauregard in the Late War Between the States 1861–1865,* Harper & Brothers, 1884.

Bell, John, *Confederate Seadog: John Taylor Wood in War and Exile,* McFarland, Jefferson, North Carolina, 2002.

Bergeron, Paul, *The Papers of Andrew Johnson*, 16 vols., University of Tennessee, Knoxville, 1994.

Bledsoe, Albert, *Is Davis a Traitor?*, The Hermitage Press, Richmond, Virginia, 1907.

Blue, Frederick, J. *Salmon P. Chase: A Life in Politics,* Kent State University Press, Kent, Ohio, 1987.

Boykin, Edward M., *The Falling Flag: Evacuation of Richmond, Retreat and Surrender,* E. J. Hale, New York City, 1874.

Bradley, Mark L., *Last Stand in the Carolinas: The Battle of Bentonville*, Savas Publishing, Campbell, California, 1996.

Brubaker, John H., III, *The Last Capital: Danville, Virginia, and the Last Days of the Confederacy*, The Danville Museum of Fine Arts and History, Danville, Virginia, 1979.

Calkins, Chris M., *The Appomattox Campaign: March 29–April 9, 1865*, Combined Books, Conshohocken, Pennsylvania, 1997

Campbell, R. Thomas, *Academy on the James: The Confederate Naval School*, Burd Street Press, Shippensburg, Pennsylvania, 1998.

———, *Southern Thunder: Exploits of the Confederate Navy*, Burd Street Press, Shippensburg, Pennsylvania, 1996.

Carr, Dawson, *Gray Phantoms of the Cape Fear: Running the Civil War Blockade*, John F. Blair Publisher, Winston-Salem, North Carolina, 1998.

Carroll, J. Frank, *Confederate Treasure in Danville*, Ure Press, Danville, Virginia, 1996.

Cashin, Joan E., *First Lady of the Confederacy: Varina Davis's Civil War*, Belknap Press, Cambridge, Massachusetts, 2006.

Clark, James C., *Last Train South: The Flight of the Confederate Government from Richmond*, McFarland, Jefferson, North Carolina, 1984.

Clay-Clopton, Virginia, *A Belle of the Fifties: Memoirs of Mrs. Clay of Alabama*, Doubleday, New York, 1905.

Cooper, Jr., William J., *Jefferson Davis, American*, Alfred A. Knopf, New York, 2000.

Cozzens, Peter, ed., *Battles and Leaders of the Civil War*, vols. 5 and 6, University of Chicago Press, Chicago, 2002.

Craven, John J., *The Prison Life of Jefferson Davis*, Carleton, New York, 1866.

Crist, Lynda Lasswell, ed., *The Papers of Jefferson Davis, vol. 11, September 1864–May 1865,* Louisiana State University Press, Baton Rouge, 2003.

Davis, Burke, *The Long Surrender,* Random House, New York, 1985.

———, *To Appomattox: Nine April Days, 1865,* Rinehart, New York, 1959.

Davis, Jefferson, *The Rise and Fall of the Confederate Government,* 2 vols., D. Appleton and Company, New York, 1881.

Davis, Varina, *Jefferson Davis, Ex-President of the Confederate States of America: A Memoir by His Wife,* 2 vols., Belford, New York, 1890.

Davis, William C., *Breckinridge: Statesman, Soldier Symbol,* Louisiana State University Press, Baton Rouge, 1974.

———, *An Honorable Defeat: The Last Days of the Confederate Government,* Harcourt, New York, 2001.

———, *Jefferson Davis: The Man and His Hour,* HarperCollins, New York, 1991.

Dickinson, Julian G., "The Capture of Jefferson Davis," speech read before the Military Order of the Loyal Legion of the United States, Jan. 8, 1889, suvcw.org/mollus/warpapers/MIv1p179.htm.

Donald, David Herbert, *Lincoln,* Simon & Schuster, New York, 1995.

Duke, Basil, *Reminiscences of Basil Duke,* Doubleday, New York, 1909.

Durkin, Joseph T., *Stephen R. Mallory: Confederate Navy Chief,* University of North Carolina Press, Chapel Hill, 1954.

Eckert, Edward, *Fiction Distorting Fact: The Prison Life, Annotated by Jefferson Davis,* Mercer University Press, Macon, Georgia, 1987.

Faust, Patricia L., ed., *Historical Times Illustrated Encyclopedia of the Civil War,* Harper & Row, New York, 1986.

Flood, Charles Bracelen, *Grant and Sherman: The Friendship That Won the Civil War,* Farrar, Strauss & Giroux, New York, 2005.

Freeman, Douglas Southall, *R. E. Lee,* vol. 4, Scribner's, New York, 1935.

Greeley, Horace, *Recollections of a Busy Life,* J. B. Ford & Company, New York, 1868.

Greeno, C. L., Talk given to Loyal Legion of Cincinnati, transcribed by Sherry Packer, August 1, 2000.

Hanna, A. J., *Flight into Oblivion,* Louisiana State University Press, Baton Rouge, 1999, reprint.

Hart, Albert, *Salmon Portland Chase—American Statesman,* Houghton, Mifflin, Cambridge, Massachusetts, 1889.

Hattaway, Herman, and Richard Beringer, *Jefferson Davis, Confederate President,* University Press of Kansas, Lawrence, Kansas, 2002.

Horn, John, *The Petersburg Campaign: June 1864–April 1865,* Combined Books, Conshohocken, Pennsylvania, 1993.

Jones, John B., *A Rebel War Clerk's Diary at the Confederate States Capital,* 2 vols., Lippincott, Philadelphia, 1866.

Jones, Katharine M., *Ladies of Richmond, Confederate Capital,* Bobbs-Merrill, Indianapolis, 1962.

Jones, Virgil Carrington, *Ranger Mosby,* University of North Carolina Press, Chapel Hill, 1944.

Lankford, Nelson, *Richmond Burning: The Last Days of the Confederate Capital,* Viking, New York, 2002.

Lodge, Henry Cabot, *Jefferson Davis, and His Complicity in the Assassination of Abraham Lincoln,* Sherman & Company, Philadelphia, 1866.

Long, E. B., *The Civil War Day by Day: An Almanac 1861–1865,* Doubleday, Garden City, New Jersey, 1971.

Longstreet, James, *From Manassas to Appomattox: Memoirs of the Civil War in America* (reprint), Mallard Press, New York, 1991.

McElroy, Robert, *Jefferson Davis: The Unreal and the Real*, Harper Brothers, New York, 1937.

McKitrick, Eric L., *Andrew Johnson and Reconstruction*, The University of Chicago Press, Chicago, 1960.

McPherson, Edward, *The Political History of the United States of America During the Period of Reconstruction, April 15, 1865–July 15, 1870*, Da Capo Press, New York, 1972.

Means, Howard, *The Avenger Takes His Place: Andrew Johnson and the 45 Days That Changed the Nation*, Harcourt Books, Orlando, Florida, 2006.

Milton, George Fort, *The Age of Hate: Andrew Johnson and the Radicals*, Coward-McCann, New York, 1930.

Parker, William H., *Recollections of a Naval Officer*, 1841–1865, Scribner's, New York, 1883.

Ramage, James A., *Gray Ghost: The Life of Col. John Singleton Mosby*, University Press of Kentucky, Lexington, 1999.

Rowland, Dunbar, *Jefferson Davis, Constitutionalist: His Letters, Papers and Speeches*, Mississippi Department of Archives and History, Jackson, 10 vols., 1923.

Sandburg, Carl, *Abraham Lincoln: The War Years*, vol. 4, Harcourt, Brace, New York, 1939.

Semmes, Raphael, *Memoirs of Service Afloat During the War Between the States*, Blue & Gray Press, Secaucus, New Jersey, 1987.

Sherman, William T., *Memoirs of General W. T. Sherman* (reprint), Library of America, New York, 1990.

Steers, Edward, Jr., *The Trial: The Assassination of President Lincoln and the Trial of the Conspirators,* University Press of Kentucky, Lexington, 2003.

Stephens, Alexander H., *Recollections of Alexander H. Stephens: His Diary Kept When a Prisoner at Fort Warren, Boston Harbour, 1865,* Doubleday, New York, 1910.

Strode, Hudson, *Jefferson Davis: Private Letters 1823–1889,* Harcourt, Brace & World, New York, 1966.

———, *Jefferson Davis, Tragic Hero: 1864–1889, The Last 25 Years,* Harcourt, Brace & World, New York, 1964.

Thomas, Benjamin, and Harold M. Hyman, *Stanton: The Life and Times of Lincoln's Secretary of War,* Knopf, New York, 1962.

Vale, Joseph, *Minty and the Cavalry: A History of Cavalry Campaigns in the Western Armies,* Harrisburg, Pennsylvania, E. K. Meyers, Printers, 1866.

Van Deusen, Glyndon, *Horace Greeley: Nineteenth Century Crusader,* Hill and Wang, New York, 1953.

Van Noppen, Ina, *Stoneman's Last Raid,* North Carolina State College Print Shop, Raleigh, 1961.

Welles, Gideon, *Diary of Gideon Welles, Secretary of the Navy Under Lincoln and Johnson,* Houghton & Mifflin, New York, 1911.

Wilson, James H., *Under the Old Flag,* vol. 2, D. Appleton & Company, New York, 1912.

Winik, Jay, *April 1865: The Month That Saved America,* HarperCollins, New York, 2001.

C. Vann Woodward, ed., *Mary Chesnut's Civil War,* Yale University Press, New Haven, 1981.

Selected Articles

Blackford, Charles M., "The Trials and Trial of Jefferson Davis," *Southern Historical Papers* (January 29, 1901): 45–81.

Deutsch, Eberhard P., "United States vs. Jefferson Davis: Constitutional Issues in the Trial for Treason," *American Bar Association Journal*, 56 (February 1966): 139–45 and (March 1966): 263–68.

Dorris, J. T. , Pardoning the Leaders of the Confederacy, *The Mississippi Valley Historical Review*, 15, no. 1 (June 1928): 3–21.

Gill, Harold, B. Jr., "Christmas Trees, The Confederacy, and Colonial Williamsburg," *The Journal of the Colonial Williamsburg Foundation* (Christmas 2005).

Hanchett, William, "Reconstruction and the Rehabilitation of Jefferson Davis," *Journal of American History*, 56, no. 2 (September 1969): 280–89.

Harrison, Burton, "The Capture of Jefferson Davis: An Extract from A Narrative, Written Not for Publication, but for the Entertainment of My Children Only," *Century Magazine*, 27, no. 1 (November 1883): 130–45.

Hart, W. O., "When Jefferson Davis Was Freed," *Confederate Veteran*, 31 (1923): 208–9.

Hertle, Richard W., and Robert Spellman, "The Eye Disease of Jefferson Davis," *Survey of Ophthalmology*, (November–December 2006): 596–600.

Hunter, R.M.T., "The Failure of the Hampton Conference," *Century Magazine* (July 1896): 476–78

Lathrop, George P., "The Bailing of Jefferson Davis," *Century Magazine*, 33 (1886–1887).

Leek, J. H., "Treason and the Constitution," *The Journal of Politics*, 13, no. 4 (November 1951): 604–22.

Louthan, Henry T., "A Proposed Abduction of Abraham Lincoln," *Confederate Veteran Magazine,* 11 (April 1903): 157–58.

Mehney, Paul D., "Capturing a Confederate," *Michigan History Magazine* (May–June 2000): 42–49.

Nichols, Roy Franklin, "United States vs. Jefferson Davis, 1865–1869," *American Historical Review,* 31, no. 2 (January 1926) p. 266–84.

Pfranz, Harry W., "The Surrender Negotiations Between General Johnston and General Sherman," *Military Affairs,* 16, no. 2 (Summer 1952): 61–70.

Sanders, Charles W., Jr., "Jefferson Davis and the Hampton Roads Peace Conference: To Secure Peace to the Two Countries," *The Journal of Southern History,* 63, no. 4 (November 1997): 803–26.

Shepley, George, "Incidents of the Capture of Richmond," *Atlantic Monthly* 46, no. 273 (July 1880): 18–28.

Stewart, William H., "The Prison Life of Jefferson Davis," *Southern Historical Society Papers,* 32 (January–December1904): 338–46.

Swallow, W. H., "Retreat of the Confederate Government: From Richmond to the Gulf," *Journal of American History* (June 1886): 596–608.

Walmsley, James Elliott, "The Last Meeting of the Confederate Cabinet," *The Mississippi Valley Historical Review,* 6, no. 3 (December 1919): 336–49.

Watson, David K., "The Trial of Jefferson Davis: An Interesting Constitutional Question," *The Yale Law Journal,* 24, no. 8 (June 1915): 669–76.

Wheeler, Joseph, "An Effort to Rescue Jefferson Davis," *Century Magazine,* 56, no. 1 (May 1898): 85–91.

Wilson, James H., Report to General William D. Whipple, January 17, 1867.

———, and William P. Stedman, "Pursuit and Capture of Jefferson Davis by the Commander of the Union Cavalry," *Century Magazine* (November, 1889): 586–94.

Index